Penn Greek Drama Series

Series Editors
David R. Slavitt
Palmer Bovie

The Penn Greek Drama Series presents fresh literary translations of the entire corpus of classical Greek drama: tragedies, comedies, and satyr plays. The only contemporary
uniform series of all the surviving work of Aeschylus, Sophocles, Euripides, Aristophanes, and Menander, this collection brings together men and women of literary distinction
whose versions of the plays in contemporary English poetry
can be acted on the stage or in the individual reader's theater of the mind.

The aim of the series is to make this cultural treasure accessible, restoring as faithfully as possible the original luster of
the plays and offering in living verse a view of what talented
contemporary poets have seen in their readings of these
works so fundamental a part of Western civilization.

Aristophanes, 2

Wasps, Lysistrata, Frogs,
The Sexual Congress

Edited by
David R. Slavitt *a n d* Palmer Bovie

PENN

University of Pennsylvania Press
Philadelphia

Copyright © 1999 University of Pennsylvania Press
Printed in the United States of America on acid-free paper

10 9 8 7 6 5 4 3 2 1

Published by
University of Pennsylvania Press
Philadelphia, Pennsylvania 19104-4011

Library of Congress Cataloging-in-Publication Data
Aristophanes.
    [Works. English. 1998]
    Aristophanes / edited by David R. Slavitt and Palmer Bovie
       p.   cm. — (Penn Greek drama series)
      Contents: 1. The Acharnians. Peace. Celebrating ladies. Wealth—
2. Wasps. Lysistrata. Frogs. The Sexual congress— 3. The New class. Clouds.
Birds
      ISBN 0-8122-3456-1 (v. 1: cloth : acid-free paper). —ISBN 0-8122-1662-8
(v. 1: pbk : acid-free paper). —ISBN 0-8122-3483-9 (v. 2: cloth : acid-free
paper). —ISBN 0-8122-1684-9 (v. 2: pbk : acid-free paper). —ISBN 0-8122-
3501-0 (v. 3 : cloth : acid-free paper). —ISBN 0-8122-1698-9 (v. 2: pbk : acid-
free paper)
      1. Aristophanes—Translations into English.   2. Greek drama
(Comedy)—Translations into English.   I. Slavitt, David R., 1935 – .
II. Bovie, Smith Palmer. III. Title. IV. Series.
PA3877.A1S58   1998
882'.01—dc21   98-8446
                                                  CIP

Contents

Introduction

Ralph M. Rosen

The plays of Aristophanes collected in these volumes, composed
and performed in Athens during the fifth and fourth centuries B.C., are the
earliest surviving record of comic drama in Western culture. Like its contemporary and cognate form tragedy, Attic comedy seems to appear suddenly as a fully formed and remarkably complex poetic genre, paradoxically
wedded to its own cultural moment yet profoundly resonant for audiences
and readers up to our own time. Indeed, the seeds of Gilbert and Sullivan,
the Marx Brothers, or Monty Python's Flying Circus are readily apparent in
Aristophanes and can easily lead one to assume that not much has changed
in comedy since antiquity. Yet the comic drama of fifth-century Athens,
known as Old Comedy, was the product of a long and complex process of
literary and cultural interactions and displays as many idiosyncrasies of its
own age as it does links to later traditions. Behind the sprightly, colloquial
translations featured in this series lie a richly varied Greek verse form and,
as the following pages will show, a comic aesthetic by turns alien and familiar to our own sensibilities.

Twice a year during the fifth century the Athenians would gather together
to honor Dionysus, god of wine and revelry. The largest and most extrava-
gant occurred in early spring, toward the end of March, and was known as
the Great Dionysia, or City Dionysia, to distinguish it from the so-called
rural Dionysia, which were celebrated on a lesser scale throughout the Attic
countryside. The other festival was known as the Lenaean Dionysia (named
after the Lenaion sanctuary where it was held), a more limited, domestic
affair that took place in January–February. Various activities occurred at
these festivals, including processions, sacrifices, and musical competitions,
but the central event at each was the performance of tragedy and comedy.
Great expense and effort were lavished on these dramatic performances, as

poets and actors competed for prizes awarded by a panel of judges drawn from ten tribes of Attica.

Tragedy and comedy were so much a part of a formal state event that the entire Athenian citizenry might, in principle, attend the performances. The Theater of Dionysus itself on the Athenian acropolis was evidently capable of holding about 17,000 spectators. The Lenaean Dionysia was a smaller and less prestigious affair than the City Dionysia, and theatrical performances were formalized there rather late in the century (about 440 B.C.). Even so, the Lenaea was as public an event as the City Dionysia, and the plots of Lenaean tragedy and comedy likewise reflect the poets' awareness that they were composing before the entire "national" community.

Drawing on a rich store of inherited myths and plots, the most skillful tragic poets crafted plays that could address issues central to Athenian political and social ideology—the relationship between rulers and their subjects, the nature of democracy, the interaction of man and woman, to name a few—and the result was that characteristically "tragic" blend of timeliness and universalizing. Greek comedy evolved alongside tragedy at the festival competitions and became equally implicated in its own historical moment, but, unlike tragedy, it was not constrained to work with mythological material, nor did it need to preserve a consistent and unbroken dramatic illusion. The comic poet was relatively free to invent plots out of whole cloth, and his imagination was limited only by his sense of what the audience would find acceptable. Furthermore, although it shared with tragedy basic compositional units, namely the alternation of spoken "episodes" with choral song and dance, comic diction was far less formal and stylized than that of tragedy. Old Comedy, therefore, could reflect the contemporary cultural climate much more directly than could tragedy: not only could the poet allude to current events or famous people through allegory or analogy but he could even name names, express indignation, and claim a personal authority (however disingenuously) to a degree wholly unavailable to his colleagues in tragedy.

The license afforded Attic comedy in the composition of plots and choice of language has a history that extends well beyond its institutionalization at the Dionysian festivals of fifth-century Athens. The exact origins of Attic comedy are difficult to trace, but the word *komoidia* itself, from which "comedy" derives, offers a useful starting point. *Komoidia* means a *komos-*

song, where the *komos* refers to a group of men, often costumed, who entertained audiences with song and dance at various festive occasions. Modern analogues to the ancient *komos* are likely to be found in the activities of Mummers, still common in certain European and American holiday celebrations. Like Mummers, *komos*-singers (*komoidoi*) performed interactively with an audience, often humorously cajoling and mocking individuals with attitudes and language that in normal circumstances would be disruptive and transgressive. Little is known about how and when *komoi* actually became comic drama, formally performed before a passive audience, but the most fundamental vestige of the *komoi* in Attic comedy can be seen in the humorously antagonistic relationships so common between individual characters and groups of characters, and between poet and audience. Fifth-century comic drama preserves some of the carnivalesque spirit of the *komos*, which rendered vituperation and satirical commentary innocuous by means of humor, irony, and a basic assumption that comic speech was ultimately fictive, no matter how "real" it pretended to be in performance.

Indeed, perhaps the central dynamic of Aristophanic comedy is precisely the tension that arises between the poet's voice, with its didactic claims and autobiographical pretenses, and the fictional demands of the genre itself. Did Aristophanes write the *Clouds*, which satirizes Socrates and his followers, because he had a genuine personal animus against him, or because Socrates was an eccentric, funny-looking man who would make a great comic spectacle? Or did the poet exploit the comic potential of Socrates, not because he had anything against him personally but because he wanted to use him to register his own sincere criticism of current philosophical trends? That seems reasonable until one notes that the play itself offers very little in the way of philosophical consistency: traditional "philosophy," which the play ostensibly endorses, ends up as comically ridiculous as the newfangled, sophistic ways that it claims to repudiate through its satirizing of Socrates.

We face a similar dilemma in assessing Aristophanes' relationship with his other famous target, the demagogic politician Cleon, who is relentlessly, often violently, mocked in *The New Class*, and mentioned with disdain at least somewhere in nearly all his fifth-century plays. Aristophanes even alludes to an actual personal feud with Cleon, a feud that supposedly began when Cleon attempted to prosecute the poet for publicly ridiculing Athenian politicians in his (now lost) play of 426 B.C., *Babylonians*. Aristophanes was very convincing: ancient commentators spoke of the feud as if it were a documented historical fact, and modern critics have followed suit, even though our only evidence ultimately comes from the comedies themselves, which have a generic obligation to create personal animosities between the poet and a target. We will probably never know for sure whether Aristophanes truly feuded with Cleon, but the question of historicity is ultimately less significant than the ways the comic poet persistently exploited the topos throughout his plays. For through the relationship with Cleon as it was developed on the stage over several plays spanning at least five years—*The Acharnians* (425), *The New Class* (424), *Clouds* (423), *Wasps* (422), and *Peace* (421)—Aristophanes could dramatize with brilliant economy the ethos of boisterous confrontation and antagonism that fueled so many plays of Attic comedy.

Any literature in which an author adopts a stance of moral indignation and undeserved beleaguerment, and engages in invective or personal mockery makes it especially difficult for the audience to separate fiction from reality, if only because the author works hard to enlist their sympathies for his allegedly urgent and topical predicament. Yet despite this implied bond with an audience in opposition to a target, a group, or even an issue, we never witness the poet's voice directly in any of Aristophanes' plays (Dikaiopolis in *The Acharnians*, is about as close as we get to this). No character ever explicitly represents the poet himself, and the poet's name is never directly mentioned. Instead, Aristophanes avails himself of a structural device known as the *parabasis*, which had become the conventional place in Old Comedy, where the poet could interrupt the flow of episodes and make personal claims through the mouthpiece of the chorus. The parabasis, which comes from the verb *parabaino*, "to step aside," was essentially a digression, a temporary halt in the main action while the chorus came forward to address the audience. Its location in the play was not rigidly fixed but tended to occur toward the middle of the play, often functioning as a kind of entr'acte. In its most elaborate form—as we see, for example, in *Wasps*—the parabasis consists of a prolonged exchange between the chorus and their leader, alternating spoken and sung verse, in which the chorus leader actually speaks on behalf of the poet.

Through the chorus leader, then, Aristophanes could take up any number of topics, including current events, the superiority of his comedy over that of his rivals, indignation at the audience for lack of support, and, of course, abuse against "personal enemies" such as Cleon. The parabasis is our main source for "autobiographical" information about Aristophanes and the primary reason it has always been so tempting to take a biographical approach to the interpretation of Aristophanes. When *Clouds* makes fun of Socrates or *The New Class* inveighs against Cleon, when Aeschylus defeats Euripides in the literary contest of *Frogs*, the relationship with the audience that Aristophanes establishes in successive parabases makes it easy to assume that the plots themselves functioned likewise as a coded, didactic message: Aeschylus defeated Euripides, so Aristophanes must therefore endorse this verdict and be trying to warn us against the evils of Euripides! But if *Frogs*, to continue with this example, were such a simplistic morality play, Aristophanes would hardly have ridiculed the literary excesses of *both* tragic poets with as much care as he does, nor would he have left the final decision to the waffling, delightfully buffoonish god Dionysus, who can barely offer a rationale for his final elevation of Aeschylus from the underworld.

Centuries of readers have had the same problem in trying to ascertain Aristophanes' views on politics or such social issues as gender relations. Do his attacks on Cleon indicate that he was "conservative"? Do his so-called peace-plays (*The Acharnians, Peace, Lysistrata*), which clearly articulated a longing for the end of the Peloponnesian War (a conflict between Athens and Sparta that lasted for nearly three decades, from 431 to 404), indicate the poet's disapproval of current Athenian war policy? Do the cluster of plays that highlight women (*Lysistrata, Celebrating Ladies, The Sexual Congress*) reveal the poet to be anachronistically enlightened about women—a protofeminist? The plays can easily suggest such conclusions, but in fact no really systematic political or social outlook is forthcoming from them. Characters will take apparently clear political stands at one moment in a play, only to undermine them elsewhere, usually for the sake of a good laugh. And when it comes to Aristophanes' sexual politics we must remain agnostic as to whether the power and status he affords women in some of his plots were received as a prescription for social change—or as an extended joke "among the guys" who made up most of the audience.

Rather than dwell on Aristophanes' personal beliefs, which we can never hope to recover anyway, let us focus on the politics and poetics of comic satire as a literary genre. In line with the antagonistic dynamic of such poetry and the poet's need to find in his surroundings something worthy of mockery, something that would strike a chord in an audience that was pitting his comic sensibility against that of his rivals, Aristophanes naturally gravitates to topics that generate controversy in nearly all societies: domestic and international politics, celebrity lives and their scandals, popular entertainment, education, and so forth. These are areas in which the slightest eccentricity can seem amusing, especially when exaggerated by caricature and incongruity. Any deviation from "the way things were" is always fodder for a satirist, and Aristophanes is famous for plots that dramatize the conflict between the "traditional old" and the "unconventional new," whether these dramatize old and new generations (e.g., *Clouds*, *Wasps*), political ideologies (e.g., *The New Class*, *The Sexual Congress*), or poetic styles (e.g., *Celebrating Ladies*, *Frogs*). This explains the general conservative feeling of so many of the plays, an almost wistful yearning for life to remain stable and ordered when the progress of time inevitably ensures that it cannot. It also explains why politicians then in office, for example, or philosopher-professors teaching for pay, were natural targets of comic ridicule: they existed in the here-and-now, and they had the potential to influence everyone's life. Any false step of theirs could cause intense anxiety within the demos, and one way the Athenians grappled with this anxiety was to reprocess it as comic performance. Comedy probably did little to change whatever views on political and moral issues audiences brought with them to the theater (it might seem remarkable, for instance, that not long after Aristophanes' unrelieved attack on Cleon in *The New Class* won first prize, the Athenians elected Cleon general), but comic poetry would certainly have encouraged them to refine their perspectives on the complex ideological forces that governed their city and their own interpersonal behavior.

As a form of public art, organized and at least partially funded by the state, Old Comedy necessarily reflected prevailing cultural norms, and its success depended largely on its ability to walk the fine line between questioning—and occasionally subverting—these norms and merely endorsing them. The generally conservative tendencies of satire were no doubt ultimately reassuring to a democracy that institutionalized the comic performances to begin with. One cannot easily imagine, after all, what group would endorse an art form that seriously repudiated its fundamental claims to legitimacy, and few looking back today on the audience of Aristophanes' time would deny that Aristophanic comedy presupposes the desirability of democracy as practiced in the fifth century. Certainly the ancient testimony mentioned earlier, even if fictional, that Cleon sued Aristophanes for slandering the demos and its politicians in his *Babylonians* of 426 suggests that there were perceived limits to comic ridicule at the time. But so far as we can tell these limits were never systematically articulated or, for that matter, rigorously enforced. It was probably less the fear of any slander laws that restricted the freedom of comic poets than a finely honed sense of what the audience—the demos itself—would find humorous.

Although we possess only eleven complete plays by Aristophanes (representing perhaps a quarter of his total output), we are fortunate that these eleven offer examples of his art from every period of his career. Readers who approach them chronologically will note that the latest plays, both from the fourth century, *The Sexual Congress* (392) and *Wealth* (388), reflect changes in structure and content from those composed in the fifth century. The most conspicuous difference lies in the diminishing role of the chorus. In its earliest stages comedy, like tragedy, was as much a spectacle of music and dance as of spoken verse, and the chorus was clearly an area in which costume, song, and gesture could be combined to create a theatrical extravaganza. Eight of Aristophanes' surviving plays, in fact, take their titles from the identity of the chorus, and in all of the fifth-century plays his choruses play an integral role in the plot (*Frogs* is a quirky exception in that it has two choruses—the frogs themselves and a band of religious initiates; the frogs appear only briefly, at the beginning, and the initiates take over the choral duties for the rest of the play). *The Sexual Congress* and *Wealth* still have choruses, but their role is, by contrast, highly restricted and at times almost obtrusive. Some of the manuscripts of these plays indicate places in the text where someone (the poet, perhaps, but we cannot be sure) was expected to add a choral song and dance as a kind of interlude. Some scholars have even suggested that these were points in the play where the chorus was expected to improvise ad libitum while the actors prepared for the next scene. The details remain uncertain, but we can say with confidence that song and dance were increasingly relegated to the sidelines, used as ornamentation and framing, but no longer deemed necessary for the advancement of the plot.

Two other changes in Aristophanes' fourth-century plays throw into relief the process by which Old Comedy gradually developed into its later forms, Middle and New Comedy. First, the parabasis all but disappeared by the fourth century, and as a result, the poet's carefully constructed relationship with his audience became necessarily less explicit. Second, even though the non-Aristophanic examples of Middle Comedy are fragmentary, it seems clear that the pointed satire, the personal, often obscene abuse we associate with Old Comedy was significantly softened. Both these changes are in keeping with a general fourth-century trend away from strictly topical, highly episodic plots, such as we find in Old Comedy, toward plots that display greater narrative coherence and linearity. Earlier concerns with specific events and personalities of the day slowly gave way to "universalizing" topics of human interest, which can be vividly seen in the popularity of stock comic characters—cooks, slaves, philosophers, misers, misanthropes, and so forth.

The shifts in public taste that Middle and New Comedy reflect are not easy to account for, but doubtless the dissolution of the Athenian empire after the Peloponnesian War and an internationalizing movement of culture in the fourth century are at least partly responsible. Were our evidence better for the period, we would probably find that the development of Greek comic drama, as well as its public reception, was hardly as uniform as we tend to construe it. Compare in this regard the state of comic drama in our own culture. Aristophanes' rambunctious, topical satire is reincarnated in late-night talk-shows, British series such as *Benny Hill* or *Fawlty Towers*, Gilbert and Sullivan revivals, Marx Brothers movies, and Three Stooges shorts. Yet at the same time, contemporary popular taste seems generally to favor the genres that look more like Middle or New Comedy, as is clear from the fact that the situation comedy has held sway on television for several decades. No doubt the Greeks of both the fifth and fourth centuries also had the capacity to appreciate a variety of comic styles, and poets could be found to cater to all tastes. We have only scattered remnants of such poets, and only a skeletal understanding of how comedy evolved, but the literary eclecticism that Aristophanes alone displays across his entire career testifies to a poetic catholicity that would be remarkable in any age.

Wasps

Translated by
Campbell McGrath

Translator's Preface

Like politics or jury duty, translation is about making informed choices. Since a work of literature—especially poetry—cannot simply be transferred from one language to another intact, a translator has to weigh meaning against musicality, form against content, seeking to balance the scales of past intention and present need. The process entails complicated trade-offs, inevitable losses, and hopefully a few compensatory gains.

The major choice I made in this translation of *The Wasps* was to preserve above all else a sense of the rambunctious energy and lyrical verve of its poetry. This seemed to me logical for two reasons: first, because I am not a classical scholar but a poet, a poet with political and comedic tendencies, a student of the Aristophanic school of satirical hyperbole, and so might my own talents best be employed; second, because the sense of poetic voice was among the weaker elements in earlier translations of *Wasps*. Most contemporary poets are not also philologists or classicists, and most translators of classical Greek are not poets (and those who are seem to have skipped over *Wasps*), so it may be this understandable schism that accounts for the wooden or didactic translations Aristophanes often receives. Or it might just be that the plays are so funny, their conceits so brilliant, their texts so loaded with information, that there is a tendency to lose sight—and sound—of the empowered poetry, line by line, speech by speech, cadence by cadence, meter by meter.

Let me add a quick caveat on the subject of meter: this is a free verse translation. I have not attempted to reproduce the metrical complexity of the original in my version of *Wasps*, nor would I have, even if it were possible to precisely reproduce durative Greek meters in our accentual language. Why not? The best justification for re-translating well-known canonical texts is the need to cast them in a contemporary poetic idiom, and for me that idiom is not metrical. Instead of the strict time-keeping of meter, I have employed variations in cadence, rhythm, and line-length to reflect Aristophanes' rich array of rhetorical modes and styles, from sing-song vaudeville patter to the elegant lyrical structures of the parabasis. Like-wise, I have not maintained the rhyme schemes of the original, but have tried to reflect those shifts in sonic texture with alliteration, assonance and some mostly-slanted rhyme schemes of my own.

And then there are the jokes. *Wasps* is a veritable minefield of satirical jabs, scatological jibes, farcical riddles, ribald dances, witty songs, incessant puns. (There should be a special service medal for the translators of jokes, whatever it is demolitions experts get for risking their lives in the line of duty.) Puns, in particular, defy translation. They depend entirely on the contextual mesh of sound and meaning in their native language, and a literally-translated pun is like a dead battery, drained of connotative spark and referential juice. The translator's delicate task is to supply an equivalent pun in his own language, or work to make the original joke explicable in context, or simply to leave it hanging for fear of changing too much the original intent—you can find examples of all three approaches in my ver-sion of *Wasps*.

In Aristophanes, just about everything depends on specific context—not merely the jokes and the politics but the social observation, the topical asides, the literary and mythological references. This dense weave of socio-political particulars is what makes his plays such famously vivid reflectors of the character of Athens and the Athenians. To fully appreciate Aristoph-anes, then, we must acquire some background knowledge of his world, in hopes of grasping as many as possible of the levels at which his satire oper-ates. Not that every place name or in-joke need be fully understood—even scholars of Athenian history tend to disagree over the precise meanings of some of Aristophanes' references. And no wonder. There are scenes in *Wasps* that operate very much like Jay Leno's joke-filled current-event monologues, and I imagine the historians of 5000 A.D. will have difficulty grasping references to O. J.'s bloody glove or Monica Lewinsky's dress (to say nothing of Jay Leno himself).

Without pretending to explain it all, let me provide at least some of the contextual background essential to *Wasps*. The play's central concern is the nature of the Athenian jury system, participation in which was one of the democratic entitlements of all citizens. *Wasps* is set during the war with Sparta, when Athens was predominantly populated by older men, veterans of earlier wars, while the young were engaged in fighting the current one. So it was the veteran warriors that composed the Athenian juries of the day, and they were famous for the severity of their judgments—hence their personification as wasps. Aristophanes was a famous enemy of Cleon, the Athenian leader, and when Cleon instituted a new practice of paying jurors a daily wage for their efforts, Aristophanes seized on the issue as the focus for this play. To some Cleon's plan seemed like a sensible form of state pension for worthy senior citizens, but Aristophanes saw it as a corruption of civic virtue and an attempt by the regime to purchase the favor of the people with public funds.

On stage, the debate falls to Philocleon and Bdelycleon, father and son, who represent both different generational outlooks and opposing political factions—pro-Cleon and anti-Cleon (their names embody this very fact). The chorus of wasps represent the Athenian jurors, and it is a remarkably modern piece of self-referentiality that they serve as literal "jurors" for a debate of the legal system staged first as an inter-generational family quarrel and then as the "trial" of a dog accused of stealing cheese. The trial scene in particular would be right at home in Ionesco or Stoppard, to say nothing of the Marx Brothers (in Hollywood terms Aristophanes resembles a cross between Preston Sturgess and Oliver Stone, with Bob Hope handling the vaudeville roles and Jim Carey the scatology). What could be more timely than Bdelycleon's diatribes against feather-bedding lawyers and suspect politicians?

Thematically, *Wasps* could almost be mistaken for a satire of our own fractious and litigious democracy, our generational disagreements over lifestyle and mores, our debate over civic responsibilities and entitlements, our concern over the corrosive influence of money on democratic institutions. Much of the time I was engaged with this translation, the O. J. Simpson trial was an ongoing national soap opera, and I often found myself wishing Aristophanes were still around to scrutinize and skewer the lunacy of that debacle. It took me several months of working with the text to realize that Aristophanes *is* still around, alive and kicking with vitality. One of the greatest testaments to the genius of Aristophanes is the paradox that his very particular satires have retained such widespread relevance over the passage of centuries and the chasms of cultural distance.

Translation, as others have said, is an intimate art. For me it was also a collaborative art. Lacking a knowledge of classical Greek, I have been entirely reliant on earlier translators for the literal meanings of the text. I am grateful to those scholars and philologists for their work, and for the historical and cultural context so vital to understanding it. I am grateful to David Slavitt as well, for inviting me to participate in the noble and much-needed enterprise of the Penn Greek Drama Series. And I am particularly indebted to Ralph Rosen of the University of Pennsylvania, who shared with me his lively original translation of *Wasps*, an invaluable resource in resolving the stubborn interpretive questions I was left with after triangulating among the sometimes quite different readings offered by other translators.

Such disagreements, it turns out, are also part of the process. This is finally neither more nor less than my own informed but subjective version of *Wasps*, my own rendering of that peculiar Aristophanic dialectic that defies any distinction between "high" and "popular" cultures, the marriage of the vulgar and the profound. In particular, I hope that the range and power of Aristophanes' poetic voice has been rendered more accessible to contemporary readers and more comfortable to contemporary tongues, especially in those longer speeches where he ups the lyrical voltage and the poetic ante to marvelous heights: Xanthias' carnival barker introduction, Bdelycleon's trial arguments, and the several sections of the parabasis where the Chorus speaks first as the playwright upbraiding his audience, and then as the proud Athenian veterans, who are suddenly humanized and rendered sympathetic and so the whole play is subtly transformed.

As befits a supporting actor, allow me to step aside and give the last word to Aristophanes himself, as voiced by his chorus of wasps:

> So let's keep an eye on the future, folks,
> and honor true poets, honor the innovators,
> honor the artisans of visionary jokes,
> the authentic voices, the impassioned creators.
> Store their words with fresh lemons in the cedar chest,
> savor their music, treasure their wit,
> that their song might last all year at its best,
> and keep your clothes from smelling like shit. (1104–11)

Cast

(The grounds and facade of an Athenian home, surrounded by fences and barricades as if for a war. The front door is piled with stones; the stable door is latched; the windows are draped with nets. Two slaves, Sosias and Xanthias, set out as guards before the house, are asleep where they sit. On the rooftop, Bdelycleon is also asleep, with his face pressed to the tiles. The time is shortly before dawn.)

SOSIAS *(waking up)*
    Hail, Xanthias, sour fruit of the omen tree. What's up?

XANTHIAS *(rising abruptly)*
Yes, I'm up—just keeping fresh for the night shift.

SOSIAS
Fresh as a daisy, with petals bruised in slumber.
Just remember what a crafty beast we're guarding.

XANTHIAS
Indeed, I can see him with my eyes closed.

SOSIAS
Good idea, I'll give it a try myself. Ah,
sweet weight of the grape unfurls the banners of my eyelids.

XANTHIAS
Is this a catnap or an out-of-body experience, Sosias?

SOSIAS *(producing a flask)*
Adrift on a river of wine, by god.

XANTHIAS *(producing his own)*
Let me join in your ablutions, my brother.   10
The armies of sleep prepare their assault,
and who are we to resist? To doze, perchance to dream . . .
(The two slaves sleep. After an interval they wake and stretch.)

SOSIAS
What a dream I have had! But tell yours first.

XANTHIAS
An eagle flew into the marketplace, massive, be-taloned,
and seized up a brass shield in triumph,
and carried it out among the sun's triumphal arches.
And it was Cleonymus' shield, cast down as he fled.

SOSIAS
Who can decipher the riddle of Cleonymus?

XANTHIAS
> What riddle?

SOSIAS
> A guy walks into a bar, says "Which animal turns tail   20
> and runs on earth, over the sea, and in the skies?"

XANTHIAS
> Smells like trouble for me, to have dreamed such disgrace.

SOSIAS
> Nothing to fear, my friend, I swear it.

XANTHIAS
> Nothing to fear but fear itself—and what could be worse
> than such cowardice? Now let's hear yours.

SOSIAS
> My dream was big—the ship of state itself.

XANTHIAS
> Begin with the keel, and spare not the least spar.

SOSIAS
> Barely asleep, I saw a flock of sheep, uncounted,
> crowded in the assembly, adorned with cloaks and staves.
> Before them stood a vast whale, voracious and rapacious,   30
> delivering a harangue of squeals and oinks
> in the voice of a scalded pig.

XANTHIAS
> Ugh!

SOSIAS
> What?

XANTHIAS

>Enough! I can smell the stink of boiled pigskin.
>It's as bad as a demagogue's leather shop.

SOSIAS

>And then the whale measured out chunks of lard
>on a pocket scale, conveniently at hand.

XANTHIAS

>How convenient—he means to weigh the lot of us,
>the people and the city, all Athens chopped and rendered.   40

SOSIAS

>And next to the whale, Theorus was seated on the ground,
>with his head become that of a crow.
>Which is when Alcibiades lisped in my ear,
>"Quoth the waven, Theoruth hath the head of a cwow!"

XANTHIAS

>Well lisped, that's Alcibiades to a hair-lip.

SOSIAS

>But isn't this a terrible omen, from man to crow?

XANTHIAS

>It's perfect, it's wonderful.

SOSIAS

>How so?

XANTHIAS

>Why, what could be better than for Theorus
>to grow feathers, take wing, and fly away like a birdie?   50

SOSIAS

>Well done, my friend, a fine interpretation.
>Consider a career in psychiatric divination.

XANTHIAS

But first, let me fill the audience in on our story,
after a few brief disclaimers:
(to audience)

expect little of us, good people.
We possess no grand Megaran hilarity,
no slaves to dispense popcorn or peanuts among you.
Here is no Heracles gone hungry,
no Euripides stuffed and roasted yet again.
Not even grand Cleon shall we take as our target,
that scion of lucky chance and blind fortune.   60
Ours is a small tale, unsubtle, yet meaningful,
no sheer vulgar farce but a comedy of wit.
(points to Bdelycleon)
You see that man asleep on the roof, face to the tiles,
that man is our master. And his father
is our prisoner, our charge shut up within these walls,
our duty to keep him under lock and key.
For this father suffers from a strange disease,
a malady unknown to any of our audience—
unless you'd care to hazard a guess.
(Sosias calls his attention to someone in the audience.)
Ah yes, Amynias, son of Pronapes,   70
guesses he's a gambler, lover of chance, a dice-aholic.

SOSIAS

And who should know better than Amynias?

XANTHIAS

At least you're in the right ballpark;
he does indeed suffer from a maniacal affliction,
though not the one you reckon.
(Again, Sosias picks someone out of the audience.)
Perhaps it's dipsomania, he is an alcoholic,
is that what you whisper to Deryclus, dear Sosias?

SOSIAS
>Of course not. It takes a gentleman to make a drunk.

XANTHIAS *(continuing to interact with the audience)*
>All right then, who's next? Nicostratus of Scambon
>wagers he's a nymphomaniac, a sexaholic,   80
>a lover of boys or strangers, sacrificial candy.

SOSIAS
>Get your mind out of the gutter, Nicostratus!

XANTHIAS
>We're wasting our time with guessing games.
>Keep quiet and let me tell you: old master is a lover
>of legal action, a lawcourt-aholic, a jurophile.
>To serve on the jury is what he lives for,
>to render daily verdicts from a front row seat.
>At night, he lies sleepless, aching to convict,
>or if he should fall to dreaming for an hour
>his soul is drawn like a moth to flame   90
>by the image of the courtroom water-clock.
>His hands are so accustomed to the pebbles of judgment
>that he wakes with fingers clawed and aching,
>like a penitent offering incense to the moon.
>If he should spy some ill-scrawled lovers' graffiti,
>*Beautiful Demus, son of Pyrilamp,*
>he scratches his own: "Beautiful verdict-box."
>Once, when the cock crowed unaccountably at evening,
>he claimed crooked officials had bribed the bird;
>it was a plot to keep him from his duty at dawn!   100
>When dinner is done he cries for his shoes
>and scurries off to the court, sleeping all night
>like a limpet fastened to the doorpost.
>He always convicts; everyone is guilty;
>he condemns with a broad stroke, the long line for all,
>wax beneath his nails like a venomous bee.

He's built a beach at home, never to lack for pebbles.
Frenzied, maniacal, he raves to serve the law.
Thus his son caged him within the house,
when neither words nor reason would contain him.   110
Indeed, it would have tested any son's patience,
the purges and exorcisms, twelve-step programs, to no avail.
When he bought him new clothes, to upgrade his image,
the old man tossed them in the garbage.
When he sent him away to the Krishnas for deprogramming,
the old man burst into court with his tambourine and mantras,
to condemn the guilty for karmic transgressions.
Finally, we crossed the Strait to Aegina,
to take the cure at the shrine of Aesclepius,
but yet again the light of dawn discovered him in court.   120
So much for sensitivity; off came the kid gloves.
Since then we've locked him up, but still he escaped
through the gutters, drains, air vents, light holes,
until we've had to caulk every crack and crevice.
Then he drove pegs into the walls
and rose through the roof like a magpie.
Now we've got the place surrounded,
circled the yard with nets no old crow will ever escape.
Philocleon's his name, the old daredevil.
Bdelycleon's his son, our tempestuous master.   130

BDELYCLEON (*from the roof*)
　　Xanthias, Sosias—sleeping on watch again!

XANTHIAS
　　Uh-oh.

SOSIAS
　　Now what?

XANTHIAS
　　Bdelycleon is up.

BDELYCLEON
>Get up here, quickly, one of you two.
>Father's in the kitchen, probing like a mouse for a hole.
>Careful he doesn't slip out the sink drain.
>And the other keep your shoulder hard against the door.

SOSIAS
>Right away, master.

BDELYCLEON
>Now what in heaven! Something's in the chimney.   140
>You, sir, rumbling the plumbing, who are you?

PHILOCLEON *(head appearing from the chimney)*
>Smoke, smoke, mere smoke escaping.

BDELYCLEON
>Smoke of what wood?

PHILOCLEON
>Fig wood.

BDELYCLEON
>Of course—the most acrid, bitter smoke of all.
>*(pushing Philocleon back down)*
>Back it up in there; I'm looking for the chimney lid.
>Here it is, and here's a log to keep you from lifting it.
>You'll have to come up with something less smoky,
>lest your fat fall in the fire, dear father.

PHILOCLEON
>Hey, boy—move aside!   150

SOSIAS
>He's at the door! He's pushing!

BDELYCLEON
> Push back, weakling, I'm coming down to help.
> Just make sure he doesn't wrench the bolts loose,
> or chew his way through hinge and pin.

PHILOCLEON *(from within the house)*
> Villains! Let me go. I'm due in court.
> I must convict Dracontides, I must!

BDELYCLEON
> Why must you? Who cares?

PHILOCLEON *(at window)*
> I must convict, it is my sacred duty.
> The Gods themselves have willed that I shall wither
> if ever a defendant escape my judgment.   160
> It was the Oracle at Delphi that told me so.

BDELYCLEON
> Apollo protect us from such gibberish.

PHILOCLEON *(tearing at netting)*
> Let me out, let me out, before I explode!

BDELYCLEON
> No, Philocleon. Never, by Poseidon.

PHILOCLEON
> Then, by Zeus, I'll gnaw my way through your nets.

BDELYCLEON
> You've got no teeth, old man.

PHILOCLEON
> Too true! I'm stuck—and how I'd like to stick you.
> Give me a sword, a stick, a legal trick.
> *(Philocleon disappears from window.)*

BDELYCLEON

    Now he's up to something extra wicked.

PHILOCLEON *(from behind stable door)*

    Not at all. My only concern is for the poor old donkey.   170
    Today is the new-moon market, and he's due to be sold.

BDELYCLEON

    Fine, then. I can sell him at market myself.

PHILOCLEON

    I'm the salesman in this family, son.

BDELYCLEON

    Only I'm not buying any. Send out the donkey.

XANTHIAS

    How craftily he's baited his hook; it's a plot to escape.

BDELYCLEON

    This fish isn't biting. I'm wise to his tricks.
    But I'll play along, to see what he's up to.
(Bdelycleon opens stable door and retrieves the donkey; Philocleon clings
to the donkey's belly.)
    Giddyup, donkey, why such grunts and groans?
    What are you crying about? Sad to be sold?
    Or is some new Odysseus dragging you down?   180

SOSIAS

    Yes—there is someone clinging to his belly! It's him!

BDELYCLEON

    Indeed, whoever could it be? Who are you, sir?

PHILOCLEON

    Noman, by Zeus.

BDELYCLEON
>   And where are you from, sir?

PHILOCLEON
>   From Attica, son of Jailbreak. I mean Ithaca.

BDELYCLEON
>   Well, Mr. Noman, the jig is up.
> *(to the slaves)*
>   Get him out from under there.
>   The old ass looks like a summoner's foal.

PHILOCLEON *(falling to ground)*
>   Let me go, or be warned, I'll resort to violence.

BDELYCLEON
>   Violence! Really, father.   190

PHILOCLEON
>   You and that jackass are two peas in a pod.

BDELYCLEON
>   Your treachery leaves a bad taste in my mouth.

PHILOCLEON
>   Wait until you taste the gall of my malice!

BDELYCLEON
>   That's enough—get back in there, you and your donkey.
> *(pushes them back into stable and latches door)*

PHILOCLEON
>   Help me, fellow jurymen! Help me, Cleon!

BDELYCLEON
>   Keep it quiet until we get the door shut.
>   Now pile up rocks to jam it closed,

shoot the bolt, slam the bar, heave the beam,
wedge the mortar stone against the whole shebang.
(Slaves proceed to bar the door. As they work, a tile falls from the roof.)

XANTHIAS
Ouch! A clod has fallen upon my head!   200

BDELYCLEON
A rat must have dislodged it from the roof.

XANTHIAS
No, by Zeus, I smell a crazy juryman,
rooting like a rat in the tiles and rafters.

BDELYCLEON
So now he's transformed into a sparrow to fly the coop!
Where's the casting net to haul him back?
Shoo, shoo, shoo there, shoo!
I swear, it would be easier to guard the whole of Athens
than such a sour and slippery sire.

XANTHIAS
We've got him bottled up now, master.
There's no way he'll get past us.   210
Perhaps it's time to consider a brief respite,
that is, ahem, a wee tiny bit of a nap?

BDELYCLEON
A nap! You fool, any moment they'll be here,
his swarm of colleagues, calling him out.

XANTHIAS
So early, sir? It's barely dawn.

BDELYCLEON
By Zeus, that means they're already late.
The middle of the night is their usual hour

for gallivanting around with lanterns and torches
and the old school songs with which they summon him.

XANTHIAS

Sir, let's drive them away with stones.   220

BDELYCLEON

Stones! Better to smash a hornets' nest!
These bitter old men are a swarm of wasps,
armed at the loins with deadly stings,
a boiling cloud of pricks and fire-sparks.

XANTHIAS

No worries, sir. A handful of stones will do
to chase this wasp nest of jurymen from the door.
*(Bdelycleon and the slaves sit by the door and gradually fall asleep. Enter
                Chorus of Old Men dressed as wasps, with deadly
                stingers protruding from their abdomens. Several
                boys accompany them, including the Chorus
                Leader's son.)*

CHORUS

Keep up, tired Komias, comrade faded
as ancient leather; Charinades outpaces you.
Hail Strymodore of Conthyle, strong as ever.
But where has Euergides gone, and Chabes of Phyla?   230
You see before you all that remain of the wild hive
that once stood watch upon the walls of Byzantium,
valiant and hungry as young soldiers are—
remember the baker's girl whose trays we stole
and split for firewood to cook our simple rations?
Buzz and march, march and buzz,
behold the swarm of righteousness!
We come to convict, we come to judge!
We come to sting, to march, to buzz!
Now we advance as one for the courtroom,   240
to try rich Laches, to punish his crimes,

for Cleon has called us to close ranks and come
with rations of anger and vindictive scorn.
Beware our venom, beware the swarm!
Come now, old comrades, cast bright the lanterns
to light our way among paths of stone.

CHORUS LEADER'S SON
Father, father, watch out for the mud!

CHORUS LEADER
Turn up the lamp. Trim the wick, you clod.

SON
I'll trim it with my finger, father.

CHORUS LEADER
Careless and wasteful, you ungrateful cur.   250
The price of oil is through the roof,
but you don't feel the pinch if it's my money spent.

SON
I've felt the pinch of your clubs and blows!
Try it again and I'm gone, with the lamp,
and you can flounder in the dark like a mud-mired duck.

CHORUS LEADER
I've beaten better men than you, my boy.
By Zeus, this is more muck than mud in which I'm stuck.
The gods will bring fresh rain in four days or less;
the crops are dry, the north wind will dampen them.
All this is foretold in the mold upon my lamp.   260
But where is our friend, our fellow juryman?
Why is he so late to join us this morning,
he in whom the passion to convict runs so high,
first among us to sing the old tunes of Phrynichus?
Come, comrades, let us gather and sing to him,
call him forth with a serenade to gladden the heart.

CHORUS *(sing)*

> Where is our friend? Why is his house dark?
> Has he lost his shoes, has he lost the spark?
> Has he stubbed his toe, is he lamed by a tumor?
> Is his dedication no more than a rumor?   270
> Banish the thought! Old Philocleon's
> a genuine mean one,
> and many's the criminal he has taught
> not to pray for forgiveness or try to atone
> to a man with a heart as cold as a stone.
>
> Is it yesterday's case that plagues our old friend?
> A rare vote of acquittal, unjustified end
> for a man who pretends to serve Athens as friend?
> Indeed we were tricked,
> and it cuts to the quick,   280
> but today we will try an undoubted spy
> from Thrace, of all places, and he's rich to the hilt,
> so let's vote for his guilt—
> come out, old friend, and watch him fry!
> Forward, boy. Move on!

SON

> Father, would you grant a small favor, a trifle?

CHORUS LEADER

> Certainly, son. What is it you fancy?
> Knucklebones, pinwheels, a handful of candy?

SON

> Figs, father. I'd like some figs.

CHORUS LEADER

> Figs! Fat chance! I'd sooner see you hanged   290
> for your insolence and ingratitude.
> Is it not enough I clothe you and feed you
> on my poor pay, but now you must have figs, too?

SON

>The only pay you've got is from the courthouse, father,
>and what if the Archon said there'd be no trial today?
>How would you feed us in those bitter straits?

CHORUS LEADER

>"Straits of Helle," indeed.
>We'd starve I suppose, or beg our bread.

SON

>Oh mother, why did you bear me
>to such a world of hellish toil?   300

CHORUS LEADER

>Spare me! The cupboard's empty of sympathy, too.

SON

>Woe, woe betide me. Suffering is my fate,
>and my little shopping bag a waste of space.

PHILOCLEON *(appearing at upper window)*

>Friends, I hear you, I appreciate the song,
>but my time of confinement endures far too long.
>Unsung, heart-broken with grief,
>I yearn to march and sow mischief
>beside you. Alas! Loud-thundering Zeus,
>send a bolt from the blue to reduce me to ash,
>pickle or smoke me, transmute me to stone,   310
>better such fate than to molder at home.

CHORUS LEADER

>Who is it imprisons you, friend Philocleon?
>Talk freely, to us who are your comrades.

PHILOCLEON

>My own son so treats me—but hush,
>let us speak softly, he sleeps by the door.

CHORUS LEADER
What pretense can he make to imprison his father,
or is this another jest, to idle or bemuse us?

PHILOCLEON
He means to keep me in complacent captivity,
well-fed but starved for the courthouse and the jury!

CHORUS
Like a tailhook he gaffs you   320
to stifle your outcry
against the scandals
that buffet and baffle
the lords of the navy.
Beware the insubmersible subversive!

It's time for you to make your escape.
Find a way to skip clear and join the swarm.

PHILOCLEON
Anything, anyway, help me to work it, old friends.
I long to stroll free, and confer, and convict.

CHORUS LEADER
A tunnel, or a loose brick, like wily Odysseus   330
you might crawl to freedom in wild rags.

PHILOCLEON
No chance. Not a hole, not a cranny, not a chink.
These walls would drive a flea to drink.
We need to come up with something better.

CHORUS LEADER
Years ago, in Naxos, you stole the skewers
right out of the fire, and drove them in the wall,
and made your way down on a hot-footed ladder.

PHILOCLEON

    Yes, once upon a time, in the glory of youth,
    I was spry as a thief, unwatched, unafraid.
    Look at me now, comrades, under lock and key,   340
    every door guarded, every way barred,
    the barbequers standing ready to skewer me
    like the cat that stole the golden canary.

CHORUS

    Nonetheless, its time to get moving.
    The moon is down. It's morning.

PHILOCLEON

    Then there's nothing left but to chew my way out.
    Forgive me, Dictynna, for the nets I destroy.
(Philocleon chews and tears the nets apart.)

CHORUS

    Spoken like a man with a plan and a will and a way.
    Chew, chew—for night gives way to day.

PHILOCLEON

    Success. I've gnawed them to shreds.   350
    Quiet now, for Bdelycleon still sleeps.

CHORUS

    Fear not, old friend.
    If he wakes we'll teach him
    to make his amends
    while he runs for his life
    from the gods he offends
    and his fear that the sting
    of the swarm may yet reach him.

    Cast a rope from the window and climb down,
    put your faith in the gods to sustain you.   360

PHILOCLEON

    But what if I'm caught, like a spider, a-dangle?
    What web will you weave to relieve me then?

CHORUS

    Stronger than oak, more supple than silk,
    our spirit will free you from walls and enemies.

PHILOCLEON *(lowering rope)*

    All right, I believe you. But promise, if I should perish,
    to bury my heart on the courthouse lawn.

CHORUS

    Have no fear. Pray to the gods,
    and the strength of your rope.

PHILOCLEON

    Good Lycus, whose shrine stands next to the courts,
    who hears the cries and tears of the defendants,   370
    who loves that wail and woe as I do,
    kindred spirit, have pity upon me and help me now,
    and never again will I squat to relieve myself
    in the cool shade, upon the mats of your temple.
(Philocleon begins to climb down the rope. Bdelycleon wakes up.)

BDELYCLEON *(to slaves)*

    Hey, wake up, wake up.

XANTHIAS

    Yes—I'm up! What's happening?

BDELYCLEON

    Voices! Could the old bird be on the wing again?

XANTHIAS

    There he is—descending the wall on a rope.

BDELYCLEON

You old reprobate, what mad scheme is this?
Xanthias, climb to the roof and find the harvest wreath   380
and strike him about the head with that branch.
We'll see if he returns, unplucked, to the limb.

PHILOCLEON

Help! Help! Lawyers, claimants, prosecutors all!
Smicythion, Teisiades, Chremon, Pheredeipnos!
He means to shut me back in the house,
and then how shall I help to turn the wheel of justice!
(Philocleon reaches the ground and is seized by Bdelycleon.)

CHORUS

Now march, now buzz, now sting we must!
Let the swarm leave the hive
with deadly resolve,
stingers to the left of us,   390
stingers to the right of us,
to punish one who would dare to detain us.
Boys, take our cloaks and flee to sound warning.
Let Cleon himself come and defend us
from one who would defile
all of Athens,
fit for death for daring to deign to
keep us from serving as jury at trial!
(Boys run off stage.)

BDELYCLEON

Listen, friends, hear my side and calm your outrage.

CHORUS

We'll buzz and shout to waken Zeus!   400

BDELYCLEON

But I shall not release him.

CHORUS
>Tyranny! Behold the face of tyranny!
>O my beloved city! O my godforsaken Theorus,
>O fawning leaders, O toadying demagogues!

XANTHIAS
>Master, by Heracles—they're armed with stingers!

BDELYCLEON
>The same with which they slew Philippus,
>son of Gorgias, tried and convicted.

CHORUS
>Now you shall know the venom of the swarm,
>the taste of our weapons, the sting
>we wield as one in battle, formed for the attack,   410
>wheeling and circling, circling and wheeling.

XANTHIAS
>May this battle be a dream or folly.
>The mere sight of their stingers brings me to my knees.

CHORUS
>Let him go! Free our comrade!
>Or soon enough you'll wish
>to have been born a hard-shelled turtle!

PHILOCLEON
>Onward, my waspy companions!
>Press the attack, front and back,
>eyes and fingers and assholes,
>sting them where it hurts!   420

BDELYCLEON
>Midas, Phryx! Masyntias! Battle stations, all!
>Hold the old man and let no one release him,

lest you enjoy the taste of chains and shackles.
Their buzzing scares me less than rustling fig leaves.
(*Servants appear and seize Philocleon; Bdelycleon dashes into house with*
Xanthias and Sosias.)

CHORUS
How scared will you be when we plunge
our stingers into your tender flesh?

PHILOCLEON
Mighty Cecrops, Hero of Athens,
dragon-willed, dragon-endowed,
save me from these barbarian slaves
whose grip is fierce as iron!   430
What ingratitude toward a master
who never beat them more than once a day!

CHORUS
Such indeed are the injustices of age, dear comrade.
See these two slaves manhandling their loving master,
what now do they remember of the clothes
he bought them, sturdy jackets and fit caps?
And the good boots he brought in mid-winter,
to save their toes from frostbite? Their cold eyes
reflect no respect for the gift of shoes, freely given.

PHILOCLEON
Won't you listen to reason, miserable creatures!   440
When I caught you stealing grapes—remember
how I whipped you, tied to the olive tree, like real men,
hard enough to make all the other slaves grow
green with envy. And this is the thanks I get!
Now let me go, quick, before my son returns.

CHORUS
> Soon enough, you two, retribution will be at hand.
> Soon enough you'll know our passionate vengeance,
> feel the wrath of the just and terrible swarm.
> *(Bdelycleon returns from the house with Xanthias and Sosias bearing*
> *sticks and smoke-makers.)*

BDELYCLEON
> Hit them, Xanthias. Drive these wasps from the door!

XANTHIAS
> Trying to, sir. I'm trying . . .   450

BDELYCLEON
> And you, Sosias, give them a blast of smoke.

XANTHIAS
> Shoo there! Be gone! Get lost! Vamoose!

BDELYCLEON
> Hit them again, Xanthias. More smoke!
> We want a stench as bad as Aeschines the windbag.

XANTHIAS
> See—they're retreating. I knew we'd drive them off.

BDELYCLEON
> Yes, but it wouldn't have been this easy
> if they'd been in tune with the songs of Philocles.

CHORUS
> Now is the truth laid bare!
> Now must the common people see
> this imperious tyranny.   460
> Beware, beware!

To bar us from the court
denies our civil right to judge uncivil wrongs.
Subversive youth, ill-kempt and uncouth,
your arguments betray your secret
wish to serve as autocrat!

BDELYCLEON

Friends, let's discuss this as men of reason,
lay down our arms and our talk of treason.

CHORUS

Discuss—with you, an enemy of the people,
hater of democracy, friend of Brasidas   470
and his traitorous, scraggly-haired monarchists?

BDELYCLEON

Lord knows I should relent.
Easier to give up the old man to these buzzards
than endure a daily dose of their waspishness.

CHORUS

This buzz is the merest hint of our anger—
we have not yet begun to wax waspish.
(Though we can parry puns till the cows come home.)
Just wait till the prosecutor indicts you for sedition.

BDELYCLEON

By all the gods, enough is enough.

CHORUS

Never! We shall not rest   480
until you're denounced as a tyrannist!

BDELYCLEON

A conspiracy of tyrannists—so you call it!
Whatever the occasion, it's all the same to you,

tyranny here and tyranny there.
You're fifty years out of date, with all the currency
of the marketplace: if sardines won't sell,
the fish-seller shouts conspiracy!
If his tuna has no takers it's due to the lovers of tyranny!
If I purchased a single onion they'd shout me down
as a teary-eyed conspirator—a tyrannist of garnishes!   490

XANTHIAS
    Even the whores are into it! At noon I attempted
    to play a game of horsy, but she
    accused me of endorsing the Hippiatic tyranny!

BDELYCLEON
    Such is our litigious society!
    They love to traffic in wild accusations.
    All I want is to help my poor old father
    give up his mind-troubling, dawn-wandering,
    legalistic lifestyle, to help him live
    like a privileged gentleman, like Morychus,
    and for this they denounce and slander me.   500

PHILOCLEON
    That's right, by Zeus, and you deserve it!
    Eels, smoked fish, the milk of doves and pigeons—
    keep all your precious gentleman's victuals.
    Feed me lawsuits al dente every day,
    and for dessert—a simple tort.

BDELYCLEON
    Your chosen diet, how typical.
    But now's the time to listen, father,
    for I can persuade you of the error of your ways.

PHILOCLEON
    Erroneous—to be a juror?

BDELYCLEON

> Erroneous to say the least.   510
> Don't you realize you've been played for a fool?
> That those you worship mock you?
> That you are a slave in your ignorance?

PHILOCLEON

> Slave! You've gone blind, son.
> I hold the whip in this world.

BDELYCLEON

> So you believe, but the facts betray you.
> You're all for Athens, all for the system,
> but tell us, what good has it done you?

PHILOCLEON

> Good question—and I'll answer.
> *(turning to chorus)*
> Let's turn to these jurors to judge my reply.   520

BDELYCLEON

> Very well—release him.

PHILOCLEON

> Hand me my sword—if I lose the debate
> I'll fall upon it in noble fashion.

BDELYCLEON

> And what if you refuse to accept their verdict?

PHILOCLEON

> Then may I never raise a glass again
> to toast the happiness of the well-paid jurist!

CHORUS

> Now we turn to you as our champion,
> speak well and with novelty,
> seek to enlighten—

BDELYCLEON
>Bring me my notebook, my briefcase, a quill.   530
>Now what was that you were saying—
>enlighten whom, and as to what?

CHORUS
>Enlighten the gloom with your arguments,
>as to whom is the better, the senior and wisest.
>All of us depend upon you, so much is at stake,
>you must defeat this impetuous snake.

BDELYCLEON
>That's right—I slither and hiss!
>And I'm taking notes so nothing goes amiss.

PHILOCLEON *(speaking to the chorus)*
>But what if he should win—please finish your thought.

CHORUS
>Then we fear our race is run.   540
>Fit to bear branches in the olive parade,
>husks of affidavits, empty, undone,
>broken-down horses sent out to pasture.

>So be brave and apply your tongue, old comrade,
>take up the cause of our sovereignty with eloquence.

PHILOCLEON *(pacing back and forth like a trial lawyer)*
>Before they can pasture us, they'll have to master us,
>and I intend to burst from the gate like a bolt
>to demonstrate the power we wield is greater than any other.
>For who could be happier than an Athenian juror?
>Who is more magnificent, more fawned upon, more fine?   550
>Though old and bent, even the strongest of men salute us
>as we trudge to the courthouse in bedroom slippers,
>trembling and pleading "mercy, oh mercy upon me, good jurors,
>have you never yourselves taken kickbacks from a contractor,

have you never put your hand into the till?"
This as he greases my palm with embezzled bills!
His was a face all too familiar from his last corruption case.

BDELYCLEON

Go slowly please, I'm taking this all down:
"criminals begging mercy on the courthouse lawn . . ."

PHILOCLEON

Once their begging is done, and my temper more cheerful,   560
I enter the courthouse and betray at once any promises I've made
to consider special pleading or bribery or what not.
I listen to the speeches of desperate men begging acquittal,
drink in their flattery, their protestations of poverty,
their tragic tales of woe so reminiscent of my own hard lot.
Some tell jokes and stories, some seek to sell Aesopean fables.
And when all else fails they bring in the teary-eyed children,
bleating like sheep, while the father begs as to Zeus himself—
"If you delight in the voice of the lamb, have pity on my son;
if it's pigs you prefer, be swayed by the sound of my daughter."   570
Which lowers my anger the tiniest bit. Such is our power:
the rich are brought before us and cast down for an hour.

BDELYCLEON

All right, second point duly noted: "rich get their
                    comeuppance."
Now, could you clarify your remarks on ruling all of Greece?
What does your power consist of, and what good does it do you?

PHILOCLEON

For one thing, we inspect all the young men when they register.
And if the great actor Oeagrus were to appear before us,
we wouldn't acquit him until he'd recited his speech from *Niobe*.
Or if it were a musician, he'd play a fine recessional
on the pipes in our honor as price of his acquittal.   580
Or let's say a loving father passed away, and bequeathed

his only daughter and heiress to a friend of the family,
frankly, we'd toss out the will with all its lovely waxen seals
and give the girl to whomever groveled most compellingly.
How many of our public officials dare to act so arbitrarily?
Alone in all of Athens we suffer no accountability!

BDELYCLEON

Here at last you make a telling point.
Though stripping this girl of her rights, and all else,
seems a bit devious, even for you.

PHILOCLEON

But that's not the end of it! Whenever the council or assembly   590
balk at a major case it comes down to our court by decree.
That's our chance to laugh at the lies Euathlus tells,
and Colaconymus, the cowardly oaf, proclaiming his loyalty
"to the common man and the Athenian people!"
And what chance does any motion stand to carry the assembly
unless it grant us a pork-barrel adjournment for the day?
Even Cleon the lordly loudmouth exempts us from his
                harangues.
More than that—he protects us, he shoos the pestering flies
                away!
I've never seen you so vigilant about your father's well-being!
Even Theorus, grand as Euphemius, if he does say so himself,   600
even mighty Theorus stoops to sponge and polish our shoes.
Such are the perks from which you seek to keep me!
Such the dominion you dismiss as bondage and slavery!

BDELYCLEON

That's right, get it all out. You believe yourself a prize pink pig,
but when I've had my say you'll see you've been wallowing
                in shit.

PHILOCLEON

I'd almost forgotten the best perk of all! Money!
When I come home with my jury-pay, everyone rushes to
                greet me.

My darling daughter washes my feet, rubs them with oil,
covers me with kisses, and weasels some cash with her tongue.
Then it's the wife's turn to wheedle and pamper me,   610
setting out the pastries as she sits down beside me:
"Try some of this, dear. Enjoy some of that, honey."
I love it! And I'm no longer dependent on you for my dinner,
you and your uppity servant, mumbling and cursing me.
If he won't fetch me a stale crust to snack on I've got my own
          "bread."
(jingles a bag of loose change)
And if that ass won't give me wine, I've got my little donkey!
(pulls out a donkey-shaped drinking vessel)
Always full, just a tip and he pours—watch him bray
at your cup and deliver a warlike fart in your face.
Isn't this splendid, the power of the purse,
power to rival the great god Zeus.   620
They speak of us both in similar tones:
"Good lord and by Zeus, how loudly
the court thunders and groans."
Like Zeus I carry myself nobly and proudly;
the rich turn pale as my lightning flashes,
they tremble in fear, and you fear me, too!
But by Demeter I'll be thrashed
if I was ever afraid of you!
(Philocleon points at Bdelycleon. He indicates his speech is over and
               receives congratulations from the chorus.)

CHORUS
Never have I heard such argumentation,
so forceful a plea, such rhetorical grace!   630

PHILOCLEON
Yes, yes, he thought to pluck poor undefended fruit,
but my eloquence renders his argument moot.

CHORUS

    Eloquent, omnivorous, your argument
    ate every grape on the vine!
    I swelled with pride at our glory,
    basked in its glow, yours and mine;
    felt, for a moment, transported with bliss
    as if to the Isles of the Blest.

PHILOCLEON

    He's scared, he's whipped, he's down.
    His tail's between his legs like a beaten hound.   640

CHORUS

    Now it's up to you, young man,
    to wriggle off the hook if you can.
    But our anger is sharp
    as a sword against your kind.
    Not even a grindstone would temper its blade
    if the spin of your argument whets our bad mood.

BDELYCLEON *(speaking in formal tones)*

    Indeed, my task will be difficult, you and I both know it—
    much too difficult for your average comic poet!—
    to cure the city of a disease ingrained by age.
    O Zeus, father of mine, son of Cronus . . .   650

PHILOCLEON

    Spare us the "father of mine" garbage!
    Get straight to the point, or I'll kill you myself
    and to hell with the consequences.

BDELYCLEON *(pacing in his turn)*

    Very well, Daddy dearest, stop glowering and help me figure
    some financial data—just count on your fingers,
    forget the smallest fractions and approximate the digits.

Let's compute the sum of Athenian wealth, its total yearly take—
the tribute paid by our allies, the sales tax, the percentage taxes,
court fees, mining revenues, rents and confiscations.
A tidy little income. Shall we say two thousand talents a year?   660
And how much of this wealth finds its way to you jurors,
the six thousand of you—"verily, not yet doth there dwell any
                    more,"
as someone or other once said. One hundred and fifty talents,
if my reckoning is right. Feel free to check my calculations.

PHILOCLEON
But that's less than a tenth of the total we tallied!

BDELYCLEON
Exactly my point.

PHILOCLEON
Where the hell does the rest of it go?

BDELYCLEON
To the politicians! "I seek only to serve the people of Athens,
I'd give my right arm for the rabble I represent."
These are the crooks you vote into power, father,   670
with their spin doctors and slogans and vacuous speeches.
Some of them have barely sworn the oath of office
before they're lining their pockets at fifty talents a pop,
extorting and intimidating the allies and subject realms
with the threat of Athenian might! "Fork it over or we'll
                    squash you
with the weight of our military pre-industrial state."
And there you are, father, dining on the crumbs of empire,
while the allies watch you starving and write you off as patsies
and funnel the loot to that bunch of bureaucratic leeches,
heaping them with wine and cheese, vats of honey and
                    sesame oil,   680
rugs, pillows, goblets, necklaces, health and wealth and pelf.

While you, father, who claim to rule o'er land and sea,
subsist on the spoils of poverty, without so much as a clove of
         garlic
in token of esteem from your loving subjects.

PHILOCLEON

By god, you're right. I bought three heads of garlic
from Eucharides' stand myself the other day!
But you're tiring me out with these minor points—
where is your proof that I've been living in slavery?

BDELYCLEON

What else can we call it but slavery, when the government
lives high on the hog while the people squeal like piglets?   690
They've feathered their nests with goose down,
and you pigeons are content with the small change they toss you,
though you've earned that money with years of service to Athens,
as young men, battling and besieging for the good of the state.
And you're so grateful to them, father, it's nauseating
how you grovel when one of those mincing primadonnas
gives you orders—like the son of Chaireas, prancing and
         wiggling
his divine little ass like an eel or a cheap whore getting laid:
"Don't be late for court or you don't get paid!"
He arrives whenever he likes, of course, keeps his legal fees.   700
Lawyers! They're all in cahoots. They split the bribes
and make the trial look good, back and forth, back and forth
like two men on a saw, stacking legalistic lumber.
And you jurors sit there with your mouths hanging open,
baffled, clueless to the ways you've been played.

PHILOCLEON

Truly? Is that how they do it?
(*tragically*)

Alas, this shakes me to the depths of my soul,
to the bedrock of my being—
I fear I've begun to see your point!

BDELYCLEON

> Good—and now imagine how rich we all might be   710
> if the fatcats and demagogues didn't keep us down!
> Consider that our empire runs from Italy to the Black Sea,
> and what do you get out of it? Jury pay! Three obols a day!
> Even that doled out coin by coin, drop by drop,
> just enough to sustain you, oil dripped from a laden swab.
> They mean to keep you poor! They want you lean and hungry!
> Because the starving dog does best his master's bidding!
> They point their hand in war, and away the armies fly.
> It would be so easy to feed the people well, to spread the wealth.
> A thousand cities pay tribute to Athens at this hour.   720
> If each of them were allotted twenty Athenians to support
> we'd have twenty thousand citizens dining on haute cuisine,
> caviar and cream puffs, with garlands of daisies in their hair.
> This is our birthright, an entitlement of the victory at Marathon.
> Yet we subsist like olive-pickers, begging favor from our masters.

PHILOCLEON

> I'm dumb-struck. I'm numb-struck!
> The sword falls from my unfeeling hand.

BDELYCLEON

> And when the masters begin to fear for their safety,
> they promise all of Euboea as a prize for the people,
> and fifty bushels of wheat per man. But they never deliver!   730
> What did you end up with—barley! Five bushels of it,
> parceled grain by grain only to those with the right papers,
> the proper forms filled out in triplicate.
>
> This is why I keep you under lock and key;
> to care for you in such estate
> as you deserve, so much finer
> than the windbags of our government. Please,
> father, name your desire
> and you shall have it,
> excepting only the entitled milk of the state.   740

CHORUS

    Wise was the man—or wasp—who said:
    don't judge the debate until both sides have spoken.
    Victory is yours, what else could be our verdict?
    We lay down our staves, our angry will is broken.
    O comrade, dear friend, hear us now!

    Trust in the words of your son;
    surrender your stubbornness.
    What luck if the rest of us had one
    like him to guide and govern us.
    Through him some god   750
    has spoken, in this your hour of need.
    Now is the time to pay him heed.

BDELYCLEON

    And I will provide what an old man requires;
    gruel, and a good coat, and a soft blanket,
    and a warm young maiden to soothe and massage
    and keep his circulation up. But—he's drawn a blank . . .
    He says nothing . . . This cannot augur well . . .

CHORUS

    His conscience has been stricken.
    At last he realizes the error of his ways,
    frenzied nights and wasted days   760
    when he refused to listen.
    He's not too bright,
    but he's seen the light at last.
    He bids farewell to his foolish past.

PHILOCLEON

    Woe is me! oh, woe is me!

BDELYCLEON

    What's the problem, father?

PHILOCLEON

> Can't you see—I don't want your gruel and overcoats!
> It's *those* I love, it's *there* I want to be,
> at the courthouse where the herald cries, "All rise!
> All jurors, cast your votes in the ballot-urn."   770
> Oh, to be the final voter, to feel the pebble of judgment turn
> at the touch of my fingers. By my soul I declare—
> where has she wandered to, my soul?—but never mind.
> No more. From now on, I'd turn Cleon himself loose,
> if he stood before me charged with theft, by Zeus.

BDELYCLEON

> Father, by the gods, trust me and give in.

PHILOCLEON

> I'll give in. I'll do anything you say.
> I'll surrender it all—except one thing.

BDELYCLEON

> Which would be what?

PHILOCLEON

> The courthouse! I'll die before I give it up,   780
> and Hades himself can render the verdict.

BDELYCLEON

> All right, father. It's clear how much you love it.
> But why trudge down to the court every day,
> when you could stay home and try some cases here,
> sit in judgment over the household slaves?

PHILOCLEON

> The slaves? You're crazy. What would I judge?

BDELYCLEON

> Judge wrongdoing, just as you always have.
> Suppose the servant girl has left the house without permission?

Fine her, as you would in court. Or you might impose
whatever sentence you saw fit, in the privacy of your chambers.   790
How is this different from what you've been doing?
And here, on a nice warm day, you'll hold court in the sun;
in the snow, by fireside; in the rain, snug within your home.
You'll start at noon, if you feel like sleeping late,
and no bailiff will admonish you or slam the courthouse gate.

PHILOCLEON

I admit, that doesn't sound all bad . . .

BDELYCLEON

And no more starving for a snack
while pompous lawyers rattle on and on.

PHILOCLEON

How can I perform my duties with my mouth
full of food? I'm a professional, you know.   800

BDELYCLEON

But the true professional always chews over the facts,
and takes time to digest a case before deciding.

PHILOCLEON

All right! You've convinced me!
But you've left out the most important detail.
Where do I collect my money on payday?

BDELYCLEON

I'll pay you, of course.

PHILOCLEON

Perfect! No more quibbling over cashed checks.
That joker Lysistratus played quite a trick on me
after court the other day. He took our obol
off to the fish seller to get it changed. Coming back,   810
he slaps down three shiny fish scales as my share,

and I pop them in my mouth thinking they were coins.
Disgusting! I spit them out and socked him one.

BDELYCLEON

What did he have to say for himself?

PHILOCLEON

He said, "You've got the gizzard of a rooster,
and you'll digest them soon enough!"

BDELYCLEON

All the more reason to stay home.

PHILOCLEON

Yes, I see it now. Go ahead and get the place ready.

BDELYCLEON

Wait here, father, while I gather what we need.
(Exit Bdelycleon.)

PHILOCLEON

It's like a miracle—the oracles are coming true!   820
For years they've said that one day Athenians
would hear cases in their own homes,
every man with a private courthouse on his porch,
like those tacky backyard shrines people build to Hecate.
(Bdelycleon returns with props to set up "court room.")

BDELYCLEON

Here I am, and look what I've come up with!
The whole kit and caboodle and plenty besides.
See, even a bedpan; we'll hang it up right here
so you don't even have to stop the proceedings to pee.

PHILOCLEON

Brilliant! Just the thing
for an old man with bladder problems!   830

BDELYCLEON

    And here are warm stones from the hearth,
    and some lentil soup to heat up when you're hungry.

PHILOCLEON

    Another fine stroke! Even when I'm sick with the flu
    I can drink down my soup and still get paid.
    But why have you brought this rooster with you?

BDELYCLEON

    In case the defendant's testimony should grow tiresome,
    the cock can crow to keep you awake.

PHILOCLEON

    This is truly marvelous, a wonderful set-up.
    There's only one thing missing . . .

BDELYCLEON

    What's that?   840

PHILOCLEON

    If only we could fashion a shrine to our patron, Lycus.

BDELYCLEON *(contriving a statue that lacks a comic phallus)*
    Uh-huh . . . Here he is, the great hero himself!

PHILOCLEON

    O my patron, my master, good Lycus—
    but you seem to be missing a little something!

BDELYCLEON

    Yes, he looks suspiciously like that coward Cleonymus to me!

PHILOCLEON

    Indeed—a hero who's tossed his weapon aside!

BDELYCLEON

All right then, father. Sit down
and let's proceed to the first case.

PHILOCLEON

I've been ready for hours—let's go.

BDELYCLEON

Now, who will our first victim—   850
I mean our first defendant—be?
What's happened in the house lately?
Didn't Thraetta burn one of the pots yesterday?

PHILOCLEON

Stop! What are you trying to pull here?
What kind of trial can we have without a bar,
the foremost and holiest object of the courthouse!

BDELYCLEON

By Zeus, we haven't got one!

PHILOCLEON

Never fear—I'll be back with one in a second!
(Exit Philocleon.)

BDELYCLEON

Amazing what's come over him!
His love for the courthouse has no limits.   860
(Enter Xanthias.)

XANTHIAS

Damn that mutt to hell! We should put that cur to sleep!

BDELYCLEON

What's the problem now?

XANTHIAS

It's your dog, Labes. He's been skulking around the kitchen,
and now he's eaten the entire wheel of Sicilian cheese.

BDELYCLEON

Excellent! A perfect crime for my father to prosecute!
Of course you'll have to testify, swear out an affidavit.

XANTHIAS

But, I don't think I can, that is—the other dog
said that he intended to press charges!

BDELYCLEON

I see—then bring both dogs here at once.

XANTHIAS

Yes, sir!   870
(Exit Xanthias. Enter Philocleon, dragging a large cage full of pigs.)

BDELYCLEON

And *what* is *this*?

PHILOCLEON

The pig-pen from hearth side. Its railings are perfect.

BDELYCLEON

But it must be a sacrilege against Hestia?

PHILOCLEON

No. It just goes to show that a man's home is his castle,
and home is where the hearth is,
and if you want to hit them where it hurts
hit them from the hearth. So let's get to it. First case!

BDELYCLEON

Right. I'll just collect the notices and list of indictments.

PHILOCLEON
>Delays upon delays. You'll bore me to tears.
>I'm ready to plow the wax and harrow the guilty.   880

BDELYCLEON
>Voilà! . . .

PHILOCLEON
>Proceed . . .

BDELYCLEON
>Indeed . . .

PHILOCLEON
>. . . to name the first defendant!

BDELYCLEON
>Damn! Forgot to bring the voting urns!

PHILOCLEON
>Where are you off to again?

BDELYCLEON
>To get the urns.

PHILOCLEON
>Then take a seat. I've got it covered.
>Why else have I kept these old jugs at my side?

BDELYCLEON
>Bravo! I can't think of anything else we lack,   890
>except, of course, the famous waterclock.

PHILOCLEON (*pointing to the bedpan*)
>And what would you call this? A species of waterclock, no?

BDELYCLEON

Marvelous! Ingenious! You're a true Athenian, father.
Now let's call for the fire and incense and myrtle,
to offer a prayer in supplication to the gods.

CHORUS

We raise a prayer for you,
an auspicious dedication
of your new communication,
an end to quarreling between you.

BDELYCLEON

Let there now be silence.   900

CHORUS

O Phoebus Apollo, Pythian one,
let this scheme succeed here in this yard,
bringing fortune upon us, and rest
for those who have labored long and hard.

Hail, Paean, the Healing Apollo! Io Paean!

BDELYCLEON

O Lord Apollo, neighbor, lord of the streets, god at my gate,
grant us your benediction and shine upon my father,
suffer him to soften, bank the fires of his rage,
sweeten with wild honey the sour wine of his heart.
Let him look with compassion upon his fellow man,   910
let him pity the suffering of the defendants,
let him weep at their pleadings,
let him sheathe the sting of his judiciary art.

CHORUS

Well said. We join you in your prayer,
and sing along in hopeful celebration.
This youth deserves our adoration,

for the love he bears the people,
unique in our experience
of those in his jaded generation.
(Enter Xanthias with Labes, a dog, and Cyon, an actor dressed as a dog.)

BDELYCLEON
Any and all jurors, come forward now!   920
There will be no late seating once the show has begun.

PHILOCLEON
Where's the first defendant! I'm ready to convict!

BDELYCLEON
Attention!
(reading the indictment)
              Whereby it is charged
by the dog of the first part, Cyon of Cydathenaion,
that the dog of the second part, Labes,
did steal and eat the Sicilian cheese without sharing one bite!
Whereby the audience is reminded that any similarities
between the dogs of the first and second parts
and our glorious Athenian leaders, living or dead,
and any allegorical implications therein, are entirely
              coincidental.   930
Whereby it is urged that the penalty for this crime
should be a fig-wood collar to be worn by the defendant.

PHILOCLEON
I say death—a dog's death to the guilty!

BDELYCLEON
Here stands the accused, Labes.

PHILOCLEON
The thief! Guilt is written all over his face!
That little smirk and smile act doesn't fool me.
Now where's the plaintiff, the dog from Cydathenaion?

CYON
>   Woof!

BDELYCLEON
>   Uh . . . present.

PHILOCLEON
>   Lord, he looks as bad as the other one,   940
>   barely fit for licking out the cooking pots.

BDELYCLEON *(to Labes)*
>   Shush! Sit!
(to Cyon)
>>   Stand and make your case.

PHILOCLEON
>   Proceed. And I'll enjoy a nice bowl of soup while I listen.

CYON
>   Men of the court, you've heard the charge I bring
>   against this dog. His crimes are most heinous,
>   committed against me and my fellow sailors of the fleet.
>   He stole the great wheel of Sicilian cheese,
>   and gobbled it down by himself in a dark corner . . .

PHILOCLEON
>   Guilty! He's just belched a whiff of cheese
>   right at me, the guilty devil!   950
>   You must do something about that halitosis, Labes!

CYON
>   . . . nor would he share the least scrap, even when I begged!
>   Sirs, how can you expect to be cared for properly,
>   when I, your faithful dog, don't get my share of the scraps?

PHILOCLEON

And he didn't share any with me, either, his countryman.
The fellow's a hot felon—hot as this soup!

BDELYCLEON

Father, by the gods, you're convicting the poor dog
before you've even heard his side of the story.

PHILOCLEON

The case is as plain as your face. He's guilty.

CYON

Yes, yes, you must convict him and send him away for good!   960
He's scarfed every crumb! He's the greediest dog of them all!
Why, if it were the whole of Sicily itself he had before him,
and he the very admiral of our great Athenian fleet,
I wager he'd plunder every city on the island
and share not a bit of the loot from that boot with his betters!

PHILOCLEON

There's not even a penny left to mend my pitchers!

CYON

He must be punished! Remember: one pantry's not big enough
for two dogs; one bush won't hide two thieves!
If I don't get my share of the spoils, why, I might stop barking
when I hear footsteps, or bark all night for no reason.   970

PHILOCLEON

Wow! The charges against him are grave, indeed!
He's a born thief, obviously. Old rooster, what do you think?
By god, he winked! Even the birds find him guilty!
Excuse me—bailiff—hey, someone, hand me the bedpan!

BDELYCLEON

Take it down yourself, father. I've got to call the witnesses.
Witnesses for the defense, please stand and be recognized:

the Cup, the Pestle, the Cheese-grater, the Fireplace, the Pot,
and all the other fire-blacked resident utensils.
*(Bdelycleon places the articles on the bar. Philocleon stands and urinates
in the bedpan.)*
Father! Goodness, finish your business and be seated.

PHILOCLEON
I'll give him the business, soon enough!   980

BDELYCLEON
Your bark is as mean as your bite, father.
Don't you ever take it easy on a poor old defendant?
(Xanthias leads Labes forward.)
Step forward, and make your defense.
Come now, say something.

PHILOCLEON
Ha! He's speechless! He can offer no defense!

BDELYCLEON
No, I think he's suffering that same strange paralysis
that froze Thucydides' tongue at his trial.
Sudden lockjaw syndrome, we might think to call it.
Well then, step aside and I shall take up the defense.
(Xanthias steps back with Labes.)
Gentlemen of the jury, it is no easy trick to speak   990
for a dog so rudely slandered, but I will do my best.
He's always been a good dog, quick to chase away the wolves.

PHILOCLEON
He's a thief! A treacherous villain!

BDELYCLEON
By Zeus, he's the best dog alive!
He can shepherd an entire flock single-handed.

PHILOCLEON

> What use is a shepherd who eats up the sheep?

BDELYCLEON

> What use! He fights for and defends you;
> he guards the door; he's an all-around wonderful dog.
> If he did steal something, let's cut him a break.
> He can fetch a bone, but he can't conduct a symphony.   1000

PHILOCLEON

> But his conduct is precisely the issue at hand!
> I wish he was no more a linguist than he is
> a musician, to spare us this long-winded defense!

BDELYCLEON

> The witnesses have been called, my good sir, pay heed.
> Cheese-grater, step forward please, and speak up.
> You were the quartermaster of the cheese, is that correct?
> Answer clearly, please. Did you or did you not
> distribute the great wheel of Sicilian cheese among the sailors?
> *(bending to listen)*
> He answers, "Yes!"

PHILOCLEON

> By Zeus, he's a liar!   1010

BDELYCLEON

> Please, sir, have pity on a hard-worked soul.
> Poor old Labes lives on table-scraps and bones,
> running all day on a thousand tasks and errands.
> But this one, his accuser, is a veritable lap-dog!
> He lolls on the rug all day, and demands a share
> of whatever comes in the house, or else—he bites.

PHILOCLEON

> Oh no, it's happening again! I'm growing soft!
> My resolve to punish is weakening, weakening . . .

BDELYCLEON
    Yes, father, I beg you to have pity.
    Do not destroy this loyal hound.   1020
    If the mutt don't fit, you must acquit!
    Bring in his children, the pitiable things.
    Come up on the stand—let's hear you beg,
    and cry, and whimper, and plead.

PHILOCLEON *(weeping)*
    Get down, get down! I can't take it anymore.

BDELYCLEON *(standing down from the bar)*
    I will get down, father, though you've often
    used that trick to stifle a defense.
    I will get down. And so, the defense rests.

PHILOCLEON
    Damn these lentils! This is what I get for eating on the job!
    For the first time, tears have clouded my judgment.   1030

BDELYCLEON
    Still, father, you will acquit him, won't you?

PHILOCLEON
    It's difficult to say, so difficult . . .

BDELYCLEON
    Be strong, father! Do the right thing, for once.
    Take your voting pebble, rush over to the urn of acquittal—
    and cast it in with your eyes closed! You can do it.

PHILOCLEON
    Never! That is, one never knows, do one?

BDELYCLEON
    Let me help you, father. I'll lead you by the hand.

PHILOCLEON
Is this the first urn, wherein are cast the votes for conviction?

BDELYCLEON
Yes, father. Here it is . . . but . . .

PHILOCLEON
Good—and here goes my pebble!   1040

BDELYCLEON *(aside)*
I've tricked him! That was the urn of acquittal!
All right, father, let's pour out the votes and count them.

PHILOCLEON
Tell me, how did it come out?

BDELYCLEON
Still counting . . . Now, Labes—the verdict is: not guilty!
(Philocleon faints.)
Father, what's wrong? Oh, father, by the gods!
Someone get me some water! Now, sit up carefully . . .

PHILOCLEON
Say it again, son: did he get off, really, did he?

BDELYCLEON
Yes, father. Labes was acquitted.

PHILOCLEON
My heart can't take it!

BDELYCLEON
Don't take it to heart, father. Stand easy, now.   1050

PHILOCLEON
How can I ever look myself in the eye again?
Acquitting a defendant—what will become of me now?

O Great Gods above, forgive me, please.
I was overcome, somehow. I didn't mean to do it!

BDELYCLEON

    Put your mind at rest, father. This is for the good.
    I'll care for you well, keep you by my side,
    take you to parties, dinners, the theater.
    From now on, it's a life of leisure, fun and games.
    Goodbye to Hyperbolus laughing behind your back.
    And now, let us go inside.   1060

PHILOCLEON

    All right, then. I surrender. Whatever you say.
(The actors file off stage, leaving the chorus.)

CHORUS

    Goodbye and good luck,
    wherever you are bound!
(to the audience)
    But you are bound to stick
    with us, O numberless crowd,
    for it's your task to fathom the truth of what follows,
    not to allow it to fall through the cracks,
    as can happen in a theater full of hollow-hearted hicks!

    Attention, good listeners, for the unvarnished truth is at hand!
    Hear it now: the poet is angry—angry at you, his audience.   1070
    For all his hard labor in the mines of verse, you've minted false
        ingots.
    At first, it's true, he toiled in shadows, ghostwriter, invisible
        presence,
    like the ventriloquist who speaks from the belly of an idiot,
    caging his comic genius in lesser poets' voices.
    But in time he rode forth for all to see, assumed the reins of
        rhyme
    to guide the horses of meter, poetry's chariot, fleet and joyful.

And then your praise knew no measure, your accolades no
        bound,
but the poet was unchanged, never arrogant or vain, unswollen
        by fame,
not one to cruise the gyms for muscle-bound groupies,
not one to fill his plays with inside jokes, with gibes to mock or
        shame   1080
some lover's jilted boyfriend. Purity was his byword,
his muse would never pimp for love nor chum for the shark of
        lucre!
Fearless and ambitious, he dared from the start
to tackle the prickliest subjects, the most Herculean of creatures.
Nor even did he shrink from attacking the dread Beast of the
        State,
befanged and bejeweled, dazzling as a fat whore in its finery,
circled in sycophantic splendor, its army of meek yes-men,
and its voice like a mountain torrent flush with destructive
        energy,
and its filth and its stink and its stench of a dead seal's asshole.
Not once, not ever, did your poet tremble in the face of the
        Beast,   1090
and his courageous voice could not be bought or silenced,
and even now he battles on your behalf. Lastly, and not least,
there is the issue of last year's composition, an assault on the
        fears and errors
that beset the generations of our fathers, things that go bump in
        the night
and things that go bump in broad daylight, writs and
        summonses, legal terror,
enough to chase a man from his bed in search of protection.
A protector such as your poet, casting a light against the fog of
        suspicion . . .
for which you repaid him, how?—with ignorant betrayal!
Thereby betraying your own ignorance, and relegating his work
        to oblivion.

And yet it's true, by Bacchus, so our poet swears, knocking them
        back,   1100
there never was a play as funny, or as verseful a comedian.
Thus it is a badge of shame for his audience, and no reflection
        on him,
that a wit which surpasses all rivals should be disdained by you
        on a whim!

So let's keep an eye on the future, folks,
and honor true poets, honor the innovators,
honor the artisans of visionary jokes,
the authentic voices, the impassioned creators.
Store their words with fresh lemons in the cedar chest,
savor their music, treasure their wit,
that their song might last all year at its best,   1110
and keep your clothes from smelling like shit.

Once upon a time we were the strongest of men,
strong of heart, strong in song,
strong in war, strong of dong!
But that was a golden age, long gone, amen,
and now our hair has grown whiter than swans.
Yet even the little spark left in us, what juice
still swims in our veins, even this
is like a fine old wine compared to the piss
of today's long-haired, prancing, dissipated youth!   1120

Spectators! Perhaps you have wondered at our curious shape,
puzzled at our slender, waspish waists,
pondered the length and point of our stingers.
Now comes our explanation, plain and simple as it is.
Only those so marked with the sign of the wasp
are true and authentic Athenians!
Behold the bravest race the world has ever known!
Our deeds are legendary in the annals of war,

how the barbarous Persians descended upon us
to smoke out the city, to burn and trample our beautiful nests!   1130
Shield to spear, spear to shield, so we met them on the
                battlefield,
drunk on love and hatred, gnawing our lips in rage.
The sun burned black beyond the storm of their arrows.
Still we moved forward, grimly, mercilessly, against them.
By evening we had thrown them back, with the gods' help,
foretokened by the owl that passed above our ranks.
And then we chased them from the field, stinging and stinging
in eyes and ears and ass and heart, until at last they fled.
To this day the memory burns in the minds of all barbarians:
fiercest of all foes is the Attic wasp!   1140

The past! The past! Those were the days!
Fearless destroyers, we sailed to the land of the Persians,
praising those best who worked hardest at the oars,
never whining or casting aspersions.
One by one we vanquished their cities,
created the wealth this new generation so liberally squanders,
for richer or poorer, in sickness and health.

So hear it now, citizens, the buzzing of the swarm,
in sound and manner every inch the wasp.
Stirred to a fury, none can match our wicked wrath.   1150
And see how we arrange to conduct our campaigns,
like clouds around nests, invidious pests,
one great swarm bound for criminal court,
another to high court, yet another to pack the Odeum
until the benches of justice are fit to burst
with the weight of our opprobrium,
until every cell of the system is packed with our bodies,
slow-moving grubs, immersed in caustic honey.
We forage for ourselves; we sting whom we want and thrive.
But beware the drones that clog the hive,   1160
home-bound, lazy, useless and wingless,

content to suck the nectar we've labored to provide.
This is our complaint: that the stingless
should share equally with we who once were warriors.
We propose a new decree: only veterans of war
shall receive the pay of jurors; only those whose lives
have been risked in defense of the noble Acropolis;
those with stingers; the few, the proud, the wasps; us.
(Philocleon and Bdelycleon come from the house, followed by a slave
carrying a thick coat and a pair of boots.)

PHILOCLEON

Stop! Unhand me! This tunic will never be taken from me!
It saved my life in battle with the great north wind,   1170
and I will not be stripped of it!

BDELYCLEON

Is there nothing new and stylish that appeals to you?

PHILOCLEON

No. I don't want it. It isn't me.
I'm plain and simple, meat and potatoes.
Last time you fed me those elegant herring
I tossed my cookies, and then who pays the cleaning bill?

BDELYCLEON

Just try it on, father. I'm willing to do my part,
but you're going to have to work with me.

PHILOCLEON

All right, what would you have me do?

BDELYCLEON

Take off that ancient tunic, and put on this new coat.   1180

PHILOCLEON

For this I raised him from a baby!
To be smothered and swaddled like a babe myself!

BDELYCLEON

Here's the coat, father—cut the palaver.

PHILOCLEON

Gods alive, what in hell is this monstrosity?

BDELYCLEON

Some call it a Persian coat, some a "Caunacian mantle."

PHILOCLEON

More like a throw-rug woven by some backwoods granny.

BDELYCLEON

Your ignorance is typical, father.
This is the very latest thing, it's hip and au courant,
which you'd know yourself if you'd ever been to Sardis.

PHILOCLEON

I'm not too ignorant to recognize it   1190
as one of Morychus' burlap food bags.

BDELYCLEON

Hardly, father. These tassels were woven in Ecbatana.

PHILOCLEON

Ecbatana—home of the all-wool sausage, I believe.

BDELYCLEON

What are you babbling about?
This was woven in Persia, at great expense.
The wool alone is worth hundreds.

PHILOCLEON

Quick then, lets sell it back
to the Caunacians for a couple of bills
before they come to their senses!

BDELYCLEON
   Stand still, now, and put this thing on.   1200
   Yes, there you go . . .
   (The slave attempts to help Philocleon put on the coat.)

PHILOCLEON
   Disgusting! It's belching hot air at me!

BDELYCLEON
   Just try it on.

PHILOCLEON
   I refuse!

BDELYCLEON
   Do it!

PHILOCLEON
   If you want me asphyxiated just toss me in the oven!
   It would be easier, cheaper, and it wouldn't smell like sheep!

BDELYCLEON
   That's it, I'll do it myself.
   (to the slave)
                    Take off.

PHILOCLEON *(donning coat)*
   All right, but you'd better keep a meat hook handy.

BDELYCLEON
   What?   1210

PHILOCLEON
   Yes—to pull me out when I'm fully cooked!

BDELYCLEON
Very good. Now, take off those horrible shoes,
and put on these lovely Spartan boots. Hurry up.

PHILOCLEON
Ha! I'll have no part of that hated foe.
That would be consorting with the enemy.

BDELYCLEON
Courage, brave soldier of Athens!
Now get your foot into the boot!

PHILOCLEON
Forcibly carried into enemy territory—what cruelty.

BDELYCLEON
And now the other foot.

PHILOCLEON
What, this foot here? Oh no. He's a diehard   1220
patriot, a hater of anything Spartan.

BDELYCLEON
Too bad. Give it here.

PHILOCLEON
More suffering. Now I'm to be denied
the pleasures of cold feet in my golden years.

BDELYCLEON *(forcing foot into boot)*
Hurry it up; get the boot on there.
Now give me the walk of a rich man,
put a little swagger in it, a little shake and bake.

PHILOCLEON *(finishes tying the boots)*
Ok, then. Now see how I look in them,
tell me which of the rich and famous I most resemble.
(Philocleon strolls back and forth.)

BDELYCLEON
> That looks like an injured man hobbling 1230
> on blisters bandaged and salved with garlic.

PHILOCLEON
> It's all part of the plan. I'm moving and grooving.

BDELYCLEON
> Very nice, father. But can you talk the talk
> as well as you walk the walk?
> Can you carry a conversation among those wits?

PHILOCLEON
> Oh, certainly, certainly . . .

BDELYCLEON
> Ok, show me what you've got.

PHILOCLEON
> Well—I've got plenty. Let's see. I could start
> with the legendary farts of Lamia.
> And then there's the one about Cardopian and his mother . . . 1240

BDELYCLEON
> Stop! Forget myths and legends entirely.
> We need human interest, local news, guy stuff.

PHILOCLEON
> Oh, I get it. Something like—
> "There once was a boy from Euboea,
> whose nose was as long as . . ."

BDELYCLEON
> Moron!
> *(checking his temper)*
> More on this later,

I mean, as Theogenes said to the dung-collector.
But truly, father, are schoolboy limericks really appropriate?

PHILOCLEON
Well, give me some other suggestions.

BDELYCLEON
The notion is to discuss weighty and impressive matters.   1250
Like when you went on that diplomatic mission
with Cleisthenes and Androcles, the scoundrels.

PHILOCLEON
Good suggestion—only I've never
gone on a mission, except to Parus—
for which I received exactly two obols.

BDELYCLEON
I see. All right, then you could tell them how Ephoudion
wrestled so brilliantly against Ascondas in the pancration.
He was old by then, of course, a white-haired man,
but his ribs were steel, his legs mighty columns,
his chest as strong as a great shield.   1260

PHILOCLEON
Stop! You've lost your senses entirely.
No shields were allowed in the pancration.

BDELYCLEON
Indeed . . . right. My point is that the in-crowd love
this kind of spirited talk. Let's hear something else.
Imagine you're drinking with your host, and you want
to wow him with your most amazing youthful escapade.

PHILOCLEON
Of course. I know just the one, a moment of great daring,
when I stole the vine-posts from old Ergasion's vineyard.
I suppose I was six or seven at the time . . .

BDELYCLEON

Vine-posts! I'm starting to lose faith in you, father.   1270
What about hunting wild boars—or rabbits, anyway?
What about the torch-races you ran?
You must have something dashing to brag of?

PHILOCLEON

Oh—I've got it! Just the thing. Most impressive.
When I was just a wee boy, many years ago,
I took on the great and famous runner Phayllus.
Yes, indeed. It was quite a contest, nip and tuck,
but in the end I won by the smallest of margins.
Two votes! By just two votes he was convicted of slander.

BDELYCLEON

Enough! No more tales of legal action, please.   1280
Just lie down here on the couch,
and let's learn how to be a fashionable dinner party guest.

PHILOCLEON

How should I lie, exactly?

BDELYCLEON

Umm, gracefully, with dignity.

PHILOCLEON (*flopping down on a rough bench*)

Is this it?

BDELYCLEON

By no means!

PHILOCLEON

How, then?

BDELYCLEON

Bend your knees, and stretch and slink yourself
along the fine fabric, like it was second nature to you.

And then admire all of the artwork on the walls,   1290
and the ceiling, and the hanging tapestries.
And then give some orders: "Water for my hands!"
"Bring in the tables!" "Let's wash up, let's eat and drink . . ."

PHILOCLEON
Bring on the feast—don't tell me I'm dreaming!

BDELYCLEON
The flute-girl has begun to play some dinner music.
Your fellow guests include Theorus, Aeschines, Phanus, Cleon,
and a foreign visitor, Acestor's son, beside you.
Now, can you handle yourself in a situation like this?

PHILOCLEON
Certainly! I can sing better than some foreigner, at any rate.

BDELYCLEON
We'll see about that. Imagine that I'm Cleon,   1300
and I begin with a song about Harmodius, the tyrant-slayer.
Now it's your turn to complete the tune:
"Oh, never has Athens seen such a man . . ."

PHILOCLEON
"If he can't steal it, nobody can!"

BDELYCLEON
That's your song? Well, it's the last you'll ever sing.
He'll fight you, he'll bite you, he'll cite you
for treason and have you expelled from the city!

PHILOCLEON
That's just fine—if he threatens me,
I'll try this little ditty out on him, by Zeus:
"Athens is on the brink of destruction, Jack—   1310
you power-crazed megalomaniac!"

BDELYCLEON

And how will you respond when Theorus,
lying at Cleon's feet, takes his hand and sings:
"Love only the good, as the tale of Admetus shows we should."
How will you match that verse?

PHILOCLEON

With lyric wit, of course:
"Only the duplicitous fox plays that fiddle;
to work both ends against the middle."

BDELYCLEON

Fine. Next comes Aeschines, son of Sellus.
He's clever, a fine musician, and so he sings: 1320
"Mighty we were, and rich as hell,
the best of all the men of Thessaly,
great Cleitagora, and I as well—"

PHILOCLEON

"Indeed we was swell, just you and me."

BDELYCLEON

All right then, you've caught the hang of it.
Now it's off to dinner at Philoctemon's.
Boy! Chrysus! Prepare our dinner;
we're off to drink ourselves under the table.

PHILOCLEON

Oh no, not me! Drinking is wrong, it's evil!
Think what it leads to: smashing down doors,   1330
assault and battery, hangovers the next morning
as the costs are reckoned and the fines are paid.

BDELYCLEON

That may be so for the common herd, father,
but not for the class of gentlemen we'll be with!

Either you buy off the victims from pressing charges,
or you can spin a clever and witty tale
to joke it all away, something from Aesop or Sybaris,
like those we'll hear at the party. That's how gentlemen
do it: they laugh it off and the world laughs with them.

PHILOCLEON

I can't wait to hear those stories! I'll learn them all,   1340
and so be free to misbehave without fear.
Let's move along, then, what are we waiting for?
(Exit Philocleon and Bdelycleon.)

CHORUS

I've always thought myself
a fairly clever man,
never one to play the fool for long,
unlike Amynias, son of Sellus,
with his long hair tied in a thong.
I remember the time he dined with rich Leogoras,
hardly his usual poor man's food,
apple and pomegranate.   1350
Now he's poor as Antiphon again!
Even his time as ambassador did little good,
that trip to Pharsallus
where he rested in solitude among the Penestae,
himself their brother in penury.

Congratulations to you, Automenes! Happy the father
of such remarkable children, one after the other.
The eldest is much loved, a bright and gifted musician.
And the second son, so charming, a noted thespian.
And then there's Ariphrades, perhaps the most distinguished,   1360
famous among our prostitutes as the cunningest of linguists!
No common school-boy, his dad says he learned it on his own,
figured it out all by himself, somehow, in the dark, alone.
[several lines are missing here]

Cleon and I, some say, have long since buried the hatchet.
But look how he continues to harass me! Nothing could match it,
    the insults and abuse, and when he'd delivered his public
            reaming
    how funny you found it to watch me screaming.
See the comedian, feel his agony! Little you cared
    except to hear what jokes I might drop, what witty retorts
            I dared,
    and I did dare a few, here and there, playing along for awhile.   1370
    But now the pole has abandoned the vine, as a joke betrays
            its smile.
(Enter Xanthias.)

XANTHIAS

    Lord, turtles are lucky to live within hard shells!
    Just as you all are lucky for the hard-tiled shell
    of the roof above you. It keeps you from harm's way,
    while my ribs have been whacked both blue and black.

CHORUS

    What's wrong, boy—if boy we may call you,
    yes, a man of years but still beaten like a child.

XANTHIAS

    The old man has flipped! He's a hellhound,
    he's drunker then the rest of those drunken skunks,
    Hippylus, Antiphon, Lycon, Lysistratus,   1380
    Theophrastus, and even the Phrynichus set!
    He was the very worst of all! Out of control!
    He stuffed himself with food and drink,
    and jumped up prancing and farting and giggling,
    like an ass fed on green corn and barley.
    He called to me—"Boy, boy!"—and whipped me good.
    Observing it all, Lysistratus began one of their fey
    party games, a round of poetic comparisons:
    "Old man, you're like a wine drunk before its time;
    you're a donkey lacking reason or rhyme."   1390

And of course Philocleon shot back with something:
"Well then you, you, you are like a locust
that has shed his shell, or better yet you're like
an actor without costume or makeup or focus."
At which they all applauded, except for Theophrastus,
too snooty to join in, thinking himself the best wit of all.
So of course the old man takes Theophrastus as his target:
"Hey, Mr. High and Mighty, Mr. Ass Kisser—
drop the attitude, you sycophantic boot-licker!"
Thus it went. He insulted them all, in the crudest terms,   1400
with the dumbest jokes, the worst songs,
a vaudeville routine of witless one-liners.
Finally, at the peak of drunkenness, he left for home,
molesting and assaulting whomever he met en route.
Oh no—here he comes now, still falling all over himself.
I'm gone, before he lets fly with the lash again.
(Enter Philocleon, drunk, with a torch in one hand and a scantily-clad
                    flute-girl on the other arm; an angry crowd is in
                    pursuit.)

PHILOCLEON
    Step aside! Gangway!
    I'm coming through and you
    won't stop the likes of me today,
    morons, idiots, fools!   1410
    Out of the way
    or I'll torch the lot of you.

MAN FROM THE CROWD
    You won't get away with this!
    Whatever your age, you'll have to pay!
    We'll sue! We'll take you to court tomorrow!

PHILOCLEON
    Hi-ho, hi-ho, it's off to court we go!
    Old news, my friends!
    The court and I have come to the end

of our relationship, can't even stand to speak of it,
suits and countersuits—   1420
egad!—zut!—
to hell with those pebbles and urns,
take off before you fry and burn!
(to the flute-girl)
Come up here beside me, my tasty little morsel.
(extending his comic phallus)
That's right, just grab the rope firmly.
Careful, though, it isn't what it once was,
older and weaker, but always eager for a helping hand!
Haven't I carried you off quite cleverly now,
in the midst of your libidinous cocktail duties?
Speaking of cocks, I'd say you've taken the bull by his horn   1430
and now's the chance to do the dance you're famous for,
or will it be another tease and tickle job,
and a flirty smile as you dash away?
Listen, I'm ready to deal for what I want;
you take care of me and when the time comes
I'll buy your freedom and you can be my mistress.
We just have to wait for my son to kick the bucket!
At my age, I haven't got control of the money yet—
I'm too young! And he's my keen-eyed guardian,
on the lookout night and day, and a tightwad   1440
to boot, a son who'd squeeze blood from an obol.
He fears for my well-being, doesn't want to spoil me.
I'm his only father, you see, a singleton.
Speak of the wolf, I see his tail a-wagging this way!
He's after us, no doubt. Here, take this torch, stand thusly.
Let's see how he likes a taste of his own medicine!
(The flute-girl stands like a statue, holding the torch.)

BDELYCLEON

So there you are, you skirt-chasing old satyr!
You've got a taste for the young stuff, eh?
I'll have you in a fine young coffin if you keep this up.
I won't stand for it, by Apollo!   1450

PHILOCLEON
>Sound like a legal pickle to suck upon.

BDELYCLEON
>I'll pickle you! You think it's a joke
>to steal flute-girls from dinner guests?

PHILOCLEON
>Good heavens—a flute-girl? Where?
>You seem to have taken leave of your senses.

BDELYCLEON
>She stands beside you like Dardanis, old fool.

PHILOCLEON
>This? It's merely a torch burning in the marketplace.

BDELYCLEON
>A torch!

PHILOCLEON
>Of course. Observe the shape, the coloration.
>*(Philocleon pretends to examine the flute-girl.)*

BDELYCLEON
>What's this, then—black in the middle?   1460

PHILOCLEON
>Some pitch the wood exudes as it burns.

BDELYCLEON
>And this—as fine an ass as one could wish for!

PHILOCLEON
>No, it's not. I mean, it is a knot! Knotty wood.

BDELYCLEON *(grasping the flute-girl by the arm)*
>Knots in your head! You, girl, come with me.

PHILOCLEON
>What are you doing with my torch-bearer?

BDELYCLEON
>Taking her away from you—not that
>an impotent old man could do her much harm!

PHILOCLEON
>Remember how Ephoudion fought at the Olympic games,
>how he knocked young Ascondas to the ground with his fist?
>Careful, son, or you'll find yourself similarly situated!   1470

BDELYCLEON
>You've become a regular Olympian, father.
>*(Enter bread seller with Chaerephon.)*

BREAD SELLER
>There he is! He's the one, by the gods!
>He practically killed me—knocked over my wares
>with his torch, trampled the loaves in the dirt,
>a whole day's worth, ten obols at least.

BDELYCLEON
>Now look what you've done, father!
>See where your drinking leads to—trouble and lawsuits!

PHILOCLEON
>Trouble—not at all. Let me show you how
>a gentleman handles these things,
>with a clever story to wriggle off the hook.   1480

BREAD SELLER

    Oh no! By the gods you'll not get off the hook
    of Myrtia, daughter of Ancylion and Sostrata!
    My entire inventory has been destroyed!

PHILOCLEON

    Yes, of course, my dear girl, of course—
    and I have a rather charming and amusing tale to offer,
    I'm sure you'll find it recompense enough . . .

BREAD SELLER

    Oh no! I'm not buying it!

PHILOCLEON

    Once upon a time, Aesop was on the way home
    from a dinner party when he met a woman,
    and this old bitch starts yapping and jawing and giving
                 him grief,   1490
    and wise old Aesop says, "Listen here, bitch! You'd do better to
                 leaven that senseless tongue of yours!"

BREAD SELLER

    You're laughing at me, eh old man?
    Well, I hereby accuse you before the Market Officials
    of ruination and despoliation, and Chaerephon is my witness!

PHILOCLEON

    Oh no you don't! Just listen to this, and see
    if it doesn't set things to right: Once upon a time
    Lasus and Simonides staged a song competition.
    And then Lasus says, he says . . . "I don't give a fuck!"

BREAD SELLER

    So that's the way it is!   1500
(She turns to exit but runs into Chaerephon, who falls at her feet.)

PHILOCLEON

> Ho, Chaerephon! Is this what you've fallen to,
> serving as witness for a woman—why, you're as abject
> as Ino, groveling at the feet of Euripides!

(Exit bread seller and Chaerephon.)

BDELYCLEON

> By the gods, I see another victim approaching
> to accuse you; at least he's got a better witness.

(Enter Complainant, battered and bruised, with crowd.)

COMPLAINANT

> Oh misery, oh woe! Old man, I summon and accuse
> you of outrageous usage against me!

BDELYCLEON

> Outrage! By the gods, allow me to make it up to you,
> and convince you to withdraw the charges,
> whatever it takes, name your cost, and I'll thank you.   1510

PHILOCLEON

> No, no—I'd like to make my own amends,
> without compulsion or bribery.
> I admit to the charges, outrage, assault and battery,
> call it what you will, but tell me only this:
> would you prefer to name your own compensation,
> or allow me to determine it, and so fix our friendship?

COMPLAINANT

> Very well, I see no need to take this to court.
> Tell me what you'll give me, and let's be done.

PHILOCLEON

> Once upon a time, there lived a man of Sybaris,
> who fell from his vehicle to the roadbed one day,   1520

injuring himself quite seriously, cracking his skull,
and thus unable to proceed any farther. Now,
a friend of his stood by, who in his wisdom said:
"Stick to what you know, buddy. Seek professional help."
So do I offer you this same pearl of wisdom,
and suggest you run off to see Dr. Pittalus forthwith.

BDELYCLEON
Your answer to the charge of outrage
is equally outrageous, father!

COMPLAINANT
Witnesses, attend! Remember his very words!

PHILOCLEON
Stop, friends, and listen to this one: 1530
There once was a girl of Sybaris, who broke her jug—

COMPLAINANT
Again I call you to bear witness to this travesty!

PHILOCLEON
That's just how it was in Sybaris, too!
A travesty! Why, the broken jug called his friends
to bear witness against the girl, and she said:
"Hey, this calling to witness is really quite witless;
use your head, and buy some glue!"

COMPLAINANT
That's right, keep jeering until the judge summons you.
Everything you've said can be used against you.
(Exit Complainant and crowd.)

BDELYCLEON *(hoisting Philocleon)*
That's it, father. By Demeter I'll not let you loose   1540
out here one minute longer.

PHILOCLEON
>   What is this!

BDELYCLEON
>   This is the end of the line!
>   If I don't get you inside, they'll soon run out
>   of witnesses to testify against you!

PHILOCLEON
>   That's just how the Delphians testified against Aesop . . .

BDELYCLEON
>   I'm not listening!

PHILOCLEON
>   For stealing the sacred vessel from the temple.
>   But cunning Aesop swore a giant beetle had taken it . . .

BDELYCLEON
>   Say goodbye, father, beetles and all!   1550
> *(Exit all but chorus.)*

CHORUS
>   Buzz and march, march and buzz,
>   we envy the comrade we're here to judge.
>   Philocleon has changed his tune,
>   from gibbous sickle to ripe full moon,
>   swollen indulgently, wanton he waxes,
>   a new babe swaddled in luxury taxes!
>   Such transformation is rare indeed,
>   and we praise the one whose deed
>   it was, his sweet-tongued son, Bdelycleon.
>   Praise him, all! Light his name in aqua neon,   1560
>   that we may view his character clearly,
>   how kind and sensible he is, how dearly
>   he dotes on his dear old father.

In this debate he has proven the victor,
with standards to uphold and tastes to raise.
Buzz and march, hail and praise!

XANTHIAS

By Dionysus! Some god has loosed chaos
to rule in our house! It's the old man again.
He's been drinking all night, and when
he heard the flute music he was transported!   1570
He's a dancing fool! All night long he's danced,
those weird ancient dances of Thespis,
and now he says he's ready to challenge
the best of our tragic dancers, and beat them all!

PHILOCLEON *(entering)*
Hark! Who waits upon my doorstep?

XANTHIAS
As if on cue—he's back, and better than ever!

PHILOCLEON
Unlatch the door, come out or come in,
the dance has at last begun to begin.

XANTHIAS
That is, the *insanity* is about to begin.

PHILOCLEON *(dancing as he speaks)*
Yes! . . . move your body backward, forward,   1580
twirl and turn, gyre and pern,
joint and sinew, burn baby burn!

XANTHIAS
He needs drugs! A sedative!

PHILOCLEON
A-ha! Old Phrynichus clucks like a scared hen . . .

XANTHIAS
   Stone him! He's gone mad!

PHILOCLEON
   . . . my wild dancing will give him a licking!
   I wag my ass! I'm kicking and kicking!
   Now I'm doing the funky chicken.

XANTHIAS
   Take care! Watch out!

PHILOCLEON
   I'm loose as a top, a limber rocket,   1590
   my joints spin freely in their sockets.
   (He brings the wild dance to a conclusion.)
   Now that's what I call dancing!

XANTHIAS
   The dance of a madman!

PHILOCLEON *(to audience)*
   So then, who will accept my challenge?
   Show me a tragic actor who dares to contest me
   in the dance—step right up, please!
   Are there no takers? None brave enough?

XANTHIAS *(pointing to first Dancing Brother in audience)*
   I see only one—over there.

PHILOCLEON
   A puny wretch. Who is he?

XANTHIAS
   It's one of the Crabbes, the middle son.   1600
   (Enter first Dancing Brother, dancing, from audience.)

PHILOCLEON

> So small I can swallow him whole!
> I'll crack his shell with my devilish dancing!
> Poor shrimp—he's got no rhythm!

XANTHIAS

> Not so fast, old man, here comes another
> dancing Crabbe—his brother!
> *(Enter second Dancing Brother.)*

PHILOCLEON

> By Poseidon, a seafood banquet!

XANTHIAS

> It's true, we're hemmed in by crabs—
> here comes one more!
> *(Enter third Dancing Brother.)*

PHILOCLEON

> What sort of creature now—owl or mole?

XANTHIAS

> Of course not. It's the baby of the family,   1610
> the littlest Crabbe; take pity,
> for he aspires to be a tragic poet in his time!
> *(The three brothers perform a tragic dance.)*

PHILOCLEON

> O Crabbe, proud Carcinus, what a father you must be,
> to raise up three such sons as these!
> Alas, I'll have to beat them, and then I think I'll eat them,
> nicely boiled, with all the trimmings, if you please!
> *(Philocleon dances wildly.)*

CHORUS

> Make room, clear the way, the dancing must proceed,
> by spin and by leap, by whirl and by turn, o marvelous
> > crustaceans,

brothers of the brine, by the shore of the salt-sown sea,
lift your legs, fling your heels, kick the kick Phyrnichean!   1620
Leap and cavort, slap your thigh! Whack your belly, whirl
       and spin
like whizzing tops propelled by the applause you earn
with each circle you circle and each turning you turn!
Now the proud father, Ruler of the Sea, joyously joins the fray.
To hell with tragedy, I say! Lead us out the comedic way!
Another first: the chorus exits dancing. And so ends this play.
(Exit Philocleon, followed by Dancing Brothers, followed by chorus in a
conga line.)

Lysistrata

Translated by
X. J. Kennedy

Translator's Preface

Lysistrata must have greatly lifted the spirits of its first audience during the gloom of war, after news had reached Athens that her navy had been destroyed. The archon, the official in charge of the Lenaea, the drama festival in which the comedy was probably first staged early in 411 B.C., imposed no stern wartime censorship. Aristophanes appears free to poke fun at the government of Athens, its diplomats, generals, and leading statesmen, including Demostratos, who had persuaded the Assembly to launch the disastrous Sicilian campaign. The playwright even speaks well of the Spartans—the enemy—and gives them the final word.

Like many works of hopeful playwrights today, *Lysistrata* was written as a contest entry. We don't know whether it won first prize in its day, but it has lasted for twenty-four centuries. Of all the plays of Aristophanes, it is the one most often translated, most often assigned in college, and most often staged. That may be because it is a strong and shapely play, funny and fresh and full of living people, crammed with slapstick, insult-contests, and watchable bits of stage business.

Perhaps, too, its sexual candor seems to us contemporary, and its notions strike us as liberal and avant-garde—that is, if we misread it slightly. True, the play affirms a respect for women that we might think Gloria Steinem had invented; and in having two nations—the city-states of Athens and Sparta—rise above their differences for the greater good, it may seem ahead of its time. But aside from these bold notions the play is not all that radical. Though its women possess basic wisdom, though Athens might best be governed in the way a housewife combs her wool, Aristophanes voices no doubts that a woman's place is in the home. For a young mother like Myrrhine to run away from her nursing baby and barricade herself in the Acropolis is, to him and his audience, a hilariously goofy idea. His play satirizes married life, yet firmly defends it. Repeatedly he suggests that men ought to be better husbands, and gentler ones.

As her name indicates ("she who disperses armies"), Lysistrata stands at the center of things. She is a determined leader, yet she can make mistakes (as in proposing to swear an oath for peace on a battle shield), and she suffers chagrins and doubts. Only for a moment does her power waver— when her henchwomen start backsliding, yearning for home. But it is she who unites her team again, by whipping out a favorable message from an oracle. We may well suspect her of having written it herself.

Lysistrata has been called a licentious play, but I think its humor is similar to that of the innocently bawdy British music hall, so given to double entendres. Its comic turns remind me of the sweet and harmless burlesque shows of Minsky and the Old Howard, with their lowbrow comedians facing raucous audiences who, as George Jean Nathan once put it, "worshipped at the shrine of progressive corporeal revelation." Even today, some may be offended by the manifest priapism of Aristophanes' sex-starved husbands, but nothing in the play is clandestine or sniggering. I can't imagine anyone getting a pornographic kick out of *Lysistrata*. Much of its humor depends on seeing concupiscence thwarted, as in Lysistrata's arrest of the escaping wives and in the long and agonizingly funny encounter between Kinesias and Myrrhine. We may flatter ourselves that we are more open-minded than those Victorians who left bits of the play untranslated. Still, perhaps few of us share the ancient Greeks' whole-spirited acceptance of the human body, and their willingness to laugh heartily at tumescence, in the sun-drenched open air.

Shortly after agreeing to do a new version of the play, I felt like a fool rushing in. I know no Greek, and my credentials as a classicist are sketchy. I can claim only to have seen Greek plays performed in English, to have taken one course in Greek drama from Moses Hadas, and once to have spent an afternoon sitting on a stone bench in Aristophanes' Theater of Dionysus. I was somewhat relieved to find that all translations of Aristophanes are rough versions. *Lysistrata* survives, as Matt Neuburg has noted in the preface to his valuable Crofts Classics edition of the play, only from "handwritten copies of handwritten copies of handwritten copies," most of them medieval, made sixteen or eighteen centuries after the original production. Translators must either fill in a great deal by guesswork or else supply footnotes to explain their uncertainties. Because stage directions do not exist and must be inferred from what happens on stage, because the characters uttering the speeches are not identified, because there is no exact indication of where a speech begins and ends—all these lacks tempt a foolhardy ignoramus to try his hand.

I was further relieved to discover ample help. Let me acknowledge my deep debt to previous translators and annotators whose work I have studied but not stolen from: Gilbert Murray, Benjamin Bickley Rogers, Dudley Fitts, Douglass Parker, Kenneth McLeish, Alan H. Sommerstein, Charles T. Murphy and Bernard Knox, Matt Neuburg, an anonymous translator for the Athenian Society in London in 1912, and more scholars than I can name, among them Kenneth J. Reckford, author of *Aristophanes' Old-and-New Comedy*.[1]

Aristophanes conceived his play for his theater; I have tried to reconceive it for our own. Like the *Tonight* show, Aristophanes relies heavily on topical humor, poking fun at celebrities in the news. Several allusions to people and events, now lost in the mists of time and irretrievable, have been tacitly dropped. In a few places where an allusion might call for a footnote, I have instead added a few words in the hope of making it clear. Several lines have been invented for transitions and three or four stanzas of song that have little or no textual support. One of the old men, Drakes, offered comic possibilities, so I gave him a few lines to sing. I felt more freedom in rendering the choral songs than in the speeches. Though its music has been lost, *Lysistrata* is after all a musical.

The most flagrant liberty I have taken occurs at the end of Act I, where a one-line allusion to an Aesop fable has been expanded into an entire song. The less familiar fable of the eagle and the dung-beetle seemed well worth spelling out. In the theater of today, the play clearly falls into two acts, the first slightly longer, the second beginning five days later, after the women's occupation of the Acropolis.

The whole of the original play is in verse, in metrical patterns of some complexity. What to do? Robert Frost said that English has only two meters, strict iambic and loose iambic. At certain moments, usually more formal occasions, the loose iambic becomes blank verse. Even in English it will be

---

[1] Chapel Hill: University of North Carolina Press, 1987.

clear that Aristophanes loves variety in language, ranging from barracks-room repartee to the high tragic mode of Euripides, which he parodies in the dialogue that opens Act II. (It may be interesting to compare this parody with the *Frogs*, in which the comic playwright declares Euripides a bantam-weight while hefty Aeschylus tips the scales.) Because Aristophanes distinguishes between Attic and Doric speech, it is customary for translators to make the Spartans speak in dialect: a Southern drawl, a hillbilly twang, a Scottish burr, a Russian growl, or some other accent remote from Ohio standard. I have opted for a dialect likely to strike most Americans as barbarous, that of the streets of Brooklyn or Jersey City. On the other hand, a more formal and elevated tone for Lysistrata's speech might help her stand high above the crowd.

Another challenge was the symbolic figure of Reconciliation, or Peace, whose body serves as a map for the negotiators to haggle over. Should she be represented on stage by a statue, a picture, a masked man, or a naked woman? I have done what I suspect Aristophanes very probably did: made her a burlesque piece of pulchritude, to be played by a man in drag.

That is only a short summary of my high-handedness. I hope the result will be a fairly readable, possibly playable version, one that will outrage the learned only occasionally.

Cast

LYSISTRATA ⎫
KALONIKE ⎬ women of Athens
MYRRHINE ⎭
LAMPITO, chief of the Spartan women
CHORUS OF OLD MEN
CHORUSMASTER
DRAKES, member of the men's chorus
CHORUS OF OLD WOMEN
STRATYLLIS, leader of the women's chorus
COMMISSIONER, an Athenian bureaucrat
THREE WOMEN, from chorus
KINESIAS, husband of Myrrhine
BABY
SPARTAN MESSENGER
THREE SPARTAN ENVOYS
THREE ATHENIAN NEGOTIATORS
GATEKEEPER
NONSPEAKING
    Spartan and Athenian women
    Ismenia, a Boeotian woman
    Beauty queen, a Corinthian
    Scythian policewoman, archer
    Policemen, Scythian archers
    Manservant
    Kleisthenes, a gay queen
    Senator
    Reconciliation

ACT I

*(Athens, a public square. In the background the Propylaea, main gate to
the Acropolis. Lysistrata, a young matron, is alone,
walking up and down impatiently.)*

LYSISTRATA

No doubt if I'd asked them over for an orgy
in honor of Dionysus, Pan-pipes and drinks,
a little Aphrodisiacal wild party,
they'd be here with bells on—you couldn't
move for the mob of them. But now,
not a woman in creation shows her face.
(Kalonike enters.)
Aha! Here's one, my neighbor Kalonike.
Good morning, Kally.

KALONIKE

Morning, Lys.
How come you're so hot and bothered?
Quit beetling your brows—you'll get wrinkles.   10

LYSISTRATA

Oh, Kally darling, this just burns me up.
What a disgrace! That women won't turn out
to save their reputations! Menfolk say
we're just a pack of conniving schemers.

KALONIKE

Ain't it the truth!

LYSISTRATA

And now, when I invite
all the girls here for an important conference,
the dumb clucks stay home dozing.

KALONIKE

    Don't worry your head, honey, they'll show.
    You know how hard it is for housewives
    to get out in the morning. Aren't we always   20
    bending over backward to serve our husbands' needs?
    Giving some lazy slave a kick in the slats,
    giving the baby a bath, giving it tittie?

LYSISTRATA

    I know, I know, but other things count more.

KALONIKE

    So why did you call this meeting?
    What's up?

LYSISTRATA

               Something huge.

KALONIKE

    Hmmmm, the plot thickens.

LYSISTRATA

                        It's thick, all right.

KALONIKE

    Thick? Stiff? Sticking straight out?

LYSISTRATA

    Nothing of the kind. If it were,
    all the girls would have been here in a jiffy.   30
    No, this thing is worrisome. It's cost me
    many a night of turning and tossing.

KALONIKE *(to herself)*

                      Obstinate thing,
    to need whole nights of diddling!

LYSISTRATA
> Listen to me, Kalonike. The fate
> of the Greek world rests on us women.

KALONIKE
> Oh no! Then the Greek world is a goner!

LYSISTRATA
> It's up to us women to govern, pass laws,
> make treaties. Either we take matters
> into our own hands, or Sparta will be destroyed—

KALONIKE
> Now you're talking! Trash the bastards!   40

LYSISTRATA
> And the Boeotians, every one—

KALONIKE
>   Only let's save
> those yummy Boeotian eels. They're great on crackers.

LYSISTRATA
> And, unthinkable though it is, Athens itself
> will perish. But if the women of our cities unite—
> Boeotians, Spartans, and ourselves—
> we can still save Greece from catastrophe.

KALONIKE
> But how can women help? Us babes aren't used
> to brainwork. All we're good for is doing our faces,
> dolling up in gauzy gowns and Oriental slippers.

LYSISTRATA
> Yes, by the gods, and that's exactly what   50
> we'll save Greece with—silks, slippers, rouge,
> peek-a-boo bras, perfumes, and see-through shimmies.

KALONIKE
>But how—?

LYSISTRATA
>>No man in Greece will lift
>a warlike lance—

KALONIKE
>>I'll help! I'll get me
>a new low-cut gown—

LYSISTRATA
>>>Nor buckle his shield—

KALONIKE
>And a lacy negligee—

LYSISTRATA
>>>Nor draw his sword—

KALONIKE
>Persian sandals, maybe. Paint my toenails gold.

LYSISTRATA
>So you see, these women really should be here.

KALONIKE
>They should, if they only knew what's good for 'em.

LYSISTRATA
>Isn't this just like Athenians? Always late.   60
>Where are the women from the Coast? And those
>from Paralus?

KALONIKE
>>Something tells me they've been
>mounted and saddled since the crack of dawn.

LYSISTRATA
And where's that true-blue friend that I expected
to be the first one here?

KALONIKE
Oh, sure, you mean
Madame Theogenes? I think she's flying
the red flag this time of the month.
I can imagine why she'd stay at home.
Hey, look, here comes a flock of people now.
*(Enter several women, gaudily dressed, chewing gum, walking as if trying
to look seductive.)*

LYSISTRATA
At last!

KALONIKE
P-U! Where are those polecats from?   70

LYSISTRATA
From Anagyra.

KALONIKE
Of course. I should have guessed.
I smelled their cheap perfume a mile away.

MYRRHINE *(rushing in breathlessly)*
Oh golly, Lysistrata, am I late?
Don't look at me like that. Say something!

LYSISTRATA
Oh, Myrrhine, when fate hangs in the balance,
how could you dawdle so?

MYRRHINE
I'm sorry, Lys,
truly I am. When I got up at dawn
it was so dark I couldn't find my girdle.
Anyway, I'm here. Why did you summon us?

LYSISTRATA

    Let's wait a minute more. The other girls   80
    from Sparta and Boeotia should arrive.

MYRRHINE

    Ah, so they should. Why, here's Lampito now.
    (Lampito enters, a husky Spartan in running clothes, followed by
               Ismenia, a slighter woman in more formal attire,
               and a large-figured woman from Corinth.)

LYSISTRATA

    Lampito, darling, I'm so glad you came.
    Why, you're the picture of health! What a tan,
    what muscles! I suspect you could strangle
    a bull bare-handed.

LAMPITO *(flexing her biceps)*
               Soitainly I could, honey.
    I woik out wit' weights. And I do duh dance
    where yuh kick yuh own hiney—like dis, see?
    (She demonstrates, kicking her rear end.)

KALONIKE

    Wow, what a bust. Is all of that for real?
    (She extends a finger to touch Lampito's bosom.)

LAMPITO

    Aw right, youse, coib dat feely-feely stuff.   90
    I ain't no cow, and dis ain't milkin' time.

LYSISTRATA

    And your pretty companion—where's she from?

LAMPITO *(urging Ismenia forward)*
    Dis here is a genu-wine swell from T'ebes.
    She's duh Boeotian Ambassadress.

LYSISTRATA
I might have known. Boeotian women
are such blooming flowers.

KALONIKE
                    Yeah, and they all
have neat, trimmed pansy-patches.

LYSISTRATA
                              And who's this?

LAMPITO *(pushing another woman forward)*
Dis here is duh foist-prize beauty queen
from Corint'.

KALONIKE
                    She must have been
Miss Big Boobs of 400 B.C.   100

LAMPITO
So all us goils is here.
Whose idear was dis meetin', anyway?

LYSISTRATA
                              Mine.

LAMPITO
Ok, give us duh lowdown, kid.
I'm just boinin' to find out.

MYRRHINE
Yes, Lys, what's so urgent?

LYSISTRATA
I'll tell you. But first, one question.
All of you have husbands away at the war.
Don't you miss them?

KALONIKE

> Damn right we do.
> My old man has been at the front
> for the last five months—at the front   110
> of General Eukrates' long retreat.

MYRRHINE

> And mine's spent seven months camped
> in Pylos, in the red-light district.

LAMPITO

> And mine, dey no sooner give him a foilough home
> dan—wham, bam, t'ank yuh, ma'am—
> and back he goes to duh front again.

KALONIKE

> And lover-boys? Scarcer than hen's balls.
> Besides, ever since the Miletians broke
> with Athens and shut down the sex-toy trade,
> you can't find a decent dildo in the shops   120
> for love nor money.

LYSISTRATA

> What if I have a plan to end the war?
> Will you support me?

KALONIKE

> Honey, count me in.
> If it would end this crummy war I'd sell
> the shirt off of my back. Might have to buy
> a few drinks out of the proceeds, though.

MYRRHINE

> And *I*'m with you! I'd cut off my right arm
> to bring peace again. I'd split myself
> like a mackerel.

LAMPITO

Youse bet I'm in. Hell,
I'd climb Mount Taygetos on muh hands and knees   130
if peace was at duh top.

LYSISTRATA

Now here's the plan. Ladies, our husbands
will have to end the war if we will just—

KALONIKE

If we'll just *what*?

LYSISTRATA

You'll do whatever I say?

KALONIKE

Darned right we will! We'd even *die* for peace.

LYSISTRATA

All right then. What we must do
is stop letting our husbands lay us.
(Stunned silence. Murmured protests. Some of the women turn away.)
Wait—what's the matter? Aren't you with me still?
Why this head-shaking, pallor, sad looks, tears?
Won't you do it?

KALONIKE

I—I don't know.   140
Maybe the war ought to just keep on going.

MYRRHINE

That's too high a price to pay. Even for peace.

LYSISTRATA

But Myrrhine, weren't you ready to sell
the shirt off your back? Kally, didn't you say
you'd die for peace, my little fish-fillet?

KALONIKE

> Sure, I would. For peace, I'd walk through fire.
> But—give up sex? There's just no substitute.

LYSISTRATA

> And you, Myrrhine?

MYRRHINE

> > I'd sooner walk through fire
> than give up fucking.

LYSISTRATA

> > Weak as water,
> weak as water, that's what women are!   150
> The tragic playwrights painted us quite right.
> Our lives are nothing but pathetic tales
> of love and babies. And you, Lampito,
> my dearest Spartan, would you fail me too?
> Stand fast with me—the two of us can triumph!

LAMPITO

> A goil not gettin' dick, she's nuttin' but
> a boid wit'out no woim. But,
> *(holding out her hand)*
> > > shake, kid,
> I'm wit' yuh. We soitainly do need peace.

LYSISTRATA *(hugging her)*

> Oh, Lampito, gods bless you, you're the one
> true woman of the lot!

KALONIKE

> > Now, look here, Lys,   160
> supposing we *did* give up—just shut it off—
> quit putting out? How would that end the war?

LYSISTRATA

It's simple. Here's exactly what we do:
we go home, get made up, and slather on
sweet-smelling oil, put on see-through gowns,
and, pussies plucked, we sit without our panties.
Our men get horny as hat-racks. We refuse.
Mark what I say, they'll make peace in a jiffy.

LAMPITO

It just might woik. Remembuh Menelaus,
he t'rew his sword aside, after he took   170
only one squint at Helen's candy-apples.

KALONIKE

Yeah, but what if our men divorce us?

LYSISTRATA

How could they be such fools, to throw away
something that they've already been denied?
As Pherecrates puts it in a play,
"It makes no sense to skin the same dog twice."

KALONIKE

What if they rape us? Haul us off to bed
by the hair?

LYSISTRATA

We'll hang on to the door-handle.

KALONIKE

And what if they start beating up on us?

LYSISTRATA

We'll give in, but just lie inert as stones.   180
They'll quickly see the error of their ways.
No fun for men if women don't take part.

KALONIKE

Well, Lys, if you insist—Ok, I'll do it.

LAMPITO

Our healt'y Spa'tan men, dey'll be pushovers.
But dese At'enian blabbermout's of you's—
how yuh gonna make 'em quit talkin' war?

LYSISTRATA

Ah, we'll find methods, dear. We know them well.

LAMPITO

Yeah? Well good luck, honey. Poisonally,
I t'ink yuh gonna have a tough time tamin' 'em
as long as dey got ships, and all dat cash   190
stashed in duh temple.

LYSISTRATA

                              True, I've thought of that,
and so right now our Senior Citizen
Ladies' Auxiliary are on the march
to the Parthenon as if to worship. Once inside,
they'll occupy it.

LAMPITO

                              Honey, yuh make
ever't'ing sound like a cinch.

LYSISTRATA

                              Very well then,
let's bind ourselves together with an oath.

LAMPITO

Shoot dat oat' to us, baby. We'll swea-uh to it.

LYSISTRATA
　　Good girl. Oh, Policeperson!
(She calls to a Scythian, a tall woman who strides in holding a bow and
a shield.)
　　　　　　　　　　　　Don't stand there gawking,
　　lend us your shield for a bowl, will you,　　　　　　　　200
　　and find us some lamb's guts to sacrifice.
(The Scythian sets down her shield and runs off.)

KALONIKE
　　Good heavens, Lys, what kind of oath is that?

LYSISTRATA
　　It's like the one in that play by Aeschylus
　　where a battleshield does service as a bowl,
　　filled to the brim with victims' foaming blood.

KALONIKE
　　But how can we swear an oath of *peace* on a shield?

LYSISTRATA
　　Oh dear. You're right. Whatever should we do?

KALONIKE
　　How about we get a big white horse—you know,
　　a symbol of peace—and dab us with its dung?

LYSISTRATA
　　Too messy.

MYRRHINE
　　　　　　　　I've got it.　　　　　　　　　　210
　　Set a bowl on the ground and fill it full
　　of wine. We can all swear on it.
　　We'll drink it straight, not even water it.

LAMPITO
  Honeybuns, I t'ink youse got foist-rate idears.

LYSISTRATA
  A bowl! Some wine!
(The Scythian policewoman reenters, bearing a large bowl and a
  large wine-jug.)

KALONIKE
  Now *there's* a decent drink. I'm getting crocked
  just from a whiff of it.

LYSISTRATA *(to the women)*
                         Set down that bowl.
  Sisters, let's kill this sacrifice!
(She takes the bowl, holds it aloft and prays.)
  Persuasion, heavenly goddess, hear our plea,
  and you, O wine who numb if you fail to cheer,   220
  receive our solemn sacrifice and grant
  glorious success to the women of Greece!
(The bearer of the jug pours wine into the bowl.)

KALONIKE
  It pours like real red blood!

LAMPITO
  It sointainly squoits like duh gen-yoo-wine ahticle.

MYRRHINE
  Hand me the bowl—let me be first to swear!

KALONIKE
  Oh no you don't. We ought to all draw lots.

LYSISTRATA
Hold on. Let every woman of us here
touch right hand to the bowl. Someone repeat
the oath after me. The rest of you swear.
(All obey. Kalonike steps forward to repeat the oath. Lysistrata holds aloft
the bowl. The others surround her, touching it.)

LYSISTRATA
From this moment forth, I shall let no man,   230
whether husband or lover—

KALONIKE
From this moment forth, I shall let no man,
whether husband or lover—

LYSISTRATA
Come at me with prong protruding in front of him—

KALONIKE
Come at me with prong protruding in front of him –
ye gods, Lys, this is a *terrible* thing to swear.
I'm getting the shakes!

LYSISTRATA
I'll lock my loins and stay home looking pretty—

KALONIKE
I'll lock my loins and stay home looking pretty—

LYSISTRATA
Made up like Venus, in my sexiest gown—   240

KALONIKE
Made up like Venus, in my sexiest gown—

LYSISTRATA
To drive my man out of his mind for me.

KALONIKE
>   To drive my man out of his mind for me.

LYSISTRATA
>   I shall not yield to him, unless I'm forced—

KALONIKE
>   I shall not yield to him, unless I'm forced—

LYSISTRATA
>   And if I am, I'll lie cold as a fish
>   and passive as a cheese beneath a grater.

KALONIKE
>   And if I am, I'll lie cold as a fish
>   and passive as a cheese beneath a grater.

LYSISTRATA
>   I shall not point my slippers at the ceiling—   250

KALONIKE
>   I shall not point my slippers at the ceiling—

LYSISTRATA
>   I shall not crouch above him like a lioness.

KALONIKE
>   I shall not crouch above him like a lioness.

LYSISTRATA
>   To seal this oath, I set lips to this bowl.

KALONIKE
>   To seal this oath, I set lips to this bowl.

LYSISTRATA
>   If I should break this vow, may all my drinks
>   henceforth be only water.

KALONIKE
If I should break this vow, may all my drinks
henceforth be only water—*ugh!*

LYSISTRATA
Do all of you swear?

WOMEN
                    We swear!   260
*(Kalonike takes a deep drink from the bowl, Lysistrata sips, then
              Myrrhine grabs it and drains it. From offstage
              come the voices of women, shouting in triumph.)*

LAMPITO
I t'ought I hoid a yell.

LYSISTRATA
What did I tell you? The old ladies
have done it! The Parthenon is ours!
And now be off with you, Lampito,
go work on your Spartan men. Your friends
can stay as hostages. The rest of us will climb
to the Acropolis. To begin, let's bar the gates.

KALONIKE
But won't the men soon organize a charge
and try to throw us out?

LYSISTRATA
                    Who cares?
Their empty threats will prove of no account.   270
They'll fight with fire, but we shall never yield.
We'll dictate terms, and triumph in the field!

KALONIKE
Step lively, girls! We're young and in our prime
and good at giving husbands a hard time.

(Lampito runs off. Lysistrata and the others enter the Acropolis. The gates close after them. A Chorus of Old Men enters. They move slowly, burdened with firewood and pots of glowing coals.)

CHORUS OF OLD MEN *(to the tune of "The Volga Boatman")*
Aching shoulder! *(Groan)*
Coals that smolder! *(Groan)*
   Old dogs
   have to lug logs
till we molder!

CHORUSMASTER *(to first man in line, who staggers under his burden)*
Hey, Drakes, old buddy, don't tell me   280
a little green firewood's too much for you?
Look alive, you feeble futzer!

DRAKES *(sings)*
I used to be a flaming youth
but now I only fizzle.
   This lumberjack
   work breaks my back—

CHORUS OF OLD MEN *(sing)*
Not to mention balls and pizzle!
Ye gods, what a miserable day!
There's a curse on our metropolis!
   Every married man   290
   is an also-ran,
for the women have copped the Acropolis!

DRAKES *(sings)*
I'm nothing but a stay-at-home at heart.
Peace and quiet—them's my favorite way of life.
   These foggy old eyes
   hadn't had a surprise
since the first time I slept with my wife.

Here I thought the little woman was at home
baking the bread and stomping grapes for wine.
  But, ye gods, what a switch!   300
  Where's that two-timing bitch?

CHORUS OF OLD MEN *(sing)*
  In the army of occupation at the shrine!
  (Repeat: "Ye gods, what a miserable day," etc.)

CHORUSMASTER *(sings)*
  Philourgos, stack that firewood high!
  Step lively, move your britches!
    We're gonna set fire
    to a funeral pyre—
  asphyxiate the bitches!

CHORUS OF OLD MEN *(sing)*
  We'll tickle 'em with a torch!
  We'll feed 'em a load of lumber!
    Where's Lykon's wife?   310
    Upon my life,
  she's a sizzling little number!

CHORUSMASTER *(sings)*
  Does anybody here recall
  old King Kleomenes?
  He too once seized our holy hill
  till brought down to his knees.
  He'd occupied our sacred shrine,
  holed up for six whole years,
  but when at last the fool came out
  you couldn't see his ears   320
  for all the hair. His bones stuck out,
  he hadn't washed, poor feller.

CHORUS OF OLD MEN *(sing)*
    One whiff of him, historians say,
    would overload your smeller.

CHORUSMASTER *(sings)*
    Well, we routed out that stinking wretch,
    our shields massed sixteen-deep,
    but the bloody siege went on so long
    that I caught up on my sleep!

CHORUS OF OLD MEN *(sing)*
    On to the sacred temple!
    We'll all do daring deeds   330
        till those dames are gone,
        as at Marathon
    we made mincemeat of the Medes!

DRAKES *(sings)*
    The gods hate women, I declare!
    So does Euripides,
    and as for males, the ones he likes
    are pretty boys who tease.

CHORUS OF OLD MEN *(sing)*
    On to the sacred temple!
    Oh, swing those pots of brass.
    We've got no donkey to help haul   340
    so let's keep hauling ass.
    We've hot coals live and steaming,
    we'll show 'em that braziers
    are piping hot and, like as not,
    far mightier than brassieres.

CHORUSMASTER *(sings)*
    O holy Pallas, hairy Pan!
    I faint, I fail, I choke!

Some mangy mongrel
bites my eyes—
it's this motherhunching smoke!   350

CHORUS OF OLD MEN (*sing*)
    On to the sacred citadel!
    The goddess calls!
    Let's give 'em hell!
    Owoooo, this lousy smoke!

CHORUSMASTER
    Ah, the coals are glowing still. Lay on the wood.
    Dip your torches in them pots, men, get 'em blazing.
    First, let's charge the gates. If that don't work,
    we'll set the damn gates on fire, smoke
    the bitches out. Hey, we could use a hand
    from them no-good generals sitting on their duffs   360
    over in Samos. You out there—any top brass
    in the audience? Come on, pot, light my torch.
    There. O Goddess Victory, help us kick the piss
    out of these dames and we'll set up a statue to you,
    not too expensive, soon's we win the day.
(*Enter Chorus of Old Women, led by Stratyllis, carrying buckets, jugs,
                    and water pitchers.*)

STRATYLLIS (*sings*)
    What filthy smoke! There must be fire!
    Come, sisters dear, walk faster
        before they fry poor Kalyke,
        Nikodike, Kratylia—
    we must avert disaster!   370

CHORUS OF OLD WOMEN (*sing*)
    These codgers with their shriveled cods,
    these ancient draft-resisters,
        are stacking hunks

of green tree-trunks—
they plan to roast our sisters!

Athena of the golden plumes,
befriend us now in battle!
Come to the aid
of our bucket brigade
and drive 'em forth like cattle!   380
(Old men surround Stratyllis.)

STRATYLLIS
Get your mitts off me, you dried-up mummies.
Decent men don't manhandle a lady.

CHORUSMASTER
Gods deliver us! A pack of old crows!

STRATYLLIS
We'll throw the fear of gods into you.
And you haven't seen half of our army.

CHORUSMASTER
What are we listening to this drivel for?
(to one of his men)
Hey, Phaedrias, smack her with a log.

STRATYLLIS *(to the other old women)*
Set down your water vessels, ladies.
Keep your hands free for throwing punches.

CHORUSMASTER
Sock her in the jaw. Muffle her gab.   390

STRATYLLIS *(thrusting out her chin)*
Go ahead. Hit me. Right there.
Do it, and you can say goodbye
to your lovelife.

CHORUSMASTER

    Shut your trap, you old mud-turtle, before
    I kick the daylights out of you.

STRATYLLIS

    Why you piss-complected puddle of puke,
    you couldn't kick your way out of a paper bag.
    You lay one finger on me, and—

CHORUSMASTER

                     And what?

STRATYLLIS

    I'll yank your tongue right out through your rear exit.

CHORUSMASTER

    By Zeus, Euripides was right: 400
    "Of all beasts, woman alone is shameless."

STRATYLLIS

    All right, girls, better grab your jugs.

CHORUSMASTER

    I'll grab your jugs, you old shrew.
    What did you bring that water for?

STRATYLLIS

    And what you bring all that firewood for,
    you limp-dicked old fart? For your own cremation?

OLD MEN

    We're going to parboil your pals.

OLD WOMEN

    And we have water that says you won't.

OLD MEN

    How can a little water stop us?

OLD WOMEN

> Try lighting those fires. You'll find out.   410

CHORUSMASTER

> Maybe we ought to grill you alive.

OLD WOMEN

> Got any soap? You could use a bath.

CHORUSMASTER

> What? *You* wash *us*, you vile old harridan?

OLD WOMEN

> Yeah, we'll clean you up for your honeymoon.

CHORUSMASTER

> Of all the brass-assed, impudent—! You dare
> address a senator like that?

STRATYLLIS

> Damn right I dare. I'm a free woman.

CHORUSMASTER

> Too free in the mouth. I'll shut it for you.

STRATYLLIS

> Just try. Maybe in the Senate you're a big shot,
> but here in the street you're a bum.   420

CHORUSMASTER

> Give her a taste of torch! Singe her bald!

STRATYLLIS

> Water brigade—action!
> *(The women raise their buckets, jugs, and pitchers and slosh the men.)*

OLD MEN
Ow! Wow! Holy Hell, that water's freezing!

OLD WOMEN
Warm enough for you?

OLD MEN
What's the big idea?

OLD WOMEN
Just rinsing you off.

OLD MEN *(shivering)*
Br-r-r-r-r!

OLD WOMEN
You've brought all those pots of coals—
why don't you warm your old bones with 'em?
(Enter Commissioner, a man in late middle age, attended by four
policemen, Scythian archers carrying bows
and quivers.)

COMMISSIONER *(talking to himself)*
Women! Dippy dames! Jangling their tambourines,
worshiping foreign gods—Sabazios,
Adonis, for Christ's sake! What screwy times!   430
Everything's bass-ackwards, like the crap
I had to listen to in the Assembly. That idiot
Demostratos urging the campaign against Sicily,
and all the while, his nitwit wife, skunk-drunk,
freaking out on the roof, wailing "O woe!
Adonis has croaked! O woe, O woeful omen!"
And Demostratos talking the dumb Assembly
into drafting the Zakynthosians,
raising a giant army, while his wife's

dervish-dancing on the roof, hollering, "Woe!   440
O woe!" So Demostratos—damn the fool!—
railroads his proposals through. That's the result
of ever letting women have their heads.

OLD MEN

Oh, Commissioner, haven't you heard? Those dames
went wild. They sloshed us with ice-cold water.
You'd think we'd peed our dickies.

COMMISSIONER

Why, by the sacred sea-god's slimy scales,
you had it coming! We men work our own
downfalls. We teach our women to be harlots.
We go to the goldsmith's shop—what do we say?   450
"Hey, smith, you know that brooch you made my wife?
She was out dancing, and didn't the little pricker
pop out of her slot. Now, me, I'll be away
on business to Salamis, but she'll be home.
Drop by the house, will you, and give her
a good tight screw?" Or we go to the cobbler's
and tell some lusty stud, "I say, young man,
my wife has a hurting sandal. Can't you take
a long lunch break, work on her sensitive spot?
You know—come stretch her straps, take down her thongs,   460
put her out of her misery?" And just look
at the upshot of it all. Why, look at me,
Commissioner of Naval Procurement, come for cash
to buy some timber, and these dippy dames
lock me out of the treasury! By the gods,
let's take some crowbars to these gates!
I'll stop this madness here!
(to the policemen)

You klutzy clowns,
what are you gawking at? Don't roll your eyes
at that bistro down the street, damn you! *Crow*-bars

is what I said, not *wine*-bars. Work those gates!   470
Jimmy the suckers open! Here, I'll help.
(Abruptly, the great gates swing wide, knocking policemen sprawling. In
the center of the doorway stands Lysistrata. She
wears a half-veil.)

LYSISTRATA
I'm coming out. You won't need crowbars now,
you'll need only a little common sense.

COMMISSIONER
Why, you insulting hussy! Grab her, cops!
Grab her and tie her hands behind her back.

LYSISTRATA
If any of your flunkies lays a hand
on me, by holy Artemis, he'll regret it!

COMMISSIONER
Aha—too scared to fight? Hop to it, cops!
Truss her with ropes—come on, you assholes, move!
(The policemen advance cautiously.)

STRATYLLIS
You lay a finger on that woman, creeps,   480
and we'll stomp you flat as doormats.

COMMISSIONER
Oh, you will, will you? All right, cops,
grab that one first—she has a mouth the size
of the Colossus.

OLD WOMEN
We're telling you, just touch
either one of them and you'll all rate black eyes.

COMMISSIONER

    Arrest them too. And don't let any more
    damned women out of the Acropolis.

OLD WOMEN

    You try, bud, and I'll scalp you. Oh, you'll howl
    like Hell when your hair and head part company.
    (The policemen draw back in fright.)

COMMISSIONER

    Something tells me I've got a cop shortage.   490
    Now, officers—all together—grab 'em!

LYSISTRATA

    And by the way, we've four or five platoons
    of woman warriors standing by inside.

COMMISSIONER

    Their hands, tie their hands!

LYSISTRATA

TO ARMS, TO ARMS!

(Women pour forth from within the temple, brandishing bunches of
carrots and celery, loaves of bread, a cake,
shopping baskets.)

LYSISTRATA

    Come help us, noble women, you generals
    of the greengrocery, majorettes of the marketplace,
    captains of cake-bakery, sergeants of the garlic baskets!
    Flail 'em, flay 'em, knock 'em down and slay 'em—
    CHARGE!

(The women swat policemen with their bread, baskets, and vegetables.
One policeman takes a cake in the face. The
women overcome the policemen and sit on them.)
    Lay off them, now. No scavenging
the battlefield.

COMMISSIONER
Migods! My cops got creamed   500
by a pack of dames!

LYSISTRATA
Why, don't you realize
you deal with freeborn women? Women of courage?

COMMISSIONER
I thought all your courage came out of a bottle.

CHORUS OF OLD MEN
O wise Commissioner, why squander words
on these dumb brutes? Remember that cold bath
they gave us with no soap, our clothes still on?

STRATYLLIS
That's what you get for lifting hostile hand
against your neighbors. Gladly would we sit
as tame as tabbies, sweet as honeybees,
stinging no man but him who raids our hive.   510

CHORUS OF OLD MEN *(sing)*
The world's turned upside down!
Why did this pack of scary
Amazons take up arms
and seize the sanctuary,
the crown of Athens town?

CHORUSMASTER
Interrogate these dolls, Commissioner!
Get to the bottoms of 'em!

COMMISSIONER *(to Lysistrata and her women)*
Speak up, you!
Why did you take over the Acropolis?
Why did you lock me out of the treasury?

LYSISTRATA
> To stop your cash supply and end the war.   520

COMMISSIONER
> You don't think money is what causes war?

LYSISTRATA
> Indeed it does. And it's the basic cause
> of many another evil. Do you think
> that Peisandros, who looks out for himself,
> and other hawks keep advocating war
> out of the goodness of their hearts? No, war
> makes them a tidy profit. From now on,
> they shan't dip into the treasury.

COMMISSIONER
> And why not?

LYSISTRATA
>   Because, starting now,
> we women hold the purse-strings.

COMMISSIONER
>   Women?   530
> You women can manage *money*?

LYSISTRATA
> Of course we can. We're good at keeping track
> of household budgets.

COMMISSIONER
>   That's a different thing . . .

LYSISTRATA
> Oh?

COMMISSIONER
This is *big* money. Money to make war with!

LYSISTRATA
Ah, but there won't be any more war.

COMMISSIONER
What? No more war? Then how the blooming hell
is Athens to be saved?

LYSISTRATA
By women.

COMMISSIONER
You?

LYSISTRATA
Of course.

COMMISSIONER
I never heard such crap in all my days!

LYSISTRATA
You're growing hot and bothered. Anyhow,
our duty's clear, we have to follow through.   540

COMMISSIONER
This is against the law!

LYSISTRATA
Nevertheless,
like it or not, you're going to be saved.

COMMISSIONER
Over my dead body!

LYSISTRATA

               Too bad, sir,
you feel that way.

COMMISSIONER

           And how did you dumb dames
all of a sudden get so damned involved
with war and peace?

LYSISTRATA

             You really want to know?

COMMISSIONER

Explain yourself, you shameless thing, or I'll—
(reaching out, threatening)

LYSISTRATA

Listen, will you? And keep your hands to yourself.

COMMISSIONER

Gods help me! I'm so mad I could spit nails!

STRATYLLIS

You keep your mitts off her, or you'll be sorry.   550

COMMISSIONER

Quit cawing, you old crow. And as for you,
(to Lysistrata)
I want a full explanation!

LYSISTRATA

             Very well.
It wasn't long ago that every woman
suffered in silence. Anything men did,
we stood for it, and didn't say a word.

Maybe we seldom got out of the house,
yet we kept up with what was going on.
Many a time we'd hear of some catastrophe
you men had caused, but then, when you came home,
we'd put on smiles and sweetly ask, "What happened   560
today in the Assembly, darling? Did they pass
the peace agreement?" You, you'd snarl and say,
"What do you care, you woman? Shut your trap!"
And we'd keep still.

STRATYLLIS

                     Not me. *I* didn't keep still.

COMMISSIONER *(to Lysistrata)*
You behaved wisely. Otherwise, your man
would have beaten you up.

LYSISTRATA

                    Just so. But before long,
you men would make another mess of things.
And if I asked, "Darling, why don't you try
a new approach?" my husband would just scowl
and say, "Enough! Back to your weaving, woman,   570
before I belt you in the two front teeth.
Tend to your loom, let men attend to war."

COMMISSIONER
That's excellent advice.

LYSISTRATA

                Is it indeed?
How then, Commissioner, can it be right
that, no matter how badly men mismanage things,
we women aren't allowed to say a word?
We've heard men ask each other in the streets,
"Where's the great man to lead us?" and then say,

"There's no one." So we womenfolk of Greece
banded together, and have taken charge.   580
How much longer were we to wait? Now *you* keep still
and listen for a change. For we shall soon
set this benighted city-state to rights.

COMMISSIONER
This is an outrage!

LYSISTRATA
Please be quiet!

COMMISSIONER
What, you, a woman, in a woman's veil,
dare tell *me* to be quiet? I'd sooner die.

LYSISTRATA
Oh, is that your problem? Welcome to my veil!
(Lysistrata removes her veil and hands it to another woman, who places
it on the face of the Commissioner. Other women
drape him in a shawl and hand him a sewing
basket and a skein of yarn. They dance around
him, taunting.)

LYSISTRATA *(sings)*
Ah, Commissioner, how fitting
for you to sit with veil on, knitting
like a housewife, keeping quiet,   590
munching beans, your weight-loss diet.
Lucky you—transformed to woman!
Changed in sex, you seem more human.
Stay a woman evermore!
It's women now who'll wage the war!

STRATYLLIS
We'll do it! Rally round me, girls!
Let's help our young sisters-in-arms!

CHORUS OF OLD WOMEN *(sing)*
> Now in sweet accord, we seniors
> wheel and whirl to celebrate
> these young leaders—aren't they lovely?—   600
> saviors of our city-state!
>
> Though our bones be old and creaking,
> though the obstacles loom large,
> we'll support dear Lysistrata
> in her valiant forward charge!

LYSISTRATA
> O Aphrodite and your sweet infant Eros,
> breathe your seductive charm into our breasts,
> harden our husbands' out-of-practice loins.
> Force them on bended knees to come to terms,
> that we be known as Pan-Hellenic peacemakers!   610

COMMISSIONER
> And what exactly do you plan to do?

LYSISTRATA
> Well, for a start, we'll do away with all
> those macho types who stride the city square,
> in battle dress with swords out, scaring people.

KALONIKE
> Arrest the pests!

LYSISTRATA
>   Aren't they a common sight
> in the marketplace these days, clanging about
> like the armored priests of Cybele?

COMMISSIONER
> As soldiers have a perfect right to do!

LYSISTRATA

    Absurd, I say: a soldier with a shield
    emblazoned with an awful gorgon's head,   620
    dickering over a half-pound of sardines?

STRATYLLIS

    It's true. Why, just the other day I saw
    an armed lieutenant hold his helmet out
    to have it filled with oatmeal, and a wild
    Thracian infantry captain scare the girl
    who sells the fruit, and gobble all her grapes.

COMMISSIONER

    Knotty problems, these. Can you untangle them?

LYSISTRATA

    Easily.

COMMISSIONER *(sarcastically)*

    Tell me more, lady. I'm all ears.

LYSISTRATA

    How do you fix a tangled skein of wool?
    Any good housewife knows. When it's all snarled,   630
    you take your spindle and you draw the strands
    this way and that, until the muddle's gone.
    In just that way, we'll fix your muddled war.
    We'll bring envoys from Boeotia, from Sparta—
    this way, that way—and let them sort it out.

COMMISSIONER

    You ninny, do you think you're going to stop
    wars between city-states as if they were
    bunches of yarn?

LYSISTRATA

My dear Commissioner,
you might be wise to govern in the way
that a housewife works with wool.

COMMISSIONER

How do you mean?   640

LYSISTRATA

To start, do just as any housewife does
when given fleece. Spread out your citizens,
inspect them well. Officials taking bribes,
you comb them out and throw the lot away
like bugs or burrs that creep into a skein.
Those who make secret pacts—conspirators—
you separate, as a woman pulls apart
tough, tangled strands. Keep lopping off the heads
of power-cliques, for they cause snarls. And when
they've all been nicely carded, they'll become   650
a true community of citizens,
freeborn Athenians, debtors, immigrants
like multicolored wool, all in one basket.
Consider our neglected colonies
that lie like useless scraps. Take up and weave
the lot together in one bolt of cloth.
Tailor them well. Give Athens a new cloak.

COMMISSIONER

Bolts of cloth? Tangled wool? What far-fetched crap!
What do you knitters know about a war?

LYSISTRATA

Idiot! We know more than you ever will.   660
It's we who bear the sons whom you send off
to slaughter on the battlefront.

COMMISSIONER

                        For shame!
Don't rub salt in old wounds!

LYSISTRATA

                     And that's not all.
For while we lonely wives are in our prime,
all ripe and ready for the feast of love,
your vile war steals the men out of our beds.
But it's the *young* girls I feel sorry for.
They wither to old maids.

COMMISSIONER

                   So what? Don't men
grow old as well?

LYSISTRATA

               For men, it's not the same.
A man may be as dried-up as an old   670
persimmon, and still find a juicy virgin.
But woman's flower is brief. Her chance to wed
goes by, and she's left lying on the shelf,
paying a fortune-teller to be told
she'll meet some tall dark stranger.

COMMISSIONER

Hell, she can still sleep around,
same as a man.

LYSISTRATA

             Commissioner, I fear
you're brain-dead. For the sake of all the gods,
go get yourself a coffin! Here, put on
this funeral wreath.

STRATYLLIS

            Here's another!

SECOND WOMAN

                  And another!   680

(They drape the Commissioner with wreaths and black ribbons.)

LYSISTRATA

> Your ferryboat will take you up the Styx.
> It's pulling out—take pennies for your fare.
> The hounds of Hell are howling to be fed.
> Take honeycakes for hushpuppies. Be off!

COMMISSIONER

> Zeus in the skies! Am I supposed to stand
> for this? I'll get me to the Assembly
> and show the other men what these damned dames
> have done to me!

LYSISTRATA

>   What? Aren't you satisfied?
> Haven't you been embalmed? We'll drop around
> in a day or two and pay you our respects.   690

(Exit Commissioner, wearing his funeral togs. Lysistrata and the other
> *younger women go back into the Acropolis, leaving*
> *the two choruses on stage. The doors swing shut*
> *once more.)*

CHORUSMASTER

> All right, soldiers! Up off your duffs!
> Take them cloaks off, get ready for battle.

(The Chorus of Old Men remove their robes. Underneath, they
wear tunics.)

CHORUS OF OLD MEN *(sing)*

> Oh, there's something gone rotten in Athens.
> You can tell by one hell of a smell.
> Old Hippias, the city's last tyrant,
> must be back on a furlough from Hell.
>
> It's entirely the fault of those women
> that we've come to this terrible pass.

We're taking a bruising like Spartans out cruising—
Hey, Kleisthenes, lend us your ass!   700
(Kleisthenes, an aged gay queen swinging a purse, hobbles quickly across
*   stage on high heels, blowing kisses to the Chorus of*
*   Old Men.)*
So beware of political females,
How they prance and they pray and they prate.
Next thing, they'll abolish our pensions
and declare they've perfected the state!

CHORUSMASTER
      Imagine it! A bunch of women—*women*, mind you—
      yakking and yammering about war! They intend
      to make peace with Sparta? My gods, you can trust Sparta
      about as far as you'd trust a wolf with open jaws
      to guard your lambchops. This is tyranny!
      But I won't let 'em get away with it.   710
      I'll take my stand next to Aristogeiton
      the tyrant-killer.
(He imitates Aristogeiton's statue: right arm lifted, fist clenched.)
      I'll strike a blow for freedom! Think I'll give
      this old crow a boot in the boobs, a bust in the mouth—
(punches Stratyllis)

STRATYLLIS
      Ohhh-h-h! You try that again, baby,
      and *I'll* give *you* a bust in the mouth!
      You don't know what it's like to be a woman.
      Let me give you a little piece of my mind.
(sings)
      When I was a girl, I performed the rites
      of goddess-worship. I set my sights   720
      on becoming the bearer of the sacred chest
      to the temple of Athena. I surpassed the rest
      and they made me a grinder-girl, knowing I'd take
      pride in grinding flour for the sacred cake.

CHORUS OF OLD WOMEN *(sing)*
> Oh, it's great to be a grinder-girl in Athens,
> the city that to grow up in can't be beat.
>> When you're just a budding teen
>> serving Pallas Athene,
> you're sitting in the catbird seat!

STRATYLLIS *(sings)*
> At the festival of Artemis, young and fair,   730
> I wore the saffron costume of a sacred bear.
> Then I totally succeeded as a pious maid—
> I bore the sacred basket in the spring parade.
> The people all cheered—what a beautiful sight!
> In Athens, little fatcats are brought up right.

CHORUS OF OLD WOMEN *(repeats the refrain)*

STRATYLLIS
> So I think I'm qualified to offer
> a bit of advice. Forget that I'm a woman.
> Already, haven't I given this state far more
> than you geezers ever have? I've given sons.
> What good are you? All the rich loot   740
> our granddads brought home from Marathon
> you fools have pissed away. You tax-dodgers,
> thanks to you, we're looking at bankruptcy.
> Don't mutter at me like that! What you need
(removes her slipper)
> is a good slipper-slap!
(wallops the Chorusmaster)

CHORUS OF OLD MEN *(sing)*
> Holy gods on high, what treason!
> Are we men or are we mice?
> Into battle, boys! Let's show 'em!
> No more being Mister Nice!

Gird your loins for action, comrades!   750
Strip your shirts—and years—away!
Give these janes a whiff of armpit!
Forward, brothers! To the fray!
(Old men take off their tunics, revealing brightly colored undershorts.)

CHORUSMASTER
Don't give these hags an inch, boys, or they'll take
a yard. Smash 'em before they launch a fleet
against us, before they light out after us
on horseback. You know, when a woman
gets in the saddle, she'll ride you to death!
Remember those Amazons in the painting,
mowing down men. Come on now, grab 'em   760
by their necks, clap 'em in stocks!

STRATYLLIS *(sings)*
Beware! Provoke me one inch more,
I'll loose the tigers of my wrath.
Don't try to run, don't call for help—
they're death to any in their path!

Come on, sisters, strip for action!
Off with our robes! Off with old age!
Give these billygoats a noseful—
Give 'em a whiff of women's rage!
*(Chorus of Old Women remove their robes. Underneath, they wear
brief tunics.)*

CHORUS OF OLD WOMEN *(sing)*
Old mummies, don't you mess with us   770
or you'll kiss your teeth goodbye.
You'll gum your garlic, suck your beans.
You'd take us on? Don't try!
*(Two of the chorus women grab the old men's Chorusmaster and set him
down on his rump. They dust their hands
in triumph.)*

STRATYLLIS
    Why should I give a hoot in Hell
    what old men do, as long as my sisters are
    Lampito of Sparta, Ismenia of Thebes?
    Old men, you shall be powerless, for all
    the votes you cast in the Assembly.
(to one of the old men)
    Hey, Senator, even your best friends
    hate your guts. Why, only yesterday   780
    I threw a little religious hen-party,
    poured a few libations to Hecate,
    and asked an old chum over from Boeotia—
    she's a dear, cute as an eel canape—
    only she couldn't enter Athens. You'd imposed
    a ban on foreign visitors. Enough
    of your foolishness, old man! You pass
    too many laws. What do you say, sisters?—
    let's set him on his butt.
(Two other women pick up the Senator and rudely seat him. They dust
                    off their hands.)

CHORUS OF OLD WOMEN *(sing)*
    Remember Aesop's fable?   790
    A big dumb eagle didn't know
    enough to fear a little foe,
        a beetle born in dung,
        and so, to raise her young,
    she built her nest in Zeus' lap,
    but there the beetle took a crap—
        oh, wily trick!
        Zeus jumped up quick—
        in getting to his legs
        he smashed the eagle's eggs.   800
    Men, keep in mind this fable.
        The moral should be clear:

though not your size, we're able
to set you on your rear!
(Chorus of Old Women exit dancing, leaving the humiliated chorus-
master and the Senator sitting where they were set.)

ACT II

(The same scene, five days later. The Chorus of Old Women stand before
the great gates of the Acropolis. The gates swing
wide. Lysistrata comes out.)

CHORUS OF OLD WOMEN *(with mock-tragic solemnity)*
Chief architect of our successful coup,
why look so solemn? Why do you come forth?

LYSISTRATA
Traitorous women's deeds and flighty minds
give me to grieve and ramble restlessly.

CHORUS
Whatever do you mean?

LYSISTRATA
                                        I dare not say.

CHORUS
Out with it! We're your friends.   810

LYSISTRATA
I can't keep still, and yet I'm loath to speak.

CHORUS
Do not conceal what weighs upon us all.

LYSISTRATA
Well, to be blunt, we women grow hard up
for erections.

CHORUS
        Zeus deliver us!

LYSISTRATA
    Why cry to Zeus? Old dears, our cause is lost.
    I can't prevent our feeble, love-starved troops
    from deserting. Just now I caught one
    sneaking through a crevice in the wall,
    heading for another hole in the wall,
    that pick-up joint, Pan's Grotto. Another one   820
    was slithering down a rope, and yet another
    high-tailed off like a dicky-bird in heat,
    bound for Orsilochus' whorehouse.
    Gods! I had to drag her back by the top-knot.
    So badly do they hanker to go home,
    they're pulling every excuse in the book.
    Oh-oh. Here comes another.
(to a woman tiptoeing out of the gates)
                        You there, halt!
    Going somewhere?

WOMAN
    Oh, I simply must run home this minute!
    Gotta see about my good Milesian wool   830
    that the moths must be murdering.

LYSISTRATA
    Moths? Tommyrot! You'll stay right here.

WOMAN
    Honest, I'll just be a minute. All I want to do
    is spread my wool out on the bed.

LYSISTRATA
    You *will* not. Back to your post!

WOMAN
> What? And let my wool be wasted?

LYSISTRATA
>   If need be.

SECOND WOMAN *(running out of the gateway)*
> O Gods above, I've simply got to dash!
> My husband's coming, and his loaf of bread
> is rising. All the dough is puffed up huge—
> I've got to punch it down for him.   840

LYSISTRATA
> Another limp excuse. Bread? *Bread*, you say?
> Your husband mustn't get a single crumb!

SECOND WOMAN
> But it won't take me any time at all.
> Let me go! That poor loaf needs my hands on it!

LYSISTRATA
> Duty first!

THIRD WOMAN *(waddling out, clutching her belly)*
>   Help, help, holy Eilithyia,
> protectress of us mothers-to-be! Don't let
> me drop this baby in this sacred shrine!

LYSISTRATA
> What on earth are you babbling about?

THIRD WOMAN
> Labor pains! I've got labor pains!

LYSISTRATA
> Since when? Last night you weren't even pregnant.   850

THIRD WOMAN

That was last night. Oh, Lysistrata, dear,
let me run home. I've got to call the midwife.

LYSISTRATA

What are you trying to hand me?
(thumping the woman's belly)

Say, what's this?

This big hard thing down here?

THIRD WOMAN

My baby boy!

LYSISTRATA

What a hard child! He must be made of bronze—
he's hollow. Why, you miserable wretch,
it's the helmet of Athena you have here!
(pulls out helmet and holds it up)
What? Were you planning to give birth to it?

THIRD WOMAN

I'm about to give birth, all right.

LYSISTRATA

Then how do you explain this helmet?   860

THIRD WOMAN

Oh. *That.* You mean that helmet? I took it
in case the baby started coming out
in the holy Acropolis. If he did, you see,
I was going to nest in the helmet like a pigeon
and lay my egg.

LYSISTRATA

You're caught red-handed.
You'll stay here, faithful to your post until
your baby boy's true birthday.
(Fourth and fifth women run out.)

FOURTH WOMAN
> I can't sleep in the Acropolis! This place
> gives me the whim-whams! Nightmares day and night!
> I just now saw the sacred temple snake.   870

FIFTH WOMAN
> Me, I can't sleep either. Athena's owls
> keep hooting all night long. I've such a case
> of insomnia—aaaagghh! I'm going batty!

LYSISTRATA
> You people, stop! You'll be the death of me!
> You sorely miss your husbands, to be sure,
> but don't you see? They sorely miss you, too.
> Your sleepless nights and nightmares are sweet dreams
> next to the sleepless nights they undergo.
> Take courage, sisters. Promise to endure
> for only a little longer. I've received   880
> a red-hot message from an oracle.
> It says we'll win, if only we hold out.
> Look, here it is in writing.
> *(produces a rolled-up scroll)*

WOMEN *(in a jumble of voices, as they crowd round)*
> Read it!
> > Let's hear it!
> > > Tell us—what's it say?

LYSISTRATA
> Be quiet and I'll read it to you.
> *(opens scroll and reads)*
> > "When it shall come to pass that swallows fly
> > far from the stuck-up hoopoe's handsome plumes,
> > when fair hens stay far distant from their cocks,
> > their troubles shall be ended. Mighty Zeus
> > will set on top whatever lies below."   890

FIRST WOMAN
Oh, wow, we'll be sitting pretty!

LYSISTRATA *(continuing to read)*
"But should the swallows yield, and quit the shrine,
they'll be a flock of no-good twittering twits."

SECOND WOMAN
That's crystal clear, for an oracle.

LYSISTRATA
Come, then, dear sisters, back to the temple.
Fight on! Let's keep our unity unbroken.
We're bound to win—the oracle has spoken!
*(Lysistrata and the younger women turn and reenter the Acropolis. The
gates close. The Chorus of Old Men enters.)*

CHORUSMASTER *(sings)*
When I was a boy in kneepants,
they used to tell the tale
of a hero named Melanion,   900
a true blue supermale.

CHORUS OF OLD MEN *(sing)*
He was wise, you'd better believe it.
He said, "Marriage?—that's a load!
I'll go off and be a hermit.
Just show me the mountain road."

DRAKES *(sings)*
So he left home, gave up women.
Oh, he put aside bad habits,
went ahunting with his hounddog,
and skinned him a mess of rabbits.

CHORUS OF OLD MEN
    Yes, he washed his hands of women.   910
    He consigned 'em to perdition.
        And, men, that's why
        let's you and I
    stay true to his tradition!

CHORUSMASTER *(to Stratyllis)*
    What do you say, old bat, how's about
    a little kiss?

STRATYLLIS
                Fat chance, garlic breath!

CHORUSMASTER
    Say, how'd you like a flat bum?
    (He aims a kick at her, which misses.)

STRATYLLIS
    Ha ha, I saw your crotch! What a bush!

CHORUS OF OLD MEN *(sing)*
    Our long hair proves we're heroes
    like Myronides and Phormio.   920
        We're bold, we're brave,
        so we never shave—
    we gotta have whiskers to show!

STRATYLLIS *(sings)*
    Let me tell you the tale of Timon—
    Ye gods, how that man did roam!
        In a bramble patch
        full of bites to scratch,
    he set up his home sweet home.

CHORUS OF OLD WOMEN *(sing)*
>Timon turned his back on Athens,
>he wandered in bog and fen   930
>>and with a bitter tongue
>>he dumped verbal dung
>all over his fellow men.

>Yes, he damned the whole male gender,
>he hated 'em through and through.
>>He called 'em fools,
>>rascals, simple tools—
>hey, that's how we see 'em, too!

>So let it be said for Timon,
>he called 'em by their right names.   940
>>He hated men's guts
>>like crazy, *but*
>he simply adored us dames!

STRATYLLIS *(to Chorusmaster)*
>So you want a smack in the kisser, huh?

CHORUSMASTER
>Haw haw! You scare me!

STRATYLLIS *(lifting leg high)*
>How about a kick in the jewels?
>*(She aims a kick at him, which fails to land.)*

CHORUSMASTER
>Don't show me nothing, cutie.
>I seen better fur on rats.

CHORUS OF OLD WOMEN *(sing)*
>>Don't strain your eyes, you geezers,
>>don't hope for a peep at our hair.   950

We know how to use our tweezers,
> so you won't see anything there.

(The two choruses exit, men to the left, women to the right. Atop the
> *great wall, Lysistrata appears. She stands, shading*
> *her eyes with a hand as if scanning the horizon.)*

LYSISTRATA *(shouting)*
Man ho! Man ho! Take your battle stations!
(Kalonike, Myrrhine, and other women join her.)

WOMEN *(eagerly)*
A man?
> You mean it?
What man?
> Where?

LYSISTRATA
He's coming, and he looks all ripe and ready
for the rites of love.

KALONIKE *(fervently)*
> O Lady Venus,
presider over the orgies at Cyprus, Paphos, and Kythera,
you who make our menfolk upright and firm,
have mercy on us! Bring us a good man, now!   960
Where's this hunk at?

LYSISTRATA
> On the road from the south.

KALONIKE
Now I see him. Who is he?

LYSISTRATA
Look hard. Anybody recognize him?

MYRRHINE
> Do I ever! It's my husband, Kinesias!

LYSISTRATA
> All right, Myrrhine, you know what to do.
> Tease him, love him up, turn on the heat,
> do anything—just don't give in to him!

MYRRHINE
> Leave him to me. I know how to handle him.

LYSISTRATA
> I'll stay right here and help work him up
> to the sticking point. Quick, out of sight, everybody!   970
> *(All except Lysistrata disappear from the wall. Kinesias enters, his tunic*
> *poked out in front as if covering a gigantic erection.*
> *A manservant holding a baby follows him.)*

KINESIAS
> Ye gods on high, this thing is killing me!
> It's like I'm tied to the torture wheel!

LYSISTRATA
> Who goes there?

KINESIAS
>   Me, that's who.

LYSISTRATA
>   Are you a man?

KINESIAS
> For Zeus' sake, lady, isn't it obvious?

LYSISTRATA
> Be off with you!

KINESIAS

And just who in hell are you,
to give me the bum's rush?

LYSISTRATA

The captain of the guard.

KINESIAS

Captain, I'm on my knees begging you,
bring Myrrhine out to me!

LYSISTRATA

Bring you Myrrhine?
And just whom do you think you are?

KINESIAS

Kinesias of Marathon, her husband, dammit.   980

LYSISTRATA

Ah! Welcome, sir! Your name's a household word!
Your wife has it in her mouth constantly.
Every time she sucks a ripe fig, she cries,
"This reminds me of Kinesias!"

KINESIAS

Oh, gods! Bring her out to me, before I—!

LYSISTRATA

Yes, and when the topic of men comes up,
Myrrhine always says, "Next to Kinesias,
other men aren't worth a candle."

KINESIAS

Puh-lease, won't you send her out here?

LYSISTRATA

And what will you give me, if I do?   990

KINESIAS *(with a pelvic thrust)*
 Everything I've got.

LYSISTRATA
 I'd better go fetch your wife.
 (She disappears.)

KINESIAS *(calling after her)*
                              Hurry up, will you?
 (musing aloud)
 What a drag it's been since Myrrhine ran out on me.
 It hurts to go home to an empty house.
 I eat my dinner alone, go to bed alone.
 All the time, I'm alone—and petrified!

MYRRHINE *(appearing atop the wall, to herself)*
 Oh, Goddess Venus, how I love him, love him!
 But I'm not supposed to love him.
 Oh no, I'd best not see him!

KINESIAS
 Myrrhine, honey! What are you doing to me?   1000
 Get your sweet ass down here on the double!

MYRRHINE
 No. I won't.

KINESIAS
                Don't you know me, cookie?
 This is your husband asking you! I need you bad!

MYRRHINE
 You don't *really* need me.

KINESIAS
                        Don't I?
 Just look at me, honey—I'm a nut case!

MYRRHINE
Bye bye. I'm going.

KINESIAS
Hold on—stop! Listen to your baby!
Come on, kid, holler.
(gives baby a pinch)

BABY
Mama! Mama! Mama!

KINESIAS
There you are.
Myrrhine, dearest, has your heart gone hard?
The poor little kid hasn't had a change   1010
or a square meal in practically a week.

MYRRHINE
I'm hard-hearted? *Me?* You big oaf,
you're the one who's neglected the child.

KINESIAS
Well then, come on down and take care of him.

MYRRHINE *(to herself)*
I'm weak. Gods help me, mother-love
forces me to give in every time.
(She disappears from the wall.)

KINESIAS
Oh, wow, she's younger—lovelier—sexier than ever!
She's the girl I married. Her little frown—
oh, gods, it just fires me up all the more!
(Gates open, Myrrhine rushes out, folds baby into her arms.)

MYRRHINE

    Poor ittle sweetums, is bad old Daddy mean to oo?   1020
    Ummmmm! Mommy's gonna kiss you, lambie-pie!

KINESIAS

    Honey, will you kindly tell me why
    you're treating me this way? Why lock yourself
    in the Acropolis, holed up with all those dames?
    You're only hurting both of us.
(He tries to fondle her.)

MYRRHINE

    Get your big meathooks off of me!

KINESIAS

    And the house is going to Hell in a handbasket.
    It's all your fault.

MYRRHINE

              I should care.

KINESIAS

    Doesn't it even matter that the chickens
    are pooping all over your best bedspread?   1030

MYRRHINE

    Let 'em poop!

KINESIAS

              And what about you and me?
    We haven't had any Venus-worship together
    in a dog's age. Please, honey, come home!

MYRRHINE

    Not till you men stop fighting and make peace.

KINESIAS

> Oh. Is that all you want? We'll do it!

MYRRHINE

> Then do it. But I'm not coming home
> until you do. I've sworn a sacred oath.

KINESIAS

> Well, can't you give me a little loving?
> It's been forever.

MYRRHINE

> > Sorry. No way.
> Kin, dearest, it's not that I don't love you,   1040
> you understand?

KINESIAS

> > Then how about doing it? Now!

MYRRHINE

> *What*, you big jerk? In front of the child?

KINESIAS

> Oh, yeah. Hey, I didn't mean—
> *(to manservant)*
> Manes, get the kid out of here!
> *(Manservant exits, taking baby.)*

KINESIAS

> Ok, sweetpuss, now Baby's bound for home.
> Let's you and me hop to it!

MYRRHINE

> > Are you nuts?
> There isn't any place to do it here.

KINESIAS

How about Pan's Grotto? There's a back room—

MYRRHINE

And if we did it there, how could I reenter
the shrine? I'd need to get re-purified.   1050

KINESIAS

Just douche off in that spring, the Klepsyora.

MYRRHINE

Surely you wouldn't make me break my oath?

KINESIAS

Break the damned oath! You can blame me.
Don't fret about it.

MYRRHINE

Wait here. I'll get a cot.

KINESIAS

Don't even bother, honey. Let's just flop
right here in the dirt.

MYRRHINE

In the dirt?
Darling, you know I love you like my life,
but—ugh!—not in the dirt!
(*She goes back into the Acropolis.*)

KINESIAS

Hot damn! At least she loves me!
(*Myrrhine reenters with a cot, which she sets up slowly and carefully,
while Kinesias waits impatiently.*)

MYRRHINE
>All right now, dearest, you stretch out on this.   1060
>*(Kinesias lies down on the cot, on his back.)*
>I'll slide my slip off—just you wait. Oh, darn.
>Where's the mattress?

KINESIAS
>Mattress? Who needs a mattress!

MYRRHINE
>Well, we can't do it on a bare cot.

KINESIAS
>The hell we can't! Give us a little kiss.

MYRRHINE *(gives him a quick peck)*
>Don't go away. I'll only be a second.

KINESIAS
>Yum! Hurry back! Honey, I'm dying for you!
>*(Myrrhine reenters the Acropolis. Kinesias, in her absence, writhes on*
>>*the cot in agony. Myrrhine returns with mattress,*
>>*makes Kinesias get up, spreads out mattress on*
>>*the cot.)*

MYRRHINE
>There, that's better. Now lie down, darling,
>   get all comfy.
>*(He stretches out on the cot again, holds out his arms to her.)*
>Oh-oh. No pillow.

KINESIAS
>Gods blast the pillow! Who needs a pillow anyway?   1070

MYRRHINE
   Well, *I* need a pillow. Hold on, be right back.
(Exits again.)

KINESIAS
   My poor dick's starting to feel like Heracles
   robbed of his dinner.

MYRRHINE *(reentering, with pillow)*
                           Now. Let's just slide
   this pillow under your head. Anything else you need?

KINESIAS
   Nothing but you, dammit! C'mere!

MYRRHINE
   I'm getting ready! I'll slip my undies off!
   Now, dear, don't forget about that peace treaty.

KINESIAS
   May the gods blast me blind if I do!

MYRRHINE
   Hold on—we don't have a blanket.

KINESIAS
   Screw the blanket!

MYRRHINE
                           Poor darling, I must take   1080
   good care of you. Back in a flash!
(Exits.)

KINESIAS
   Cot. Mattress. Pillow. Now it's blankets.
   This woman's driving me bonkers!

MYRRHINE *(returning with blanket)*
    Here we are. Now let me just arrange
    it nice. Get up a second, dear, will you?

KINESIAS
    Get up? I've been up for days.
    (Kinesias groans, reluctantly getting to his feet while Myrrhine spreads
               the blanket on the cot. He lies down again.)

MYRRHINE
    How about a nice long rub-down with some oil?

KINESIAS
    Oil? Oil? OIL, you say?

MYRRHINE
    Well I'm going to give you a nice rub-down,
    a little teensy-weensy one.

KINESIAS
                    Father of the Gods,   1090
    make her spill the damn-blasted oil!

MYRRHINE
    Now hold out your hand and I'll give you some.
    You smear it on good.

KINESIAS
                Yuk! This oil stinks!

MYRRHINE
    Oh dear. I brought the fish oil by mistake.

KINESIAS
    I don't give a damn, it smells great!

MYRRHINE
> No, no, darling, this won't do.
> I'll just go get some lovely aloe lotion.
> *(Exits.)*

KINESIAS
> Great Zeus and all the gods!
> Won't you please send to everlasting Hell
> whatever silly bastard invented rub-downs!   1100

MYRRHINE *(returning with a new bottle)*
> Here we go, dearest. A nice fresh bottle of lotion
> all for you.

KINESIAS
> I've already got a lotion bottle,
> dammit, and it's ready to pop its cork.
> *Woman!* Will you kindly stop running around
> and plant your butt down here on this cot?

MYRRHINE
> I'm coming, darling. See, I'm taking off my shoes.
> You *will* support the peace movement, won't you?

KINESIAS
> Don't worry—I need a peace, all right!
> Hey, where you going? Come back!
> *(Myrrhine dashes back into the Acropolis. The gates shut behind her.)*
> Good gods, I've just been pussy-whipped!   1110
> After all that fuss, she runs out on me!
> *(Chorus of Old Men enter and surround Kinesias.)*

KINESIAS *(sings)*
> Now what'll I do?
> I haven't a clue.
>   My heart—and my privates—are sore.
> I'm down in the dumps

with an ache in my lumps—
   doesn't anyone know a good whore?
Dear Gods above, what
must a man do for twat?
   Things are going from lousy to worse.   1120
Our kid's throwing fits
and me, I've no tits—
   I guess I'll go hire a wet nurse.

CHORUS OF OLD MEN *(sing)*
   By gum, by gorry,
  we're downright sorry
    to see you in this fix.
  These women deceive us,
  lead us on and leave us
    with prostates sore—the pricks!

KINESIAS
   Wow, how I'm hurtin'!   1130

CHORUS OF OLD MEN
   You are, for certain.
    You suffer from lover's cramp.
  That no-good bitch
  wouldn't scratch your itch,
    the tricky little tramp!

KINESIAS
   No, no, she's a honey!

CHORUS
   You being funny?
  She's a bitch, bitch, bitch, bitch, bitch!

KINESIAS
   A bitch, yes, yes, a bitch! Almighty Zeus,
  snatch her up like a handful of sand   1140

caught in a hurricane, send her
spinning across the sky, whirl her about,
and fling her down to earth again, that I
may catch her on my ever-loving spear!
(Kinesias and the Chorus of Old Men exit. Enter a Messenger from
Sparta and, from the other side of the stage, the
Commissioner. Each man has a protuberance
under his robe.)

MESSENGER

Hey youse, take me tuh your leaders, won'tcha?
I got a secret message to deliver poisonally.

COMMISSIONER *(laughs and points)*

What are you, a walking battering-ram?

MESSENGER

Ain't youse got no manners? I'm a impawtant
messenger from duh Spa'tan chiefs,
bringin' woid about duh peace treaty.   1150

COMMISSIONER

A messenger, eh? Then why are you carrying
that concealed weapon?

MESSENGER *(whirling about, trying to conceal his bulge)*

You seein' t'ings, dad. I got no such t'ing.

COMMISSIONER

Well then, why do you turn your back on me?
What's that you trying to hide under your cloak?
Are you ruptured?

MESSENGER *(aside)*

Dis shrewd old codguh's got duh goods on me.

COMMISSIONER
Why you poor bastard, you're in the same fix
I'm in—your staff's stuck upright.

MESSENGER
Nope, doc, youse got muh case all wrong.   1160

COMMISSIONER
Then tell me, what's the matter with you?

MESSENGER
Nuttin'. Dis is muh secret code message-container.

COMMISSIONER
Oh yeah? I've got one of those gadgets myself.
Listen, you can level with me. How are things
in Sparta, really? Are the people suffering?

MESSENGER
Duh men are. Dey all got awful stiffs.

COMMISSIONER
Can this affliction be a sudden plague
that Pan in godly wrath calls down on us?

MESSENGER
Naw. Lampito and duh other dames stahted it.
Dey slammed shut deir pussies. Evuh since,   1170
duh love-life's been on hold.

COMMISSIONER
                    So?

MESSENGER
So it's duh pits. All us guys walk aroun'
hunched over like we was carryin' lighted candles

t'rough a friggin' whirlwin'. Duh dames
won't give us duh goodies till we make peace.

COMMISSIONER

Aha! I see it all now, clear as day!
Those conniving females hatched a plot against us.
Scoot back to Sparta, Messenger! Tell your chiefs
to send their envoys over here right away,
ready to sign the peace. And I shall tell   1180
the senators of Athens to talk turkey.

MESSENGER

Now yer makin' sense, mistuh! I'm halfway
back tuh Spa'ta already!
(Exits running.)

COMMISSIONER

                              How to convince
the senators? Oh, I know—I'll show 'em
my secret coded message-container.
*(Exits. Enter, from opposite sides of the stage, Chorus of Old Men and
                  Chorus of Old Women.)*

CHORUSMASTER

In all the world there's no more savage beast
than woman. Not even tigers, nor a forest fire,
is half so ravenous, so unquenchable.

STRATYLLIS

If you think that, then wouldn't you prefer
we be your friends and not your enemies?   1190

CHORUSMASTER

No way! I'm a woman-hater. Always was,
always will be.

STRATYLLIS *(shrugging)*
>Well, it's a free city.
>By the way, someone should tell you—your bare chest
>makes you look like a half-plucked chicken.
>Give me your shirt, I'll help you back into it.

(Chorusmaster produces his tunic, and Stratyllis helps put it on.)

CHORUSMASTER
>You're mighty kind—well, for a savage beast.
>Maybe I should have kept my shirt on.

STRATYLLIS
>There. That's an improvement. But now why
>are you winking and blinking so? Must be a bug
>in your eye. If you act nice, I'll take it out.   1200

CHORUSMASTER
>Yeah, take it out and let me look at it.
>The pesky little thing's been driving me nuts.

STRATYLLIS
>All right, I will, although I have to say,
>you're a grouchy old fossil.

(She wipes his eye.)
>Why, Heavens above!
>What a colossal chigger you've got! No, no—
>I meant the bug. So there, it's out now. See?

CHORUSMASTER
>Thanks, dearie. So that's what was bugging me.
>Only now I'm leaking tears.

STRATYLLIS
>There, there now,
>Mama's got a handkerchief. Here. Blow.
>Let Mama kiss it and make it better.   1210

(kisses him)

CHORUSMASTER
    Now cut that out!

STRATYLLIS
                    Didn't you like it?

CHORUSMASTER
    Aw, you dames. Always going up our sleeves,
    soft-soaping us. It's like the saying goes,
    "Women! Can't live with 'em, can't live without 'em."
    But what the hell. From now on, let's make peace.
    Come on, women; come on, men, join forces and sing
    all together, shall we? Everybody ready?

CHORUS OF OLD MEN AND OLD WOMEN *(sing)*
    Athenian women, Athenian men,
    don't badmouth the opposite sex again.
    Hard times have hit us, and we all hurt,   1220
    so let's quit treating each other like dirt!
    Crones and fuddy-duddies,
    let's be bosom buddies,
    let's cultivate the gentle touch.
    Let what's mine be yours
    and what's yours, mine,
    though we haven't got anything much!

DRAKES *(sings)*
    Want to borrow a couple of thousand drachs?
    I could dig down deep in my cloak.
    Heck, I wouldn't expect you to pay me back,   1230
    but I happen to be stone broke.
(Choruses repeat the refrain, "Let's be bosom buddies . . .")

STRATYLLIS *(sings)*
    Hey, you're all invited to a party tonight.
    Come on over, you chicks and studs.

There'll be pea soup with ham and some barbecued lamb.
Bring the kids, wear your fancy duds.
Make yourselves at home—don't bother to knock,
walk right in—only don't get sore
if I happen to lose the key to the lock
that would let you bums through my door!
(Choruses repeat, "Let's be bosom buddies . . .")
(Enter three Spartan envoys from one side of the stage, the Commissioner
from the other. The Spartans wear tunics, but
hold cloaks or robes in front of them, concealing
their groins.)

COMMISSIONER

By Zeus, it's the envoys from Sparta already.   1240
Every one of 'em's got a six-day beard
and sticks out in front like a Boeotian eel.
Good day, my noble Spartans. How are you?

FIRST SPARTAN

So what's to talk about, yuh dumb bastit?
Can'tcha see how we are? We're up Shit's Creek
wit'out no paddle. We're like t'ree cawkscrews
wit'out no cawks.

COMMISSIONER

                         Indeed, I plainly see
you're hard-pressed, sorely stressed,
and hot to discharge your responsibilities.

SECOND SPARTAN

Youse ain't just whistlin' "Dixie," bub.   1250
Fuh duh love o' Zeus, let's get to duh peace treaty.
We're so hard up we'll sign anyt'ing.

CHORUSMASTER

And here come our own Athenian negotiators,
clutching their cloaks as if they're hiding

stolen hams. Look at 'em all hunched over
like wrestlers going into a crouch!

(*Enter three Athenian negotiators, in tunics like the Spartans, and also
holding cloaks in front of them.*)

FIRST ATHENIAN

Where's Lysistrata? We can't hold out much longer.

COMMISSIONER

Why, I believe you and these Spartan studs
suffer from the same complaint. Let me examine you.
Stick out your tongues. Say "Ah." Tell me,   1260
is any time of day the worst for you?
Right before dawn, perhaps?

SECOND ATHENIAN

                              Aw, rats, you quack,
this thing of ours goes on the whole day through.
The way I am, even Kleisthenes looks good to me.

STRATYLLIS

Best keep your problems hidden, boys. Don't let
the Legionnaires of Prudery see you.
Remember how they went all over town
busting the prong off every statue of Hermes?

THIRD SPARTAN

Lady, youse got a pernt.

(*Spartan envoys and Athenians don the robes they have been carrying.*)

FIRST ATHENIAN

Hail, Spartans! It's been hard to wait for you!   1270

FIRST SPARTAN

Oh, yeah? Well, don'tcha t'ink us Spa'tans, too,
we ain't been boinin' up?

SECOND ATHENIAN
                        Let's get right down
    to business. Why are we here?

SECOND SPARTAN
                        Dammit, youse knows—
    we gotta woik out duh peace.

THIRD ATHENIAN
    Then let's call Lysistrata here at once.
    That woman—she's the one we're dealing with.
    She's the enemy general.

FIRST SPARTAN
                        Call her, den,
    fo' Zeus' sake!

FIRST ATHENIAN
                    Ha!—we don't need to.
    Here she comes now.
(Lysistrata enters.)

COMBINED CHORUSES *(sing)*
    Let's stand up and cheer!   1280
    Lysistrata's here!
        A leader both brave and charming!
    She's a force for peace—
    every man in Greece
        finds her totally disarming!

LYSISTRATA *(aside)*
    And now, unless I miss my guess, these men
    should be pushovers.
(to all)
                        Where's Reconciliation?

(Enter Reconciliation, a chubby man in a long blond wig, dressed as a
naked woman. He wears huge, burlesque breasts,
buttocks, and vulva. He comes in seductively, to
slow and sultry music.)

Right this way, Reconciliation dearest!
To begin, please bring me the Spartans.
Don't lay rude hands on them like some impatient husband,   1290
but lead them here gently, in womanly style.
If they draw back, then take them by their handles.
(Reconciliation leads each Spartan envoy to Lysistrata's right side.)

LYSISTRATA
Now bring me the Athenians in their turn.
Whatever they extend, you may grasp firmly.
(Reconciliation leads each Athenian negotiator to Lysistrata's left.)

LYSISTRATA
Hear me, the pack of you. Though I'm a woman,
I've a mind of my own, a bit of common sense.
Besides, my father and many another elder
taught me a thing or two. I blame you both,
Spartans and Athenians alike. Don't you deserve
your equal shares of guilt? You both wage war.   1300
Yet, brother Greeks, you pour the same libations
to the same gods at Delphi and Thermopylae.
You fools! The Greece we love now lies surrounded
by Persians at our gates, while you lay waste
our cities, slay an entire generation
in senseless battle. Take that—my first charge!

FIRST ATHENIAN *(aside)*
How the woman runs on! I'm ready to burst!

LYSISTRATA
Next, I must scold you Spartans in particular.
Don't you recall when earthquakes cracked your streets,

when your Messenian slaves rose in revolt?   1310
Remember how your chief, Perikleidas,
in a scarlet cloak that made his face more pale,
came whining to us, begging us Athenians
to lend you an army of four thousand men?
Thanks to our noble Kimon, you survived.
Is this how you repay us for our kindness?
By coming back to set our homes on fire?

SECOND ATHENIAN
   Damned if she isn't absolutely right!

FIRST SPARTAN *(aside)*
   Maybe's she's right. But—dat Reconciliation!
   Holy balloons, ain't dat a poifect can!   1320

LYSISTRATA
   Let me not spare you smug Athenians either.
   Have you forgotten how, when the tyrant Hippias
   made you wear sheepskins, how your Spartan friends
   fought by your side, routed the tyrant's forces,
   so that once more you might wear free men's robes?

SECOND SPARTAN
   Dis dame's got brains.

THIRD ATHENIAN *(eyeing Reconciliation)*
   And this Reconciliation babe—what boobs!

LYSISTRATA
   Then, with the memory of your comradeship
   still in your heads, why carry on this war?
   Why should you not at last be reconciled?   1330

FIRST SPARTAN *(indicating Reconciliation's rear end)*
   We'll agree, if you At'enians give up your claim
   to duh back country.

LYSISTRATA
What claim, exactly?

FIRST SPARTAN
Tuh duh town o' Pylos. We been hot
tuh take a crack at dat sweet place fo' years.

FIRST ATHENIAN
Damnation! Pylos will never be yours!

LYSISTRATA
Oh, give it to them.

FIRST ATHENIAN
But it's a vital spot!

LYSISTRATA
Then make a deal. Trade them some other place.

FIRST ATHENIAN
Well, maybe we could take the double peaks
of Malia,
(indicating Reconciliation's breasts)
maybe the straits of Megara
(points to legs)
maybe Old Beaver Inlet down in Echinus . . .   1340
(points)

FIRST SPARTAN
Hold on, yuh greedy bastit! Do yuh t'ink
yuh gonna lay youh hands on *everyt'ing*?

LYSISTRATA
Why dicker so? What are a couple of hills?

SECOND ATHENIAN

 All that rich land! I'm ready to strip bare
 and plow hell out of it!

SECOND SPARTAN

       I wouldn't mind
 givin' it a little foitilizuh, m'self.

LYSISTRATA

 And so you shall. But first, you must make peace.
 Why don't you go confer with your allies?
 How do you know they'll make peace on these terms?

FIRST ATHENIAN

 No need to bother. Our allies are in   1350
 the same fix. They'll sign quick, to get to bed.

FIRST SPARTAN

 Our allies too. Dey're sperlin' for a peace.

LYSISTRATA

 Very well then. To the Acropolis, all!
 There, while you pledge an everlasting peace,
 our sisters shall pour wine, and you shall feast
 out of their bountiful baskets. Then each man
 shall take the hand of his own loving wife
 and go straight home.

FIRST ATHENIAN

       Spartans, what do you say?
 On to the Acropolis!

FIRST SPARTAN

      Just lead duh way,
 A'tenian, baby! You don't need tuh beg.   1360

SECOND ATHENIAN
    Let's go! Last man in is a rotten egg!
(They hurry into the Acropolis, followed by Lysistrata, Reconciliation,
                and the other envoys and negotiators, leaving only
                the two choruses.)

CHORUSES OF OLD MEN AND OLD WOMEN *(sing)*
    Share and share alike,
    say us geezers and dames!
        But all we can share
        is the morning air,
    'cause we don't have a thing to our names!

STRATYLLIS *(singing to Chorusmaster)*
    Need a favor, friend? Just ask it!
        Need your kid—cute little maid—
    all dressed up to bear the basket
        in the sacred spring parade?   1370

    Velvet capes with braid inside 'em,
        silken shawls with golden strings—
    wish to hell I could provide 'em,
        but who's got such costly things?

    Take my gifts done up in boxes,
        rip the wraps, undo the twine—
    if you see one damn thing in 'em,
        you've got better eyes than mine!
(Choruses repeat the refrain, "Share and share alike . . .")

CHORUSMASTER *(sings)*
    Is your household going hungry?
    Packs of kids and slaves to feed?   1380
    Has your brood no bread for breakfast?
    Let me be your friend in need!

You could bring your bags and buckets
to my granary. I'd pour
tons of wheat like golden ducats,
if I had the stuff in store.

How I'd hate to disappoint you!
Guess I'll keep my door tight shut.
Better not come by, you beggar,
'cause my bulldog, he bites butt.   1390

(Choruses repeat the refrain.)
(Lights dim, signifying that hours pass. Lights rise again on the two
choruses. The Chorusmaster, now holding a torch,
knocks loudly on the closed gates.)

CHORUSMASTER
Hey, in there! You, gatekeeper! Open up!

GATEKEEPER *(from within)*
What do you want?

CHORUSMASTER
Is it all over? Have they signed the peace?
Open up, before I burn down both your doors
and tickle your fat bottom with my torch.
Should I? I should, but that's the oldest gag
in the book. Hey, audience, want me to?

GATEKEEPER *(opening the gates and emerging)*
Out of the way, you buzzard, or I'll twist
your silly beak! They're coming out! Make way!
(Chorusmaster and choruses stand aside. Enter the three Athenian
negotiators, staggering as if slightly drunk.)

FIRST ATHENIAN
Good gods on high Olympus, what a feast!   1400
And aren't those Spartans great guys, when you get

to know them? And weren't we Athenians
the life of the whole damn' party?

SECOND ATHENIAN

                              Yeah, we're quick
to crack a joke when there's a drink in us.
If you ask me, we always ought to take
a couple of drinks before we ever try
negotiating anything. Every time
we sit cold sober at a conference table,
we fuss and fume, we hardly hear a word.
We think they said stuff that they didn't say,   1410
we read wrong meanings into everything.
Back home again, we never do agree
on what the hell we all agreed upon!

THIRD ATHENIAN
But when we're all lit up, the meeting flows.
Who cares if someone sings "O Telamon,
My Telamon" when he's supposed to sing,
"Rule Cleitagora, Cleitagora Rule the Waves"?
We clap like hell, and swear the bastard sang
the best damned song a singer ever sang.
(Choruses converge around them.)

CHORUSES OF OLD MEN AND OLD WOMEN
What's happened?
                              Give us some news!   1420
Is it all over?
                  Has the peace been signed?

GATEKEEPER
What, you pests still hanging around? Stand back,
all of you—here come the Spartan envoys now!
*(Choruses retreat. Enter the three Spartans, the first empty-handed, the
              second carrying a guitar, the third a drum or
              tambourine.)*

FIRST SPARTAN (*to his companions*)
> Play, youse bozos, play! I feel like singin'
> somet'in' for dese At'enians. I t'ink I'll do
> dat dance where I kick muh own tail.

FIRST ATHENIAN
> Yes, play! Dance! Sing! Show us your stuff.
> (*Music. First Spartan dances, then breaks into song.*)

FIRST SPARTAN
> Inspire me, Goddess Memory,
> and help me sing dis song—
> how, side by side, At'enians   1430
> and Spa'tans, we stood strong.
>
> At glorious Artemisium
> we manned duh winnin' oars.
> When Leonidas he held duh pass,
> we fought like foamin' boars.
>
> What matter if duh Persians
> come t'ick as grains of sand?
> Us Spa'tans and At'enians
> can save our native land!
>
> O holy huntress Artemis   1440
> who kills wit' silver darts,
> help rid us of our foxy wiles
> and join our hands and hearts!
> (*Enter, from the doorway, the Spartan women held hostage, together
> with Ismenia, the Corinthian beauty queen, and
> the women who had occupied the Acropolis.*)

LYSISTRATA
> Well sung, good friend. Now, Spartans, you may claim
> your women—come, Athenians, do the same.

Let each wife take her husband by the hand
and gladly lead him home, and there be manned.
Goddess Athena, on this best of days,
let dance and song contribute to your praise.
Henceforth let men and women find surcease   1450
from torments past, and live in lasting peace!

CHORUSES OF OLD MEN AND OLD WOMEN *(sing)*
Now we hasten to our dancing,
summoning the sister Graces,
three bestowers of all beauty.
sing we praise to Artemis,
virgin sister of Apollo,
and the fire-eyed Dionysus,
gallivanting with his Maenads,
Zeus, who sunders bolts of lightning,
and high Hera, queen of Heaven—   1460
every god we call to witness
that our peace be long-enduring.
Hail to gracious Aphrodite,
granter of sweet harmony!

Shout we now our victory—
    Whoopee!
    Whoopee!
Yippee! Yay!
    Evoy, evoy!
    evai, evai!   1470

LYSISTRATA
Spartans, give us one more song!

SPARTAN MEN AND WOMEN
Down from ol' Mount Taygetos,
come, Spa'tan Muse, descend!

Our song o' joy begins
wit' praise for golden Apollo.
and Tyndareus' twins.
Dey say dat Poppa Zeus
as a swan wit' quilly legs
made Leda an offer she couldn't refuse:
he laid her—and she laid eggs.   1480

So hooray for a whole lot o' lovin'
in duh good old Spa'tan style,
apushin' and ashovin'
and dancin' all duh while
on the banks of duh Eurotas
where our women gets deir quotas,
    boobies jigglin',
    bottoms wigglin',
    whirlin', twirlin',
    swiftly swirlin',   1490
    piles o' people boy-and-girlin',
    feet designed fo' kick-ass dancin'
    doin' fast and fancy prancin',
led in duh dance by Leda's child,
dat swan-necked Helen o' Troy,
    tumblin' hair
    what lets loose brightness,
    legs what leap
    wit' deer-like lightness—
dancin' for sheer joy!   1500

So—sing praises to duh goddess
wit' her armor-plated bodice!
in Spa'ta we built her a shrine
    decked with plenty o' brass—
    oh, it's real foist class
on account of she's divine.

Oh, you know the one I mean,
she's Athens' namesake queen—
so, hail,
      all hail,
           to the wisest, wiliest woman of all,
great Pallas—Pallas Athene!   1510

Frogs

Translated by
Alfred Corn

Translator's Preface

Although it's possible to translate, and well, from languages you don't know, I wouldn't have taken on the project of putting into contemporary English a full-length play of Aristophanes if Attic Greek had been a closed book to me.

I studied Latin in high school and would certainly have ended up a different person if I hadn't. Greek, on the other hand, wasn't taught. During undergraduate years I was too preoccupied with modern languages—French, Italian, German—to begin Greek. Tackling it remained a dreamed-of possibility, postponed until circumstances allowed. My first attempt came in the summer of 1971, when a classics major friend of mine initiated me into the first mysteries of the language. But vacation ended, and Greek had to be shelved in favor of enterprises less recreational. In the late 1970s, living and working in New Haven, I met Robert Fitzgerald, who had come there after retirement from Harvard. His preeminence as a translator of Homer doesn't need to be celebrated here again, but I can say that Robert's own dapper, at-ease approach to ancient and modern literature lent an added glamor to a knowledge of Greek. I remember finding in one of his own poems a line praising "Greek participial loveliness." What did he mean by that? He made no attempt to explain in so many words and asked me whether I had thought of looking into the language. I told him that I had begun it once but had now forgotten most of what I'd learned. In his characteristic musical whisper, he said, "Well, you know, our Greek grammar is like the foam on the crest of a breaking wave: one moment it's there, the next, not." I laughed, but the suggestion was clear: there were levels of knowledge, on one hand, the professional's, on the other, the layman's, which would probably always need some propping up. No need to be embarrassed if your mastery of a supremely difficult language proved less than perfect. Robert Fitzgerald could acknowledge not remembering everything? Then perhaps I, too, could learn enough Greek grammar to qualify as a respectable forgetter of it.

What I did was enroll as an auditor in one of those beginners' total immersion courses, this one taught at Yale. First I got the instructor's permission to audit and then mustered enough chutzpah to ask him whether he would consider grading my assigned work as well. Classics hadn't for decades been a popular undergraduate study; possibly he was touched by my maverick project, undertaken not for credit but simply for the intrinsic value of the subject. During the entire term, which met five days a week, three hours each day, he made no distinction between me and his regularly enrolled students (a kindness for which I'd like once again to express gratitude). At the end, he told me I would have been given an A, which was nice but nothing compared to the glimpse caught, through barely parted curtains, of a distant splendor. I learned quite a lot of Attic Greek grammar, which, even during the term, I began to forget, the difference being that I now knew how to look up what I'd forgotten. (Do they still sell those "verb wheels," printed on stiff paper, and indispensable when you're trying to get through the roulette game of obscure verb tenses and modes without losing your shirt?) To prove that I had actually learned some Greek, though, I undertook to translate Sappho's great hymn to Aphrodite, which took me months, every minute of the process a delight. Results, if anyone is curious, can be found in a book of poems titled *The West Door*.

Robert was right: Greek uses participles in astonishing ways, sometimes linking several of them in different tenses to produce a new sense of temporal relationships. I was also agog to discover that a Greek participle could describe a group of women who had laughed thus: γελασασας (in transcription, *gelasasas*), the sound giving an excellent approximation of the ha-ha-has still cheerfully pealing across an interval of more than two millennia.

I remember, too, trying to get a feeling for the aorist tense, usually translated in the past but combining both future- and past-tense morphemes. What I came up with as an approximation is the British locution used in response to occurrences whose supposed actuality is about to be revealed or confirmed. Example? A knock comes at the door; Mrs. A. says to her husband, "That will have been Lydia." We might find another approximation in the French literary habit of recounting past events in the future tense, as: "Racine composed *Andromaque*, his first play, in 1667. He will not write *Phèdre*, usually regarded as his greatest, for ten more years." It's interesting, too, that Greek aphorisms or general statements are usually cast in

the aorist: "Man was [more idiomatically, *is*] the only animal that laughs."
An alternate translation giving an aorist flavor to it might be: "Man will
prove to have been the only animal that laughs." The sense that all time,
past, present, and future, is one and the same strikes me as particularly
Greek, a culture known for its preoccupation with ineluctable fate. Possibly
it was that same intimation of fatedness that Eliot wanted the opening lines
of "Burnt Norton" to convey in *Four Quartets*, though what follows is a
Christian rather than a Greek treatment of human destiny.

Aristophanes wrote only comedies, all with serious purposes. Like Molière,
he meant *castigare mores ridendi* ("to chastise behavior through laughter"—
a postclassical phrase, incidentally). Despite broad humor and elements of
slapstick, *Frogs* is probably even more serious than the others, concerned as
it is with the very survival of Athens as a free city-state. It was first staged in
405 B.C. at the Lenaea, its author then forty years old. Athens had recently
undergone several reverses in its continuing conflict with Sparta, no one
doubting that as much as one more defeat would be final. The war effort
demanded material support from every citizen. Aeschylus had died fifty
years earlier; both Sophocles and Euripides the preceding year. As the most
important playwright still living, Aristophanes would have to do his part in
energizing discouraged Athenians for the coming confrontation. In Greek
culture, from Homer forward, it was axiomatic that poetry played an important role in the formation of the *polis*. For Plato that role was negative;
for Aristophanes, drama had the potential for kindling a militant spirit in
its audience. As a writer of comedy, he could mock cowardice and gold-
bricking. In *Frogs* he could even become a drama critic and weigh the re-
spective virtues of Aeschylus and Euripides. As critic, he cannot neglect
purely aesthetic issues, but Aristophanes is first and foremost concerned
with the contestants' comparative ability to inspire martial ardor and forti-
tude, a contest that spurs his dramatic genius even more than does the re-
hearsal of normal stylistic criteria. In any case, questions of both substance
and style produce the famous "trial" of the two great tragedians staged during the second part of the play. Discussed in the abstract, stylistic earmarks
of the two playwrights are also embodied in the roles Aristophanes has provided for them in the play. If Euripides' tragedy is perverse and verbally
elaborate, so are his speeches in *Frogs*. By the same token, Aristophanes'

Aeschylus speaks with all the Bronze Age stamina and syntactic overkill said to define him as a playwright.

At first glance *Frogs* may not seem unified, divided as it is between an opening section in the parodic form of a conventional journey to the underworld (the principal characters Dionysus and his servant Xanthias) and the concluding contest, for the most part made up of arguments spoken by the rival dramatists. After a number of rereadings we can see that the god of viniculture and drunkenness and his down-to-earth sidekick correspond in interesting ways to Euripides and Aeschylus. On one side, refined intellect sometimes overheated by delirium; on the other, practical sense and physical strength. It's notable that Xanthias has much more success than Dionysus when he dons the heroic garb of Heracles, just as Aeschylus' granitic commitment to military prowess is of more value to Athens in the moment of crisis. Aristophanes is not the sort of polemicist who puts his thumb on the scale in order to make sure his side wins. Aeschylus' faults as he sees them—and we may not always agree, by the way—are duly noted along with Euripides' strengths, although, again, we may feel that Aristophanes hasn't acknowledged all of them. Finally, the work is a play, not a rationally constructed and fully supported critical argument. Differences between the contestants must be marked in strokes broad enough to be grasped in the back rows of the amphitheater; and they must be dramatized as comedy, comedy with a serious, public purpose. A built-in surprise in the working out of the plot is that Dionysus awards the palm to Aeschylus rather than to his friend Euripides, with whom he has obvious affinities. As patron of the drama, he is called on to put aside for the moment his bacchic attributes and respond to incontrovertible evidence. If Aeschylus' verses haul down the scales and send Euripides' lighter ones up in the air, how is he to deny that they do? One way to regard the outcome is to think of it as provisional: Aeschylus may not be a better tragedian than Euripides in all ways and for all times than Euripides; but, for an Athens threatened with defeat and loss of sovereignty, he is the man of the hour and therefore must be brought up from Hades as an active force in the realm of sunlight and air.

David Slavitt, editor of this series, urged his translators to make stageworthy versions of Greek drama. In order to comply I saw that I'd need to translate not only words but human types, to experience Aristophanes' characters as living people and render them as such. It meant finding a voice peculiar to each—Dionysus' intelligent, evasive, and sometimes affected drawl; Xanthias' exasperated, practical-minded clowning; Euripides' lacy, high-strung self-regard; Aeschylus' raging-bull, congressional diatribes. Prosodic concerns also played a role. Although Aristophanes' dramatic poem is composed metrically throughout, it didn't strike me as advisable to follow suit for a play to be staged today. The first part of the comedy is on that basis reconceived as prose, with a few metrical interludes; for example, the Frog chorus and Dionysus' retorts to it, done here in iambic tetrameter with rhymes. The play's second phase, the debate between Euripides and Aeschylus, is more formal and rhetorical than the first, and I've used meter for it—blank verse for Dionysus and Euripides, dactylic tetrameter (often with anacrusis and/or truncation) for Aeschylus. Dactylics' driving *thumpeta-thumpeta* helped me give the emphatic, almost archaic quality of the old tragedian's discourse. Still, I wouldn't have used meter anywhere in the translation if I'd felt that it undermined the speechly, dramatic energy found in Aristophanes.

Many distinguished translations of *Frogs* precede my attempt. The 1924 Loeb edition of the Greek text is accompanied by a smooth, metrical Englishing, Edwardian in tone. Benjamin Bickley Rogers is credited, but I wonder whether he wouldn't have acknowledged a debt to Gilbert Murray, a translator always able to combine classicist erudition with the sophistication of the 1890s. As an undergraduate, I read and laughed along with R. H. Webb's ingenious, high-spirited version. Later on, I admired the energy and accuracy of Richmond Lattimore's, done in American English. While working on my own, I consulted the detailed scholarly edition prepared by A. H. Sommerstein, whose notes to the play were very helpful in deciphering topical references and drawing out veiled implications in the language.

I've relied on earlier scholars' unforgotten knowledge of Attic language and Aristophanic comedy to arrive at a translation that keeps faith with the original, going along even so with the series editors' assumption that a contemporary poet and novelist could bring worthwhile qualities to the enterprise. I take it for granted that Aristophanes' audience responded to the play not as a museum piece but as a theatrical experience to be enjoyed. In theater, the supreme commandment is "Thou shalt not bore." Those attempting to produce contemporary stage versions of Greek drama will have kept in mind that fidelity is sometimes paradoxical; sooner or later they'll join in with the chorus of the old standard "I'll always be true to you, darling, in my fashion." With a little assistance from contemporaneity, the fate of great dramatic works will prove to have been unfailingly aorist: belonging to the past, certainly, but also to the present and the future, at least for those able to bring humor and imagination to an encounter with them.

Cast

XANTHIAS, Dionysus' factotum
DIONYSUS
HERACLES
CORPSE, on the way to Hades
CHARON
CHORUS OF FROGS, dwelling in a lake near Hades
CHORUS, adepts in the Eleusinian mysteries
AIACUS, Hades' porter
HOUSEMAID TO PERSEPHONE
HOSTESS OF AN INN
PLATHANE, second hostess
SLAVE IN HADES' HOUSEHOLD
HADES
EURIPIDES, the distinguished playwright
AESCHYLUS, Athens' master playwright
NONSPEAKING
    Donkey belonging to Dionysus
    Porters who carry Corpse
    Two maidservants of the innkeepers
    Slaves in Hades' household
    Ditylas, Skeblyas, Pardokas, Scythian archers
    Muse of Euripides, who plays castanets

(A street in Athens. In the background, the door to Heracles' house. Dionysus enters on foot, and Xanthias, riding a donkey, with a bag on a pole slung over his shoulder. Dionysus sports a yellow robe with lion skin draped over it, like the one Heracles always wears. He also carries Heracles' signature club and wears buskins.)

XANTHIAS
    Ok, Boss, should I crack the usual jokes, the ones that always get
        a laugh?

DIONYSUS

    Go right ahead as long as it's not "I'm beat to—et cetera," just
        hold off on that one, it's too emetic.

XANTHIAS

    But maybe some other little witticism, Ok?

DIONYSUS

    Whatever, but not "Oh, my aching back!"

XANTHIAS

    Ah, come on, what about this one—
(makes a lewd gesture)
                        it's a hoot.

DIONYSUS

    That'll do fine. Just make sure you don't wag your pole, and—

XANTHIAS

    Huh?

DIONYSUS

    And whine that you've "got to dump your load."

XANTHIAS

    I can't say, "I'm so overloaded that if somebody doesn't help, I'll
        have a diarrhea storm"?

DIONYSUS

    God, no. Look, you're about to make me throw up.   10

XANTHIAS

    What, you mean I've got to carry all this around and not even get
        a chance to make groaners like the ones Amei-
        psias and Lycis and Phrynichos put in every
        comedy they write?

DIONYSUS

Don't you even dream of it! Every time I see one of their productions I'm bored a year older than I was when it started.

XANTHIAS

My poor neck, broken under its load, and it can't even crack a joke!

DIONYSUS

It takes nerve to be as spoiled as you. Here I am, Dionysus, son of Lord Winejug, hobbling along on foot, while my slave rides and doesn't have any burdens to bear at all!

XANTHIAS

Whaddya mean, no burdens?

DIONYSUS

How can you say you're burdened when the donkey's carrying *you*?

XANTHIAS

Well, I'm carrying this!

DIONYSUS

How?

XANTHIAS

Against my better judgment, that's how.

DIONYSUS

It's the donkey that carries it all, right?   20

XANTHIAS

Well he's not carrying everything by himself, for godssake!

DIONYSUS
How can you claim to carry anything if you're *being* carried?

XANTHIAS
Uhh, because my back aches and my neck hurts like hell.

DIONYSUS
All right, since the donkey's no help, why don't you get down and
carry *him*?

XANTHIAS
Sheesh, why, oh, why didn't I sign on as a sailor in that naval
slugfest where every poor fool who fought got his
freedom? Then I could tell you where to go.

DIONYSUS
Dismount, scumbag. I've kept at it, and now we've reached the
door I was trying to get to, the place where I was
going to stay tonight. Porter! Open up!

HERACLES
Who's banging on my door? Sounds like a centaur slammed up
against it. What's going on?

DIONYSUS
Whew!

XANTHIAS
What is it?

DIONYSUS
Did you see that?   30

XANTHIAS
What?

DIONYSUS
How rattled he was.

XANTHIAS
Well, sure, he thought you were loony-tunes.

HERACLES
Well, bless Demeter, now I have to laugh. I'm biting my lip, but
it's no good, I can't help it. Ah-hah-hah-hah!

DIONYSUS
If you don't mind, would you come here? I need your help.

HERACLES
A lion skin draped over a yellow dress! A club! And those
designer boots! What in god's name for? Where
were you headed?

DIONYSUS
I just finished a stint on board the *Kleisthenes*.
(*He makes a stereotypical gesture suggesting it was a "gay" cruise.*)

HERACLES
Locked in combat with the navy, eh?

DIONYSUS
Yes, and sank more than a dozen enemy ships.

HERACLES
You two?   40

DIONYSUS
Yes, by Apollo.

HERACLES (*falsetto*)
"Then I woke up and it was all a dream." Ha-ha!

DIONYSUS

Anyhow, there I am sitting on deck reading Euripides' play
Andromeda,
and suddenly, it hits me, a longing in my heart, you have no idea
how strong.

HERACLES

A really big longing, eh?

DIONYSUS

No, a small one, no more than seven feet tall and 250 pounds,
like the actor Molon.

HERACLES

A longing for a woman?

DIONYSUS

No.

HERACLES

For a boy?

DIONYSUS

Nope.   50

HERACLES

A man?

DIONYSUS

No, just drop it, will you.

HERACLES

Well, did you and Kleisthenes have a go at it?

DIONYSUS

Listen, buster, will you stop making fun of me? I have this
huge craving.

HERACLES
>What kind of craving, buddy?

DIONYSUS
>Not sure I can explain. Suppose I make a little comparison. Have you ever had a burning desire for, mm, a bowl of pea soup?

HERACLES
>Pea soup? Damn straight I have, a million times.

DIONYSUS
>Is my comparison clear, or do you need further explanation?

HERACLES
>You don't need to explain pea soup, I get that much.

DIONYSUS
>Fine, that's the kind of craving I have for dear old Euripides.   60

HERACLES
>Even though he's dead?

DIONYSUS
>Yes, and no one's going to dissuade me from my plan of tracking him down.

HERACLES
>You mean you're going all the way down there—to *Hades*?

DIONYSUS
>Um-hm, and even further down, if there's a lower level.

HERACLES
>Why do you want to?

DIONYSUS

I need to speak to a real poet,
(*declaims from Euripides' Oeneus*)
"For some are not now with us, and, of those remaining, all
inferior."

HERACLES

Well, we've got Iophon, haven't we, Sophocles' son?

DIONYSUS

All right, he's the only good one left—though even with him, the
case is moot.

HERACLES

If you really need to dig somebody up, why not Sophocles? He
tops the list.   70

DIONYSUS

Because I'd like to give young Iophon a chance to show us what
he can do on his own, without his father. Any-
how, Euripides is a clever cuss, he must already
be working on his escape plan; whereas the old
man (who was comfortable here on earth) is also
going to be perfectly comfortable *there*.

HERACLES

And Agathon, where does he stand?

DIONYSUS

He has slipped away—no longer with us. A fine poet, much
missed by his dear, darling entourage.

HERACLES

But where did he go?

DIONYSUS

To picnic with the great departed.

HERACLES
What about Xenocles?

DIONYSUS
As far as I'm concerned he can just drop dead.

HERACLES
Phythangelos?

XANTHIAS
Hey, what about me? My shoulder hurts like hell! Little you care.

HERACLES
But don't we have a whole nest of singing birds, tragedians by the
thousands, who can rattle along a country mile
ahead of Euripides?   80

DIONYSUS
Mm, nullities, chatterboxes, twittering machines, bald-faced
careerists.
They crank out their little debut and are heard no more—
a one-night stand with the Muse of Theater!
I dare you, name me *one* dramatic poet
who writes a brilliant, well-constructed line.

HERACLES
Brilliant how?

DIONYSUS
Someone original, who takes risks, something like
(*declaims*)
"Bright empyrean, Zeus' bedroom," or "Time's fateful footstep,"
or "Although my tongue was guilty of perjury,
my heart dissented from all sacrilege."

HERACLES
> You like *that*?

DIONYSUS
> Wild about it.   90

HERACLES
> Awful stuff, and you damn well know it.

DIONYSUS *(declaims)*
> "My mind's not yours to rule; put your own house in order."

HERACLES
> That's no better.

DIONYSUS
> The only thing you know about is food, so you can just stuff it.

XANTHIAS
> Nobody gives a hot damn what *I* feel.

DIONYSUS
> Anyhow, the reason I came here—and dressed up like you—was
> to ask you this: When you went down there to
> capture Cerberus, which of your friends offered
> hospitality along the way, you know, in case I
> need it, too. Also, tell me about the highways, the
> safe harbors, the springs, the food shops, the rest
> stops, bordellos, hostesses . . . and inns that have
> the fewest bugs.

XANTHIAS
> Still not one word about *me*.

HERACLES
> You dumb cluck, you're really hell-bent on going, aren't you?

DIONYSUS

    Would you please just calm down and tell me about the various
        routes, which is the fastest, I mean, so long as it's
        not going to be too hot or, for that matter,
        too cold.

HERACLES

    Which one should you hear about first, let's see . . . Well, one
        starts off with a noose and a stool. Anchors
        aweigh!—and then you swing.   100

DIONYSUS

    No thanks. Afraid I have this hangup—I like to breathe.

HERACLES

    Then there's the beaten track, a shortcut! courtesy of mortar
        and pestle.

DIONYSUS

    Fresh-ground hemlock, you mean?

HERACLES

    Exactly.

DIONYSUS

    Sorry, too cold, you catch your death that way, it starts in the
        shins and in seconds you're chilled to the bone.

HERACLES

    All right, how about a quick downhill slide?

DIONYSUS

    That's more like it. Walking's not my strong point.

HERACLES

    Well, just toddle over to the Pottery Works . . .

DIONYSUS
    And then?

HERACLES
    Then climb that tower, the tallest one . . .   110

DIONYSUS
    And then what?

HERACLES
    When the torch-race starts, just wait for the signal torch to flare
            and then, when the crowds are roaring, "Go, go,
            go!" you just let yourself go.

DIONYSUS
    Go where?

HERACLES
    You skydive. Alley Oop!

DIONYSUS
    Sure, and break out a couple of meatballs made of my brains.
            Don't think so.

HERACLES
    Well, which way *will* you go?

DIONYSUS
    The one *you* took.

HERACLES
    That's a hard road. You'll get to a huge lake, deep as they come.

DIONYSUS
    And how do I cross it?

HERACLES

An old boatman will row you over in a tiny punt, about this big.
Costs two bucks.   120

DIONYSUS

That two-dollar ticket price, no getting around *it*. Who started
that custom anyway?

HERACLES

Theseus was the first to plunk down. And once you pay, you'll
see humongous snakes and vast herds of savage
beasts . . .

DIONYSUS

Stop trying to scare me off, it won't work.

HERACLES

And then Big Muddy, with waves of eternal do-do—in which
you'll find everyone who ever did harm to a
guest, or refused to pay a hustler the fee owed, or
beat his mom or zapped his dad, or broke a vow
he'd sworn, or

(chuckles)

copied down one of Morsimos' stinko soliloquies.

DIONYSUS

Plus, I suggest, all those who've danced in the great bard
Kinesias' sword-and-shield hoedown.

HERACLES

Anyhow, the next thing you'll be basking in is flute music, and
you'll see sunlight as bright as ours up here; and
a crowd of cheerful revelers, both men and
women, will clap their hands for joy.

DIONYSUS

Who might they be?

HERACLES

> Happy initiates of the mystic order . . .

XANTHIAS

> I suppose I'm the jackass that carries the mystic paraphernalia.
> Well, don't count on my help now and
> forevermore!   130

HERACLES

> . . . who'll tell you everything you need to know, since they live
> right beside the road you're traveling. You'll be
> passing right by Hades' gate. Safe journey, my
> friend!

DIONYSUS

> And to you. Take care.
> *(Exit Heracles. To Xanthias)*
> > All right, load up.

XANTHIAS

> Hey, I never *un*loaded.

DIONYSUS

> Get a move on.

XANTHIAS

> Pleeeeze don't make me. Why not hire one of these dead people
> being carted off, considering they'll be going
> down there too?

DIONYSUS

> And if I don't find one?

XANTHIAS

> In that case, you can count on me.
> *(Enter Porters, carrying Corpse on a stretcher.)*

DIONYSUS
It's a deal. Well, well, look what's on its way, a body on a
           stretcher. Hello there! Mr. Cadaver! Would you
           be willing to carry our bags down to Hades?

CORPSE
How many?

DIONYSUS
These right here.   140

CORPSE
Say, for five bucks?

DIONYSUS
No, too steep.

CORPSE *(to porters)*
Keep moving.

DIONYSUS
Wait, can't we work something out?

CORPSE
It's five bucks or no dice.

DIONYSUS
How about two-fifty?

CORPSE
I'd just as soon be alive again as take that.

XANTHIAS
That prick! He can just go to hell. I'll manage.
(Porters and Corpse exit.)

DIONYSUS
>What a prince! Always there when I need you. Come on, let's
>catch that ferry.

CHARON
>Land ho! Pull her up!   150

XANTHIAS
>What's that?

DIONYSUS
>That? It's a lake, the one he mentioned. *And*, thanks be to God,
>the ferryboat.

XANTHIAS
>It *is*, in Poseidon's name, it is—and Charon aboard it!

DIONYSUS
>Hail, Charon! Welcome! Blessings on you!

CHARON
>All passengers for Sunset Rest aboard! All aboard for Forgetful
>Acres! For Snuff City! For Dogtown Junction!
>Anybody for Columbarium? For Inferno World?

DIONYSUS
>Me!

CHARON
>Step right up and climb aboard.

DIONYSUS
>No, seriously, where are you headed? You're really going to
>Inferno World?

CHARON
>If *you're* on board we are. Climb in.

DIONYSUS *(to Xanthias)*
>   You next, boy.   160

CHARON
>   Sorry, no slaves allowed. Not unless he bought his body back in a
>   sea battle.

XANTHIAS
>   Well, I *would* have, only I had pinkeye at the time.

CHARON
>   All right, then take a walk around the lake.

XANTHIAS
>   Where do I meet up with you again?

CHARON
>   Over by Desert Gulch Rock. Right by the Rest Stop Exit.

DIONYSUS
>   Do you follow?

XANTHIAS
>   Do I ever! Who put the hex on *me* this morning?
> *(He trudges off.)*

CHARON *(to Dionysus)*
>   If you'll just take an oar.
> *(Dionysus thinks he means "sit" on an oar, and does so. Charon
>   calls out.)*
>   Anybody else coming on board? Last call!
> *(to Dionysus)*
>   What do you think you're doing?   170

DIONYSUS
>   You told me to take an oar, and so I did.

CHARON

Sit *there*, Fat Boy! There on that bench!

DIONYSUS

All right.

CHARON

Now stretch out your arms, come on, all the way.

DIONYSUS

Like this?

CHARON

Stop your clowning. Brace your feet, and now pull hard.

DIONYSUS

You expect me to row? I'm not a sailor, crew wasn't my sport,
and I'm not one of those who commute to
Athens from across the bay in Salamis. Sorry, just
can't do it.

CHARON

Oh, you can learn. Pull your oar. You'll hear some tuneful
chanteys to help you keep time.

DIONYSUS

Sung by who?

CHARON

The Swansong Frog Choristers, and they're stupendous!   180

DIONYSUS

Ok. Let's have the countdown.

CHARON

Heave ho, and off we go!

FROGS

> *Brekekekex, ko-ahx, ko-ahx! Brekekekex, ko-ahx, ko-ahx!*
> Offspring of the spring and marsh,
> gather round and sing along!
> With clarion tones and nothing harsh,
> brothers, croak a thrilling song!
> *Ko-ahx, ko-ahx!*
> To Dionysus the Divine,
> we dedicate our Nysos lay.   190
> And to his tipsy comrades gay,
> a heady draft of festal wine!
> *Brekekekex, ko-ahx, ko-ahx!*

DIONYSUS

> *Ko-ahx, ko-ahx* my ass, which hurts like hell!

FROGS

> *Brekekekex, ko-ahx, ko-ahx!*

DIONYSUS

> But you don't give a damn!

FROGS

> *Brekekekex, ko-ahx, ko-ahx!*

DIONYSUS

> Stop it! Enough with your *ko-ahx!*
> That's your singing, eh, those squawks?

FROGS

> We sing the way we sing, Sir Knowitall,   200
> applauded by the sacred Muses nine
> and hornfoot Pan, the merry woodlands piper.
> Apollo, premier harpist, loves us, too,
> thanks to the rugged reed we cultivate
> in native swamps, for fabricating lyres.
> *Brekekekex, ko-ahx, ko-ahx!*

DIONYSUS

> I've rubbed big blisters on my hands.
> My backside's bathed in seething sweat
> and soon will bray your loud refrain:
> *Brekekekex, ko-ahx, ko-ahx!*   210
> Be quiet, philharmonic folk!
> Time for a breather, isn't it?

FROGS

> No, instead
> we'll sing still louder and even more
> if ever yet in days of yore,
> where marshland flags and rushes thrive,
> on sunny mornings we would prance,
> marking the beat of melody
> that soared and plunged with each glad dive;
> or, in flight from rain and thunder,   220
> we sought the watery depths down under,
> our plangent odes and measured dance
> a bubbling choreography.

FROGS AND DIONYSUS

> *Brekekekex, ko-ahx, ko-ahx!*

DIONYSUS

> Maybe I'll take at least your beat.

FROGS

> Think twice before you risk that feat.

DIONYSUS

> A greater risk would be to row
> until my gut split open, so—

FROGS AND DIONYSUS

> *Brekekekex, ko-ahx, ko-ahx!*

DIONYSUS
> Meanwhile, you just go to hell.   230

FROGS
> We mean to sing, and do it well,
> stretching the larynx, holding fast
> as long as froggy throats shall last.

FROGS AND DIONYSUS
> *Brekekekex, ko-ahx, ko-ahx!*

DIONYSUS
> Well, this time you won't be the winner.

FROGS
> The vain boasts of a rank beginner.

DIONYSUS
> Repeat that when the contest's done.
> I don't give up, once I've begun;
> I'll croon and shout until I've won:
> *Brekekekex, ko-ahx, ko-ahx!*   240
> So there! Who sings the last *ko-ahx*?

CHARON
> Enough! Quiet! Put up your oars. We're docking now. Pay up
>   and be on your way.

DIONYSUS
> Here: two bucks.
> *(Exit Charon.)*
>   Wait: Xanthias, where's Xanthias? Is that you,
>   Xanthias?

XANTHIAS *(entering)*
> Yo!

DIONYSUS
Come here.

XANTHIAS
Glad to see you, sir.

DIONYSUS
What was it like out there?

XANTHIAS
Total darkness. Mudville.

DIONYSUS
Well, did you see the dad-killers and perjurers he mentioned?

XANTHIAS
Sure, didn't you?   250

DIONYSUS
By God, I sure did. In fact
(looks out at the audience)
I see them right now. So, where do we go from here?

XANTHIAS
It's definitely time to move on. This is the place where Heracles
said hideous monsters live.

DIONYSUS
Oh, he's full of it. It's all a bluff, meant to scare me off. He knows
I'm a fighter and he's jealous. You'll never see a
conceited ass like Heracles. Actually, I wish we
had run into a little trouble, just to make this trip
interesting.

XANTHIAS
I bet you do . . . Wait up. I hear something.

DIONYSUS
Wha? Wh-where is it?
(Enter Monster.)

XANTHIAS
Right behind us.

DIONYSUS
Stand behind me.

XANTHIAS
No, wait, it's in front of us now.

DIONYSUS
Ok, maybe you should get in front of me.   260

XANTHIAS
Omigosh, I see it—a scary monster!

DIONYSUS
What's it look like?

XANTHIAS
Like everything. It keeps changing shape. It's a bull; it's a donkey,
        now it's a bee-utiful girl.

DIONYSUS
Oh really? Where? I'll go meet her.

XANTHIAS
It stopped being a girl. Now it's a dog.

DIONYSUS
Uh-oh, we've got Empusa, the famous shape-changing blob.

XANTHIAS
Well, now its face is on fire.

DIONYSUS
Does it have legs made of copper?

XANTHIAS
Copper? Yes, as a matter of fact, one of them is. And the other is
made of cow manure.

DIONYSUS
Eek! How do I get out of here.   270

XANTHIAS
Where can we hide?

DIONYSUS *(to the priest of Dionysus, seated in the first row)*
O priestly father, protect me, since we belong to the same club
and will dining there later on.

XANTHIAS
Sir Heracles, we're done for!

DIONYSUS
Don't call me by that name, you idiot!

XANTHIAS
Ok, Sir Dionysus, then.

DIONYSUS
That's even worse.

XANTHIAS *(to the monster)*
Get the hell outa here.
(Monster exits.)
                                    Master, master, come here!

DIONYSUS
What? What's happening?

XANTHIAS

Relax. It's all taken care of. And just like that actor Hegelochos,
we can say, "We've passed through terrible
storms and here's the cat . . . astrophe reversed by
fine weather." Empusa flew the coop!

DIONYSUS

You swear?   280

XANTHIAS

So help me God, she has.

DIONYSUS

Swear again.

XANTHIAS

Cross my heart.

DIONYSUS

Again!

XANTHIAS

And hope to die. Damn, I was white as a sheet when I saw her.
But *this* guy
(pointing to Dionysus)
he turned yellow—and he still is.

DIONYSUS

What have I done to deserve all this? Which of the gods has it in
for me?

XANTHIAS *(declaiming)*
"Bright empyrean, Zeus' bedroom, Time's fateful footstep"?
(Offstage, the sound of flute music.)

DIONYSUS

Wait!

XANTHIAS
     What's the matter?   290

DIONYSUS
     Didn't you hear that?

XANTHIAS
     What?

DIONYSUS
     The soft breath of a flute.

XANTHIAS
     Yeaaah, and a smell of smoke, a flaming torch—some occult
          ritual underway around here.

DIONYSUS
     Let's duck down and listen in on what's happening.

CHORUS *(in the distance)*
     Iacchus! O Iacchus! Iacchus!

XANTHIAS
     I know who they are! It's those New Age mystics, the ones he told
          us about. This is their turf around here. They're
          singing that hymn to Iacchus, you know, the one
          that the poet Diagoras wrote.

DIONYSUS
     I think you're right. So let's keep quiet and find out what they're
          up to.

CHORUS
     Iacchus! Almighty beloved, who dwells in these fields,
     Iacchus, O Iacchus!   300
     Come to me, come as a dancer, come down to this meadow.

Come to your loving adherents
crowned with a garland of myrtle, oh
step to the measure that fills you with pleasure—
a dance with the Graces' insouciant charm,
lightsome and lovely, and sacred to all who adore you.

XANTHIAS

Demeter's daughter Persephone, holiest queen divine!
What an aroma of barbecued pork you just sent my way!

DIONYSUS

If you'll shut up, I'll try to get some sausage for you.

CHORUS

Torches, arise, plucked to wakefulness on solid ground,   310
Iacchus, O Iacchus!
Star of fire flaming over our sacred vespers,
lighting up the meadows,
urging aged limbs to leap for joy,
throwing off old pain and sorrow,
freed from the ancient burden,
the heavy burden of the years.
Torchlight, gather the faithful all together,
lead, oh lead us onward, your sprightly chorus
trooping to the flowered glade.   320

LEADER

Let evil thoughts keep silence now. Our chosen band excludes
those who cannot grasp the meaning of our sacred rites;
whose hearts and minds are stained and blinded with impurity;
who've never seen or learned to celebrate the Muses' revels,
or chant the Bacchic prayers Kratinos wrote, the stage's most
            famous
butcher; or those who love cheap jokes that never should have
            been told;
those who fail to calm our people, or, worse, stir up sedition,

fanning the fires of enmity in hopes of easy money,
looking—even when our country's racked by storms—for graft;
those eager to betray a battleship or fort, those like   330
Thorykion, who shipped supplies the state had need of
from Aegina to Epidaurus, just across the Bay,
transporting oarlocks, canvas, tar—and duty's five percent
be damned—the traitor meanwhile funneling aid to the enemy;
likewise those troubadours who make latrines of Hecate's shrines;
or the senator who, when lampooned in these our ancient rites,
downsized our actors' salaries: To all of these I say,
I forbid you once, forbid you twice and three times. *Never*
come near our holy ceremony! But you, disciples, comrades,
arise and dance our midnight liturgies of joy and praise.   340

Onward, faithful hearts and true!
On to the happy woodland bower!
Tread the measure midst herb and flower
bathed in evening dew!
Stride on and make your satire keen
now that our banqueting is done.
And to Persephone, Hades' queen,
we chant our praises, hailing one
who vows that by her grace
our city need not fear the base   350
deeds of Thorykion.

And now let's tune our voices to a different mode,
may Demeter be praised, Our Lady of the harvest.
O goddess whom we honor in these rites,
save the congregation of your adepts;
protect us as we voice your solemn hymns,
dancing the measured strophes
of the sacred litany.
Grant, too, that all our words ring tart and witty,
with thoughts conceived to make the hearer think;   360
may we be worthy of the laurel crown

conferred upon the victor
when the festival concludes.

And now, another mode: Summon that young prince
                    among gods,
who joins with his own chorus, dancing along the sacred path.

Iacchus, come, beloved Lord,
with joyful step approach
the elder deity.
No matter if the journey's long,
your strength shall be renewed.   370
Iacchus, devotee of dancing, walk beside us!

And if our robes are torn and raveled,
and if our shoes are battered, too,
just think how much was saved!
Iacchus, devotee of dancing, walk beside us!

I glimpsed a sweet young girl among the crowd
whose robe someone had ripped in the rough and tumble.
The tear revealed a lovely, tempting breast.
Iacchus, devotee of dancing, walk beside us!

DIONYSUS
    I wouldn't mind a little fun and games   380
    myself. What if I jumped in here . . .

XANTHIAS
    Me too!

CHORUS
    Suppose we now all satirized
    that foreigner Archedemos?
    Seven years, and still no green card to cut his teeth on.

It doesn't matter, for among
the walking stiffs up there
he is the kingpin, poised to make his power grab.

And Kleisthenes, so rumor says,
weeps the whole day beside   390
a tomb, while plucking hairs from his posterior

and slapping himself silly. Poor thing,
he mourns his dear departed,
darling Sebinos, native son of Babbleton.

Meanwhile Kallias, I'm told,
has joined the navy, and
drapes his pudendum with a lionskin when he fights.

DIONYSUS

    Please, could any one of you
    kindly give directions
    to Hades' castle? As you see, we're strangers here.   400

CHORUS

    You needn't go a single step
    farther, nor ask again:
    you are already there, this is the door to it.

DIONYSUS

    Gather up the luggage, boy.

XANTHIAS

    Always the same old song—
    "Tote that bale, for God and country."

CHORUS

    Places!
    For now we must continue onward with our round-dance
    until we reach the sacred grove, where flowers bloom

for us, all glad initiates in the mysteries.   410
A torch to light the girls and women whom I walk with!

We're off to see the roses and the flowered field,
going our own way,
lovely dancers all,
skipping along as the Goodluck
Goddesses have ordained.

O sacred band, the sun sends down his splendid rays
to smile on us and bless.
For we have always striven
righteously to aid   420
stranger as well as friend.
(Exit Chorus. Dionysus and Xanthias go to Hades' door.)

DIONYSUS
    What's the proper way to knock on his door? I wonder
    how the locals go about it?

XANTHIAS
    Stop beating around the bush; just do it. Don't forget, you've got
                    the lionskin of Heracles, and, therefore, his clout.

DIONYSUS
    Porter! O porter!
(Enter Aiacus.)

AIACUS
    Who is it?

DIONYSUS
    Me, Heracles, the champion!

AIACUS
    Oh, you villain, you scoundrel, you bastard, you scumbag! You
                    took my watchdog Cerberus—my special charge,

the one you grabbed by the throat and dragged
away with you. So now I've headed you off,
you're trapped between the black rock of the Styx
and the Acheron Mountain! The dogs of Cocytus
will track you down! Echidna the hundred-
headed monster's going to chew up your balls,
the Great Infernal Eel gets your lungs, and the
Teithrasian Gorgons get your kidneys and
entrails. They're going to rip you to bits! And I'm
going to round them all up this instant.

(Exit Aiacus. Dionysus drops to the ground.)

XANTHIAS
> Whoa! What's the matter?

DIONYSUS
> Now I've done it. Please call the god who mops up after
> our sins.   430

XANTHIAS
> Hey, get up, you nut, before somebody sees you.

DIONYSUS
> How can I get up? I fainted. Would you please run a damp
> sponge over my heart?

XANTHIAS
> Ok, here's one. You do it.

DIONYSUS
> Let's see, where has it gone . . . ah, here.

XANTHIAS
> Sheesh! You're saying your heart's down *there*?

DIONYSUS
> Well, it was so terrified it flew there to find a cave to hide in.

XANTHIAS
    You get the Olympic medal for cowardice.

DIONYSUS
    Me, a coward? Now, would a real coward have ever asked you for
        a sponge?

XANTHIAS
    If not, what *would* he have done?

DIONYSUS
    He'd have stayed right where he was, wallowing like a pig. Me, I
        stood up and wiped myself off.   440

XANTHIAS
    Now there's a hero for you. God!

DIONYSUS
    Well, exactly. But now, be honest, weren't you frightened when
        he started screaming those awful threats?

XANTHIAS
    No, for godssake. Never blinked an eye.

DIONYSUS
    Ok then, tell you what. You win the hero contest, so you get to
        play me and wear the lionskin and carry the club.
        And I'll be the slave and carry the bags. Deal?

XANTHIAS
    Your word is law. Hand 'em over.
    (They exchange.)
        Hey, look at Mr. Xanthias-Heracles! Just see if I'm a coward
            like you!

DIONYSUS

What you look like is one of those wimps who used to cruise
outside Heracles' temple. But never mind, let's
hoist this pack on my back.

HOUSEMAID

Heracles, honey, it's you! Come on in! When Miss Persephone
heard you were here, why, she put bread in the
oven, made pea soup, roasted a whole ox on a
spit, and made buns and cakes. So come and
get it!

XANTHIAS

Oh, well, thank you, you're awfully nice, but . . .

HOUSEMAID

So help me Apollo, I'm *not* letting you go, I mean it! Now, we've
been roasting some chickens, and making
desserts, and getting our best wines ready. So,
here, come with me.   450

XANTHIAS

Very thoughtful of you, but . . .

HOUSEMAID

Now, don't make a fuss. I'm not going to let you go. Oh, by the
way, there's a girl who plays the flute waiting, and
a couple of belly dancers, too.

XANTHIAS

Did you say belly dancers?

HOUSEMAID

Yes, pretty young things, fresh from the bath and dressed like
models. Come *on!* They're setting up tables now
and the cook has just brought out the filet
mignon.

XANTHIAS

    Great, you just go ahead and tell those dancing girls I'll be right
        there.

(Exit Housemaid.)

    All right, boy, load up and follow me.

DIONYSUS

    Hold on a second. You didn't think I really meant it, did you?
        Just because, as a joke, I dressed you up as
        Heracles? Well, you can drop it now. Pick up
        these bags and get a move on.

XANTHIAS

    What the—. You mean you're going to take it all back?

DIONYSUS

    Not *going* to: I *am* taking it back. Get out of that skin.

XANTHIAS

    No way! As the gods are my witness—.   460

DIONYSUS

    Gods my ass. What on earth made you think that you, a slave,
        could *ever* be convincing as *Heracles*, Alcmena's
        firstborn son?

XANTHIAS

    Oh the hell with it, take it back. But you may need to call on me
        again some day, wait and see.

CHORUS

    This man is foxy, clever, keen
    of wit, we must agree.
    he's often braved the wave-tossed ocean,
    no frozen statue he!
    He has the power of motion

and a clever sense of when to lean
left and when to lean right.
Watch him snag each useful breeze—   470
they're cronies at first sight.
Why, he's just like Theramenes,
our political jumping-bean.

DIONYSUS

Oh, wouldn't that have been amusing—
"Xanthias dates a chorine."
A steamy clinch on Turkish rugs,
like a porno magazine!
And when he interrupts those hugs
to pee, his slave, not losing
time or opportunity,   480
jumps in and takes his place.
Then Bossman returns (the slave is me)
and ties knots in my face—
but not knots of my choosing.

(Enter a tavern "hostess" and her partner Plathane.)

HOSTESS

Plathane! Plathane. Here's that no-good bastard, the one that
                    barged in our tavern and scarfed down sixteen
                    loaves of bread!

PLATHANE

You're absolutely right, that's him.

XANTHIAS

Somebody better watch out.

HOSTESS

And, besides that, twenty slices of roast beef, at two bucks a shot.

XANTHIAS

Somebody's in big trouble.

HOSTESS
    Not to mention the garlic.   490

DIONYSUS
    You're off your rocker, woman. You don't know what
        you're saying.

HOSTESS
    Oh, you thought I wouldn't recognize you with those brogans on!
        I haven't even gotten to the fish, nor the fresh
        cheese, which he gobbled up *with* its cheesecloth,
        so help me. And when I dropped a few hints
        about the bill, he glared at me and started yelling.

XANTHIAS
    Yep, that's our boy. You can count on him to do that.

HOSTESS
    Yeah, and he whipped out his knife and waved it around like
        a lunatic.

PLATHANE
    That's *exactly* what he did.

HOSTESS
    He scared me and the other girls so bad we ran upstairs and hid.
        And then off he went, taking our bedding
        with him.

XANTHIAS
    That sounds just like him.

PLATHANE
    Well, we're going to do something about it.

HOSTESS
    Run and get us one of those ombudsmen who live down here
        now—Kleon, he'd do, maybe.

PLATHANE

    And while you're at it, bring Hyperbolos. We're gonna fix this
               guy good.   500

HOSTESS

    You fat-assed pig! I'd like to take a brick and knock out the teeth
        that chewed up my pantry like a mad dog!

PLATHANE

    And I'd like to put you six feet under in the city dump.

HOSTESS

    I'd like to take a scythe and rip out the guts you stuffed with *our*
        sausage.
    But I'll go get Kleon. He'll put out a warrant, he'll squeeze it
        out of you.

DIONYSUS

    Dear God, how I adore you, Xanthias!

XANTHIAS

    Yeah, right. I know what you're plotting. Forget it: I'm not going
        to be Heracles again.

DIONYSUS

    Oh, sweet man, how can you say that?

XANTHIAS

    Well then, tell me, how can I
    (mimicking)
    "a mere mortal, a slave, et cetera, play the son of Alcmena"?

DIONYSUS

    Yes, yes, I know you're annoyed with me, and you're right. In
        fact, if you punch me, I won't complain a bit. I
        swear, if I ever make you take this gear off again,

    may death strike me and my wife and kids
    (I mean, if I had any). And throw in old
    Archedemos to boot.   510

XANTHIAS
    Duly noted; I accept your terms.
(They exchange accouterments again.)

CHORUS
    Again we see you in the manly
    garments you once donned, then doffed.
    Draped in that pelt, a club in hand,
    it's time you lived up to their style,
    with virtues like his who wore them first—
    heroic fortitude and courage!
    If fear should ever make you whimper,
    betraying your lowly origins,
    your master will strip off those clothes,   520
    and you revert to what you were,
    a porter carrying heavy bags.

XANTHIAS
    Gee thanks, that's really good advice.
    Although, guess what, I half suspected
    it might turn out just like you say.
    If any bad thing comes along,
    he makes me dress like Heracles;
    but if some goody falls in my lap,
    he takes the costume back. Meanwhile,
    as long as I'm dressed up like this   530
    I'll be a tough guy, I'll eat my spinach.
    In fact, round one's about to start.
    I hear them pounding at the door . . .

AIACUS
    Get that dognapper! Handcuff him, tie him up, drag him to jail!

DIONYSUS

Uh-oh, somebody's in big trouble.

XANTHIAS

Get your mitts off me! Get away! Scram!

AIACUS

Oh, so you want to fight, eh? Hey, Ditylas, Sclebyas, Pardocas,
come here quick! Take this man out.

DIONYSUS

Isn't that something, a thief like him resisting arrest!

AIACUS

Outrageous!

DIONYSUS

It's really shocking.   540

XANTHIAS

So help me God, if I was ever in this place before now, if I *ever*
stole so much as a plug nickel from you, may I
die and burn in hell! Meantime, I'll make a deal
with you: Take this slave; torture him as much as
you like; and if that trial by fire proves me guilty,
you can arrest and execute me.

AIACUS

Torture him how?

XANTHIAS

Any way you please. Strap him on a rack, whip him with
brambles, hang him up by his heels, put a load of
bricks on top of him, pour vinegar up his nose.
But don't, whatever you do, flog him with a leek
or an onion stalk.

AIACUS

Fair enough. And if I beat him up too bad, I'll pay you
compensation.

XANTHIAS

No need for that. Take him away and whip him.

AIACUS

Might as well do it right here, so you can witness the confession.
All right, you can put down those bags, and you
better not lie.

DIONYSUS

Hold on. I'm giving you fair warning. Don't you dare torture me.
I'm a god. If you do, you'll answer for it.

AIACUS

Wha? How's that?

DIONYSUS

I'm telling you: I am Bacchus, son of Zeus, a god. And *this* one's
the slave, get it?

AIACUS

You hear what he said?   550

XANTHIAS

Sure, I heard it. That's just one more reason to torture him: If
he's a god, he won't feel a thing.

DIONYSUS

Well, since you say that you're a god yourself, Mr. Heracles, why
don't you let them torture you, too?

XANTHIAS

Ok, you're on. And whichever one of us blubbers first or cries
uncle, then he's not a god.

AIACUS
Well, I can see that you've got class: You're all for law and order.
Ok then, strip.

XANTHIAS
Now, how are you going to do this so it's an even trade?

AIACUS
It'll be a snap. I'll match you, punch for punch.

XANTHIAS
That sounds fair. On your mark! Go!
(Aiacus hits him.)
Just see if I flinch!

AIACUS
I punched you.

XANTHIAS
No way!

AIACUS
Well, in fact, it doesn't sound like I did. Now the other
guy's turn.   560
(hits Dionysus)

DIONYSUS
I'm *wai*-ting.

AIACUS
I just punched you.

DIONYSUS
You did? Why didn't I feel it?

AIACUS
No idea. I'll try the other guy again.

XANTHIAS
> Go for it.
> *(Aiacus punches him.)*
>> Ooooo!

AIACUS
> Ooooo? That didn't hurt, did it?

XANTHIAS
> Why, no, I was just thinking of that marvelous, holy ceremony—
>> the Diomean rites of Heracles.

AIACUS
> This man's a monk, can't get to *him*. Better try the other guy.
> *(Dionysus whacks him.)*

DIONYSUS
> Ohoho!

AIACUS
> Yo?   570

DIONYSUS
> Look at those horsemen there. What a sight!

AIACUS
> Why are you shedding tears?

DIONYSUS
> I smell onion, don't you?

AIACUS
> So, are you saying this didn't bother you?

DIONYSUS
> Bother me? Not at all.

AIACUS
All right, I'll have another go at him.
(*hits Xanthias*)

XANTHIAS
Owww!

AIACUS
Problem?

XANTHIAS
Would you be so kind as to pull out that thorn from my foot?

AIACUS
What's going on here? Ok, it's the other one's turn.   580
(*hits Dionysus*)

DIONYSUS (*yelling*)
Apollo! Lord!
(*quieter*)
                ". . . of Delos and of Pytho."

XANTHIAS
Aha! You hear that? He's hurting!

DIONYSUS
Not a bit. Just reciting a line from a poem by Hipponax.

XANTHIAS
You're not really working at it. Give him a good whack in
            the ribs.

AIACUS
By God, you're right. Turn your gut this way.
(*hits Dionysus*)

DIONYSUS *(screams)*
Oooh! Poseidon!

XANTHIAS
See? He's in pain!

DIONYSUS
". . . who rules supreme among the Aegean peaks and
underneath the green and silver wave."

AIACUS
Dammit to Demeter. I give up, I can't tell which of you's the god.
Both of you come inside. My master Hades and
his lady Persephone will know, considering that
they're gods themselves.

DIONYSUS
Well, exactly. I just wish you'd thought of that before beating
me up.   590
(They enter the door.)

CHORUS
Come Muse of enchantment, Oh strike up a song!
Our multitudes wait for you, row upon row.
Strong in our wits, ah, stronger than Kleophon,
that mongrel foreigner, whose Thracian babble
mimicked the swallow's nonsensical wheedling—
hear how she pleads for her countryman, who,
despite a hung jury, did not escape hanging.
It is our chorus' bounden duty to counsel the city.
That your minds might be at peace, let all free men be equal.
Because Phryníchus managed to manipulate them,   600
some of your number slipped and fell. If so, the best
policy is to overlook the sin and, then,
the moment he repents, to welcome home the sinner.
No one should forfeit, for all time, his civic status.

And it would be a grave injustice if former slaves,
because they fought (however valiantly) at sea,
should have a higher rank than free-born citizens,
with rights like those conferred on the brave Plateans.
Now, we're not blaming you for giving them their freedom;
there, at least, you've acted rightly and demonstrated,   610
in the face of tribulation, fundamental wisdom.
Still, those who also fought at sea—and not once only
but many times, just like their forefathers, our kinsmen:
because of *one* mistake, refuse them amnesty?
O Athens, wisest of cities, calm your anger, pardon
all those who've fought in our sea battles. Racked by tempests
as you are now, to take the hard line would be madness.

CHORUS LEADER

And if I'm any judge of human character,
and the fate it's likely to produce, then for Kleigenes
(that sly baboon, our little Baron of the Bathhouse,   620
who had us pay top price
for soaps, adulterated
with cheap ingredients from Kimolus)
time's running out, as well he knows—
which never stopped the weakling from carrying a stick
to fend off muggers, wheresoe'er he goes.

CHORUS

Lately we've been thinking Athens has begun
to treat patrician citizens much as she now
handles our currency. Oh yes, this sterling silver
treasure, pure Athenian from days of old,   630
honestly minted specie, beautiful in form,
accepted everywhere as peerless coin of the realm:
this we neglect to utilize, instead preferring
cheap counterfeits of brass and tin turned out last week.
Meanwhile our well-bred, unalloyed nobility,
persons of ancient stock whose rank befits their worth,

artistic, cultivated folk, keen sportsmen, too—
these we ignore and even scorn, in favor of
new money, pushy types right off the boat, trash
that in a better time we'd not have deigned to use   640
as scapegoats in our civic rites. Assign important
duties to *them*? O foolish nation, think again,
and mend your ways! In public service, only proven
value should be made use of. Thus, when Athens triumphs,
credit will go to you. And if she falls, at least
it won't be from the limbs of some ignoble tree.

(Enter Aiacus and Xanthias, the latter in his own clothes again.)

AIACUS

My God, your master's first-*class*, a true gentleman!

XANTHIAS

Course he is, chases girls and guzzles hooch with the best
of them.

AIACUS

Not to have beaten you, once it was clear that you, his slave, were
pretending to be him, the master—incredible.

XANTHIAS

Oh, he'd regret trying that.   650

AIACUS

Well put, boy, that's the way we slaves should talk.

XANTHIAS

Oh, you like that, huh?

AIACUS

Well, sure: When I can cuss my master out behind his back, it
puts me in seventh heaven.

XANTHIAS

The same thing when you go outside after he's beat up on you
and you say all kinds of nasty things about
him, right?

AIACUS

Lots of fun.

XANTHIAS

And snooping into his private affairs?

AIACUS

Love it.

XANTHIAS

My man! And do you like eavesdropping on his conversations?

AIACUS

Sheer pleasure.

XANTHIAS

And gossiping about what you've heard?   660

AIACUS

Hot damn, when I do that, woooo, it's ecstasy!

XANTHIAS

Phoebus Apollo! Put her there! Here's a big smacky for you!
Blood brothers for life! . . . Now what in God's
name is all that racket going on in there?

AIACUS

It's Aeschylus and Euripides.

XANTHIAS

Huh?

AIACUS

> Oh, some really weird things have happened. The dead people
>> are involved in a gang war, everybody choosing
>> up sides.

XANTHIAS

> What's the problem?

AIACUS

> See, we've got this old tradition that the number-one practitioner
>> in each of the arts gets invited to a big dinner
>> down at the Civic Center—in fact, he gets to sit
>> next to King Hades.

XANTHIAS

> I see.

AIACUS

> Anyhow, this goes until someone better comes along; then he has
>> to step down.

XANTHIAS

> But why has this been any problem for Aeschylus?   670

AIACUS

> He always held the throne for Tragedy, since he was the best in
>> that line.

XANTHIAS

> Who else would?

AIACUS

> Thing is, when Euripides came on the scene, of course he started
>> playing up to the lowlife types, and we've got a
>> *lot* of them: gangsters, pickpockets, cat burglars,
>> hit men, you name it. So they listened to his

fancy speeches, all the bleeding heart stuff, and
just went through the roof. They said he was the
best thing they ever heard. That swelled his head,
at which point he said that Aeschylus' throne of
Tragedy should go to him.

XANTHIAS
    Did they clobber him?

AIACUS
    No, the mob said there should be a contest, and may the smartest
        technician win.

XANTHIAS
    Those gangland types said that?

AIACUS
    Sure, they were screaming to high heaven.

XANTHIAS
    Nobody took Aeschylus' side?

AIACUS
    Good people are few and far between.
    (He looks at audience.)
    Same down here as up there.   680

XANTHIAS
    So what's Hades going to do about it?

AIACUS
    He's going to stage a poetry contest and put both of their
        tragedies to the test.

XANTHIAS
    Say, why didn't Sophocles claim the throne, too?

AIACUS

> Sophocles? Never. When he came down here, he hugged Aes-
> chylus, deferred to him, and never mentioned
> the throne at all. Now Kleidemides is saying
> Sophocles is planning to watch from the side-
> lines, and if Aeschylus *wins*, why, he'll stay
> put. But if he loses, then Sophocles is going to
> fight for his *own* artistic achievement against
> Euripides.

XANTHIAS

> So this is really going to happen?

AIACUS

> Yes, very soon, God willing. Amazing things are in the works.
> They're going to put the Muses on scales, and see
> which one comes out on top.

XANTHIAS

> You mean they're going to weigh tragedy like sides of beef?

AIACUS

> Yep, they'll get out their spirit-levels, their yardsticks, their
> casting molds . . .

XANTHIAS

> You mean, like, for making bricks?

AIACUS

> . . . their T-squares and calipers. You see, Euripides is going to
> check out *every word* of the tragedies.   690

XANTHIAS

> I'm sure Aeschylus resents all this.

AIACUS

Mmm, he lowered his head, knitted his brows, and glared at
them like a bull about to charge.

XANTHIAS

So who's going to decide the contest?

AIACUS

That's the sticky part. They've had trouble rounding up impartial
judges. Just for starters, Aeschylus and the
Athenians don't mix.

XANTHIAS

Too many crooks for his taste, right?

AIACUS

Well, and considering how stupid the rest of them are, he said
the idea that they should evaluate poetry was a
joke. Anyhow, they eventually decided to bring
in your master Dionysus to do the job because
he's considered an expert. So let's go inside; you
know how nasty bosses can be to their servants
when they've got some project underway.

(Exit Aiacus and Xanthias.)

CHORUS

Dreadful and dire shall be the wrath of him who speaks like
thunder
when he sees that word-besotted bard sharpening his fangs.
His terrible eyes shall roll in rage and frenzy.

The crests, the flowing manes of poetry shall toss and wave   700
when warriors clash, wood and metal splinters flung right
and left,
as charge meets cavalry charge of word and sentence.

His hair will stand on end like a horse's mane, when he lets fly
those verbal missiles, planks ripped up from the foredeck of
        the stage,
shivered timbers bolted and hurled at the foe.

Ah, but meanwhile that fine-tuned tongue will do its clever work,
a pun of self-regard in each malignant phrase and image,
eating away at poetry's great lungs.
(Scene change: the Hall of Hades, with Hades seated on his throne,
Dionysus beside him, Aeschylus and Euripides
stage front.)

EURIPIDES

Say what you will, I won't give up the chair.
I write much better poetry than he does.   710

DIONYSUS

You hear him, Aeschylus. What do you answer?
(pause)

EURIPIDES

Aha! the silent treatment—a stratagem
he's used a thousand times in his theater.

DIONYSUS

Now, now, calm down, no need to be so hostile.

EURIPIDES

You haven't studied him as long as I have.
An arrogant, in fact, a savage author
of unrestrained and ranting lunacy,
grandiloquent, bombastic verbiage!

AESCHYLUS

So says the son of our dirt-farmer goddess,
words from the chief of the babble collectors.   720

Rag-picker, tailor for tattered old scarecrows!
Well, you'll regret it.

DIONYSUS
Would you please calm down?
"Heat not thy soul with fury," Aeschylus.

AESCHYLUS
Oh, but I *must* show this wretch how contemptible
insolence is when it comes from a blockhead.

DIONYSUS
Bring me a lamb, a sacrificial, *black*-fleeced
lamb, to appease the storm about to break.

AESCHYLUS
You have imported debased and unnatural
passions from Crete to our noble tragedy!   730

DIONYSUS
Calm yourself a moment, Aeschylus.
And, you, Euripides, might well consider
a prudent exit from this hailstorm here,
so that no headlong piece of icy wit
makes an open-skull encephalogram
of your brain—along with your play *Telephos.*

Now, Aeschylus, if you'll practice a little
restraint, then our debate will go more smoothly.
A poet shouldn't scream like a banshee, right?
You're going at it like a house on fire.   740

EURIPIDES
I'm ready any time to face him down.
If he wants first blood, fine! If not, I'll go
for the lyric jugular of tragedy,

with *Pyleas, Aeolus, Meleager,*
all my best plays, and *Telephos* as well.

DIONYSUS

How do you answer, Aeschylus? Speak up.

AESCHYLUS

I'd not have chosen to hold our debate down
here, where I suffer a disadvantage.

DIONYSUS

How?

AESCHYLUS

My tragedies didn't expire at my death.   750
Euripides' did; you can *quote* them down here.
Nevertheless, if we must, I'll cooperate.

DIONYSUS

Good! Now, bring some incense and an altar.
Before this battle of wits begins, I'll pray
for skill to judge the contest like an artist.
Meanwhile, the chorus may invoke the Muses.

CHORUS

Daughters of Zeus, the virgin Muses nine,
who survey the subtle intellects gathered here,
when they go down to the tournament in wit's strong armor,
the various tools and techniques that help them triumph,   760
come and take part in the contest, inspire our contenders,
gifted both in magniloquence and cavil,
for the competition's about to begin in earnest.

DIONYSUS

You might both want to say a prayer first.

AESCHYLUS

>Demeter, Goddess, provision my soul;
>grant I be worthy to serve in your rites.

DIONYSUS *(to Euripides)*

>And now you may burn incense, too.

EURIPIDES

>   No thank you.
>My homage goes to gods other than these.

DIONYSUS

>You've coined your own deities?

EURIPIDES

>   Yes, I have.

DIONYSUS

>Well, pray to them, those private gods of yours.   770

EURIPIDES

>Bright empyrean, daily sustenance,
>eloquent discourse, my wit, my flair,
>help me annihilate his arguments.

CHORUS

>We, too, are longing to have heard
>disputations from these sages.
>Vigor and enlightenment
>arm their every thought and word.
>In their deadly war of wits,
>one deploys a gift for phrases,
>expression married to intent,   780
>form honed down until it fits.
>The other will assault his foe,
>cut and thrust or slash and burn,

filled with power and the rage
of heroes lofty as they go
crowned with praise that truth shall earn
uprooting trees of verbiage.

DIONYSUS

You may begin debating now. But, please,
refrain from empty verbal flourishes.

EURIPIDES

I'll postpone discussing my own merits   790
and show, instead, just what a pompous fake
he is; and how he deceived the followers
of Phryníchus, first of our tragedians.
He'd bring onstage a mourner wrapped in veils—
Achilles or Niobe, say—their faces hidden,
a mute statue that merely *mimed* bereavement.

DIONYSUS

You're right.

EURIPIDES

            Then enter Chorus, bawling no less
than *four* odes—which the statue greets with silence.

DIONYSUS

I, for one, liked that. Isn't silence better
than the chitchat we expect these days to hear?   800

EURIPIDES

Spoken like a clod.

DIONYSUS

                No doubt. But tell me,
why did he do that?

EURIPIDES

         It was a *trick*, you see,
to keep them guessing: When *would* Niobe speak?

DIONYSUS

    The grifter took us in.
(to Aeschylus)
               You seem perturbed.
    Something wrong?

EURIPIDES

         I'm revealing his trade secrets!
So: halfway through his play, he'd introduce
some thuggish phrases, brutal rant that wore
(as 'twere) a helmet over bushy eyebrows:
lines *no* one understood.

AESCHYLUS

           By thunder!

DIONYSUS

                Quiet!

EURIPIDES

                Not a word made sense.

DIONYSUS

    Hush! Don't grind your teeth.   810

EURIPIDES

    It was all Scamanders, moated fortresses,
    "The griffin-eagle brazen on a shield,"
    incomprehensible stuff.

DIONYSUS

            You've got a point.
Many a night I've sat up puzzling what
on earth "the gilt horse-cockerel" might be.

AESCHYLUS
That is a nautical *emblem*, you blockhead!

DIONYSUS
Really? I'd guessed some mythic cockfight hero.

EURIPIDES
Do we even mention such in a tragic work?

AESCHYLUS
And the monsters you've put in *your* plays, blasphemer?

EURIPIDES
Well, no "horse-cockerels," no "stag-horned goats,"   820
no nightmares borrowed from Persian tapestries.
When I picked up our art where you had left it,
I found it bloated from its feast of bombast.
I slimmed it with a special regimen:
juices and exercise, a nimble beat,
and a consommé of all the books I'd read
nourished my songs.

DIONYSUS
                    Your slave Kephison spiced it up?

EURIPIDES
My prologues *never* were abrupt or random;
the first onstage retold the story's origin.

DIONYSUS
Good thing they didn't discuss *your* origins.   830

EURIPIDES
From start to finish no one was left dangling;
the lady spoke, and just as often, her slave;
the warlord, his daughter, and the withered crone.

AESCHYLUS
    That is precisely why you should be hanged.

EURIPIDES
    Because I was, please God, so democratic?

DIONYSUS
    Given that populism's never been
    your strongest suit, you might let that one go.

EURIPIDES
    I wrote *speechlike* dialogue.

AESCHYLUS
                    So you did.
    If only you'd spilled out your guts some *other* way.

EURIPIDES
    I brought in strict verse measures—and a manner,   840
    a clever slant, oblique, seductive, agile.
    I showed how suspect all things are.

AESCHYLUS
                    So you did.

EURIPIDES
    I chose my subjects from the common life
    so people could judge the content for themselves,
    without being overwhelmed by rant and bombast
    about, what, *Kyknos, yea, and Memnon armed*
    For battle, steeds adorned with crests and bells . . .
    Look at our followers, respectively:
    His Megaenetos, his Phormisios—
    buccaneers both, addicted to the poleaxe.   850
    Meanwhile, Theramenes and Kleitophon are *mine*.

DIONYSUS
> Theramenes, our clever politician!
> When his campaign sinks—the good ship *Commonwealth*?—
> he jumps it for another named *Lies and Stealth*

EURIPIDES
> I taught the art of thinking in my plays.
> My characters work through the whys and wherefores
> of experience; the spectators, in turn,
> learn how to deal with crises facing *them*,
> including ordinary household problems:
> they pry, investigate, ask *when* and *where*,   860
> *which one* and *who*—until it all comes clear.

DIONYSUS
> That's true! Nowadays what Athenian,
> when he comes home, will ever fail to ask:
> "Well, where's the salad bowl? I want an answer!
> Who bit the head off that sardine? And who's
> been nibbling olives? All right, where's the garlic!"
> In days of yore, the lord of the manor would
> just flop down, glaze over, and say nothing.

CHORUS *(to Aeschylus)*
> "See you this, O great Achilles":
> how do you reply? Rein in your   870
> passions, lest they thrust and fling you
> beyond the bounds ordained by custom.
> Grievous charges made against you,
> you must answer with strong reasons,
> not with rabid condemnation.
> Reef your sails with timely prudence
> while you drive athwart the tempest.
> Then, when fierce winds drop and slacken,
> you will harness all their power,
> and, so speeded, your brave vessel   880
> will destroy the adversary.

DIONYSUS

First among the bards of Hellas, sublime
tragedian, let the gushing fountains flow!

AESCHYLUS

That I should contend with a fraud such as *this* is an
outrage. But lest he lay claim to the victory:
(to Euripides)
What qualities *do* we admire in the dramatist?

EURIPIDES

A mastery of craft, abundant wit,
the skill to make a moral stance persuasive.

AESCHYLUS

Since you've performed just the opposite, taken
virtuous people and made them all perverts,   890
what's the reward you deserve for your exploits?

DIONYSUS

Anyone doing that deserves to die.

AESCHYLUS

Consider what manner of men he received from me;
then what he *did* with them. *I* gave him heroes,
lofty in stature, who'd never retreat from a
citizen's duty, in peacetime or war—not these
loafers and cowards, too weak to wield weapons.

DIONYSUS

Wait! We're not here to subsidize the arms race.

EURIPIDES

How was it only *your* verse produced heroes?
(pause)

DIONYSUS
  Aeschylus? Stony silence isn't an option.   900

AESCHYLUS
  Soldierly ardor informed my work.

DIONYSUS
                          Which work?

AESCHYLUS
  Seven Against Thebes, if I must answer plainly.
  All those who watched became thirsty for combat.

DIONYSUS
  But that was awful, egging on the Thebans,
  instead of us, to fight. You should be whipped.

AESCHYLUS
  You could have done as the Thebans did, but,
  no, you had other ideas. My *Persians* came
  next. Its intention? To make us love victory.

DIONYSUS
  It was great, hearing "Darius is dead . . ."
  And then the chorus keening bizarre dirges . . .   910

AESCHYLUS
  That is the way of true poets. Recall that, from
  earliest times, they've redeemed us from savagery.
  Orpheus praised divine peace, holy mysteries;
  Musaeus, our health, and the wisdom of oracles;
  Hesiod, tillage, the plow and the seasons;
  Homer earned glory by singing of heroes
  who put on their armor and fought, did he not?

DIONYSUS

> Yes, but that was lost on Pantacles,
> who, when he struggled into battle dress,
> stuck a plume on his helmet from the *outside*.   920

AESCHYLUS

> But others revered him: Lamachus, certainly;
> a hero, and one I could use as a model for
> brave-hearted soldiers—Patroclus or Teucer—
> inspiring our people to go and do likewise.
>
> God, if I ever resorted to strumpets
> like his Stheneboea and Phaedra! In fact,
> not one of my works deals with amorous women.

EURIPIDES

> Aphrodite never laid a glove on *you*.

AESCHYLUS

> May she never! She certainly used *you* and your ilk
> for a mattress until she had flattened you all.   930

DIONYSUS

> He has a point. The marital disasters
> you dramatized for the stage came home to you.

EURIPIDES *(to Aeschylus)*

> What social problems have my Stheneboeas caused?

AESCHYLUS

> Bellerophons—well, as you staged them—led women of
> high station to swallow a lethal potion of
> hemlock because of the shame that they felt.

EURIPIDES

> And Phaedra's story didn't predate my play?

AESCHYLUS

    Yes, but a playwright should never treat subjects
    like wickedness; he should avoid them. And just as
    children have teachers to guide them, adults have   940
    playwrights, whose dramas should celebrate virtue.

EURIPIDES

    So, if your words are big as mountain ranges,
    you're giving good instruction, is that it?
    Why not hold class in a language people speak?

AESCHYLUS

    Illustrious deeds should be matched by illustrious
    diction. Besides, when a demigod speaks, we
    expect him to use grander words than *we* do,
    just as his clothing's more splendid than ours—a
    standard that you have corrupted.

EURIPIDES

                   How so?

AESCHYLUS

    You clothed noble persons in rags as a way of   950
    engendering sympathy for them.

EURIPIDES

                And why is *that* wrong?

AESCHYLUS

    For one thing, the rich will no longer support
    the war effort. Dressed up like beggars, they go around
    weeping and wailing, as though they were penniless.

DIONYSUS

    Meanwhile, by Demeter, they're got cashmere
    tunics beneath their clothes. And once they've taken

everyone in, they're off to pick up lobster
and caviar deluxe at the fish-market.

AESCHYLUS

What's more, you've encouraged the fad for "philosophy,"
which leaves the gymnasia empty, while youngsters who   960
should be in training instead let the rumps they're
sitting on atrophy. Even our *sailors*
have started to question their captains' commands.
In *my* day the most they attempted was begging
for rations, a chantey, and row-and-heave-ho.

DIONYSUS

That, and, God bless them, farting in the face
of the rower just behind, or raiding the galley
for extra grub, or robbing folks on land.
The sailors we have nowadays talk back, though,
and the ships they sail tack every which way.   970

AESCHYLUS

What depravities *hasn't* this reptile encouraged?—
a lady's-maid playing procuress, or women
giving birth in Athena's own temple, committing
incestuous acts with their brother, or claiming
that life is not life, in fact, *death* is the *true* life—
corrupting our principles, filling the city
with demagogues, monkeys whose only ambition's to
bamboozle the public. And meanwhile there's no one
to hand on the torch to; they've all become sluggards,
too weak to run relay—for *any* exertion.   980

DIONYSUS

You're right. At the last Pan-Athenian
games I saw this poor overweight slob,
pasty-faced, panting, staggering on, *crawling*
to reach the finish line—hilarious.

When he got to Potters' Gate, the spectators
whacked him in the stomach, on the ribs,
the butt—which made him fart so explosively
the torch that he was carrying got blown out.

CHORUS

So much is at stake in this clash of minds,
how do we decide between them?   990
One breaks out his fiercest thunders,
while the other parries, ducks and pivots,
launching a deadly counter-assault.
But why keep making the same contentions?
You've only just begun, and there
are many issues left to thrash out.
So reach for your differences,
move in for the attack, unsheathe
the keen blade of argument,
old and new, to carry the day.   1000
Place your bets, and winner take all!

Don't worry that your audience
won't understand you, things have changed.
They're able, so to speak, to follow
the libretto, catching every subtle
reference. These are veterans
of our Athenian theater,
smart as whip—so don't hold back.

EURIPIDES

All right. Begin with Aeschylus' prologues,
try out the opening lines of our master playwright: 1010
his murky expositions leave you guessing.

DIONYSUS

Which prologue are you going to put on trial?

EURIPIDES

    Quite a few. But first,
(to Aeschylus)
                    if you'd recite
    for us the *Oresteia's* opening lines.

DIONYSUS

    Silence! Aeschylus, you may begin.

AESCHYLUS

    "Underworld Hermes, guardian of the fathers' right
    authority, assist me, uphold my claim as I
    repatriate from exile to my native land."

DIONYSUS *(to Euripides)*

    Any faults to criticize?

EURIPIDES

                A dozen or more.

DIONYSUS

    But the whole thing was only, what, three lines!   1020

EURIPIDES

    Each one of those three lines has twenty faults.

DIONYSUS *(to Aeschylus, who is spluttering)*

    Aeschylus, please be quiet. If you don't,
    you'll be docked for more than three iambic lines!

AESCHYLUS

    I should be quiet for *him*?

DIONYSUS

                I'd advise you to.

EURIPIDES
  Right at the start he makes a cosmic blunder.

AESCHYLUS *(to Dionysus)*
  See, your advice was absurd.
(Dionysus tries to calm him down.)
                                    No, I *won't*.
(to Euripides)
  Where have I blundered?

EURIPIDES
                              Begin once again.

AESCHYLUS
  "Underworld Hermes, guardian of the fathers' right
  authority—"

EURIPIDES
  Orestes says this at his father's tomb, correct?   1030

AESCHYLUS
  Correct.

EURIPIDES
              So when his mother deceived and killed
  his father, that's a good example of Hermes
  "guarding the fathers' right authority"?

AESCHYLUS
  No, for addressing the Hermes who aids us as
  "underworld Hermes" implies that this extra
  function derives from his *own* father Zeus.

EURIPIDES
  Oh, but that's even worse. If he received
  his underworldly function from his father—

DIONYSUS
>He got the knack of robbing graves from Zeus!

AESCHYLUS *(sniffs)*
>Dionysus, the wine you've been drinking's gone bad.   1040

DIONYSUS
>Recite the next part.
(to Euripides)
>>>>And you watch out for flaws.

AESCHYLUS
>". . . save me, support my claim as I
>repatriate from exile to my native land."

EURIPIDES
>The great bard Aeschylus repeats himself.

DIONYSUS
>Oh, really? Where?

EURIPIDES
>>>>Just look at how he says it:
>". . . repatriate from exile to my native land."
>"Repatriate" *includes* "my native land."

DIONYSUS
>True. It's like saying to a neighbor, "Lend me
>a rolling-pin that rolls out dough with a pin."

AESCHYLUS
>It's *not* true you dolt! Not the same thing at all.   1050
>That's the best of all possible phrases to use.

DIONYSUS
>Oh really? Tell us why you put it that way.

AESCHYLUS
>"Returning" is one thing; *repatriation*—
>assuming no further dilemmas await you—
>terminates "exile"; the native comes *home.*

DIONYSUS
>Well said. Rebuttals here, Euripides?

EURIPIDES
>Orestes didn't "repatriate": he came back,
>disguised, without permission from the state.

DIONYSUS
>Good point.
>*(aside)*
>>Not that I really understand it.

EURIPIDES *(to Aeschylus)*
>All right. Another excerpt.

DIONYSUS
>>Aeschylus?   1060
>Continue, please.
>*(to Euripides)*
>>And you take notes on the faults.

AESCHYLUS
>"And by this funerary mound, I beg
>my father to hearken and incline his ear . . ."

EURIPIDES
>Another repetition: "hearken and
>incline his ear." Two terms for the same thing.

DIONYSUS

Don't be silly. He's talking to the dead.
They don't respond until you've begged at *least*
three times.

AESCHYLUS

And how do you write *your* prologues?

EURIPIDES

I'll say one. If I repeat myself, or if
you notice any padding, things that don't   1070
advance the plot, why, you may spit on me.

DIONYSUS

Go on, recite. We're looking forward to
the apt expression your prologues are renowned for.

EURIPIDES

"Oedipus enjoyed, at first, good fortune . . ."

AESCHYLUS

"At first"? Why, that's nonsense! His life was disastrous.
To begin with, Apollo decreed that he'd murder
his sire; it was settled before he was born.
How *did* he "enjoy, at first, good fortune"?

EURIPIDES

". . . but suffered, after, more than any mortal."

AESCHYLUS

"After"? There was never a *moment* he didn't   1080
suffer. No sooner born than they put him
in a crock, which they left in the woods in winter.
All so he wouldn't grow up and do in his
father. And then, a bit later, he managed
to hobble along with his damaged and swollen
feet to find Polybus. Then, while still young, he

married a matron—his mother, it happened.
In the end, he elected to rip out his eyes.

DIONYSUS
    Blindness would be good fortune insofar
    as it prevented you from seeing how   1090
    Erasinides was tortured after
    he returned to Athens recently.

EURIPIDES
    Enjoy your silly chatter. I write good prologues.

AESCHYLUS
    I'm not going to bother to whittle away at your
    prologues, challenging each of your phrases;
    with the help of the gods I'll dismantle them, using
    only a flask of oil.

EURIPIDES
                        A flask of oil? My prologues?

AESCHYLUS
    Just one. For, you see, with your method of writing,
    anything fits in the meter, whether a
    "sheepskin," a "flask of oil," or "little bag."   1100
    I'll show you.

EURIPIDES
                    Oh, you'll show me?

AESCHYLUS
                                    Yes, I will.

EURIPIDES
    I suppose I should recite one:
    "Aegyptus, as the old romances tell,
    took ship to Argos with his fifty sons.
    He came to port—"

AESCHYLUS

and lost his flask of oil.

DIONYSUS

"His flask of oil?" But where does that come in?
I think you'd better have another go.

EURIPIDES

"Lord Dionysus, who, equipped with torch
and wand of ivy, and clad in dappled fawnskins,
frequenting the upward slopes of green Parnassus,   1110
in sacred dances—"

AESCHYLUS

lost his flask of oil.

DIONYSUS

Struck down again with that damned flask of oil!

EURIPIDES

It's really not important. Here's a prologue
he can't attach his tiresome *flask of oil* to:
"No man enjoys all forms of happiness.
This one, though nobly born, has slender means;
that, low-born, has—"

AESCHYLUS

lost his flask of oil.

DIONYSUS

Euripides?

EURIPIDES

What?

DIONYSUS

          You'd better take in sail.
This *flask of oil* is blowing up a storm.

EURIPIDES

    By Demeter, I won't let him upset me.   1120
    This time I'll knock the props from under him.

DIONYSUS

    Let's hear a prologue, then. And watch that flask!

EURIPIDES

    "Cadmus, Agenor's son, in days of yore
    Quit Sidon city and—"

AESCHYLUS

               lost his flask of oil.

DIONYSUS

    My friend, I think you'd better buy that flask
    if you don't want your prologues chewed to bits.

EURIPIDES

    You mean, just pay him off?

DIONYSUS

              I would, because—

EURIPIDES

    Well, I refuse. I've many other prologues
    that won't let *flasks of oil* latch on to them:
    "Pelops, Tantalus' son, with his swift steeds   1130
    rode into Pisa and—"

AESCHYLUS

               lost his flask of oil.

DIONYSUS

You see! He stuck on that oil-flask again.
You'd best pay up. You'll get it for a dollar
or so, and, really, it's a nifty item.

EURIPIDES

Not yet! I've only just begun to recite:
"One day Oeneus—"

AESCHYLUS

lost his flask of oil.

EURIPIDES

Will you please allow me to complete the line?
"One day Oeneus reaped an abundant harvest
from his fields, and then, while offering the first-fruits
to Demeter—"

AESCHYLUS

he lost his flask of oil.   *1140*

DIONYSUS

While making a ritual offering? Who stole it?

EURIPIDES

Don't interrupt. Let him try to mess up this one!
"Zeus, as right opinion has maintained . . ."

DIONYSUS

Careful! He'll whip out that *lost his flask of oil.*
It plagues your prologues like sties in people's eyes.
You'd best attack the music of his verses.

EURIPIDES

All right. I'll prove his lyric gifts are nil.
Every piece he's written sounds the same.

CHORUS
It's leveled at our greatest bard,
whose plays are hailed as masterworks. 1150
His rival's taking a huge risk.

EURIPIDES
Our greatest bard? We'll check the truth of that.
I'll beat out his johnny-one-note rhythms for you.

DIONYSUS
And I'll keep score for us with these small stones.
(Flute plays offstage.)

EURIPIDES
"Achílles, Phthían lórd, when you héar the críes of the wóunded,
ah, whý will yóu not cóme to their réscue, whý won't you
sáve them?
Great Hérmes, pátriárch, we will bléss you, wé of the láke-shore.
Ah, whý will yóu not cóme to their réscue, whý won't you
sáve them?

DIONYSUS
That's two strikes against you, Aeschylus.

EURIPIDES
O lórd of gréat Acháia, the són of Átreus, héar me: 1160
Ah, whý will yóu not cóme to their réscue, whý won't you
sáve them?

DIONYSUS *(another stone)*
That's a third strike against you, Aeschylus.

EURIPIDES
"Keep sílence, áll. The bée-guardians ópen Ártemis' témple.
Ah, whý will yóu not cóme to their réscue, whý won't you
sáve them?

My skíll can téll that ómen the héroes sáw by the wáyside.
Ah, whý will yóu not cóme to their réscue, whý won't you
sáve them?

DIONYSUS

Strike, strike, strike! A lot of them today.
I think I'll go to the bathhouse and soak.
All these beats have left welts on my backside.

EURIPIDES

Don't leave before you've heard my next critique—   1170
this time, the tunes he's written for the lyre.

DIONYSUS

Fine. But please don't beat the rhythm out.

EURIPIDES *(plucks at an imaginary lyre)*
"Double-throned might of Achaians, young scions of Hellas—
Plinkety, plinkety, plinkety, plinkety, plinket.
"Sphinx, the presider, the bitch that held sway, be ye sped by—
Plinkety, plinkety, plinkety, plinkety, plinket.
"Spears and the vanquishing hand of that militant eagle—
Plinkety, plinkety, plinkety, plinkety, plinket.
"Sending ye all to be meat for the sky-roaming vultures."
Plinkety, plinkety, plinkety, plinkety, plinket.   1180

DIONYSUS

What's all this "plinkety" nonsense? A chantey
you got from Marathon? Some sandhog's work-song?

AESCHYLUS

The point is that *I* drew my music from noble
springs, with results just as noble; and never
grasped at such "flowers" as blow in Phrynichos'
"Muse-haunted meadow." But meanwhile this mountebank
drinks from malodorous wells, like Meletos'

pop songs, or Karian "country," or dirges, or
dance-tunes. I'll demonstrate, if you will bring me a
lyre . . . And yet, why should I need one? Instead, send   1190
Euripides' Muse! Castanets are her specialty!
She's the accompanist *his* lines require.
(Enter a "private dancer," not young, barely dressed, gyrating and
clicking castanets.)

DIONYSUS
Well, this "artiste" is hardly a Muse from Lesbos!

AESCHYLUS *(singing to castanet accompaniment)*
    Halcyons, you who twitter
        close by the tide-flow,
    splashing your wings with seadew;
        spiders in attics,
    Wwi-hi-hi-hinding silk to
        ply in your loomcraft;
    musical dolphins, leaping   1200
        high as the ship's bow;
    oracles, drawn toward racetracks;
        tendrils a helix,
    vine with your soothing vintage;
        girlie, embrace me!
(The dancer embraces Dionysus.)
    See how her foot goes?

DIONYSUS
                Indeed, I *do.*

AESCHYLUS
Both of her feet, you see them?

DIONYSUS
                I do.

AESCHYLUS *(turning to Euripides)*
> If that is a typical effort, Euripides,
> how dare you disparage my skill with the lyric?
> You, with your dozen "techniques"—a performance   1210
> that matches the stunts of that harlot Kyréné.

(Exit Euripides' Muse.)
> So much for your odes. Let's examine your arias.

(sings)
> O darkness of shaded Night,
> what dream, what dread have you
> sent from invisible Hades,
> what soul devoid of soul,
> the offspring of midnight darkness,
> an apparition that makes me tremble,
> dressed in cadaver's raiment,
> gazing with evil, evil eye,   1220
> possessed with huge talons.
> Yet light a lamp, handmaidens mine,
> draw dew from the streams; heat, and pour a bath
> that I may sluice away this inhuman dream.
> O genius of the ocean,
> it has indeed come to pass. My fellow tenants,
> behold a wonder: My cockerel: why,
> Glyke has spirited it away!
> Nymphs of the mountains,
> and you, divine Frenzy, help me,   1230
> me, the forlorn one,
> absorbed in my task,
> my hands wi-hi-hi-hinding
> flax on the distaff
> to make a skein that I could vend
> before dawn at the market.
> My cockerel flew up to the heavens on gossamer wings,
> leaving me to grieve, oh, grievously,
> tears, bitter tears, shed by my eyes,
> woeful creature that I am!   1240

But now, ye Cretans, Ida's progeny,
take up your bows and come to my aid.
Lay siege to her house as you dance around it,
and summon the lovely Dictynna,
her pack of puppies also,
to pace every inch of Glyke's chambers.
And you, Zeus' daughter, a bright torch
in either hand, O Hecate, light the way
through Glyke's house as I conduct a search.

DIONYSUS

As far as lyric competition's concerned,   1250
you may both rest your case.

AESCHYLUS

I've had enough.
Let's bring in the scales. It's the only objective
procedure to use. We shall weigh every word,
phrase against phrase, and measure their gravity.

DIONYSUS

All right, I'll do it—weigh your poetry,
like some no-nonsense grocer selling cheese.

CHORUS

The genius brain works overtime.
What an extraordinary method!
Who else would have come up with it?
If you'd described it to me in passing,   1260
I'd have said you were delirious.
(A balance scale is brought in.)

DIONYSUS

Both of you here, beside the scales.

AESCHYLUS AND EURIPIDES

We're here.

DIONYSUS
>   Each one holds the pan and says his line;
>   and don't let go until I say, "Cuckoo!"

AESCHYLUS AND EURIPIDES
>   We're ready.

DIONYSUS
>   Speak your line into the scale.

EURIPIDES
>   "Oh, had the *Argo*'s mainsail ne'er taken wing—"

AESCHYLUS
>   "River Spercheius, and meadows where cattle graze—"

DIONYSUS
>   Cuckoo!

AESCHYLUS AND EURIPIDES *(letting go of the pans)*
>   We're off.
> *(Aeschylus' pan sinks.)*

DIONYSUS
>   Look, this one's pan is gliding
>   straight down!

EURIPIDES
>   And why on earth should it do that?

DIONYSUS
>   Why? Because he put a river in it.   1270
>   Just like a wool-seller, who soaks his wool
>   to make it heavy. But *your* line had wings.

EURIPIDES
>   So let him speak another line, and weigh it.

DIONYSUS
    All right, grab hold.

AESCHYLUS AND EURIPIDES
    We've done so.

DIONYSUS
                Good. Now speak.

EURIPIDES
    "No temple shelters Eloquence, save language."

AESCHYLUS
    "Death is the only god who desires no tribute."

DIONYSUS
    Let go.

AESCHYLUS AND EURIPIDES
      We have.
    (Aeschylus' second pan sinks.)

DIONYSUS
             His pan is dropping again!
    Well, Death's the heaviest of all our burdens.

EURIPIDES
    But Eloquence is the strongest proof there is!

DIONYSUS
    Eloquence? Lightweight stuff, in fact, quite daffy.   1280
    You should select a line that has more weight,
    something substantial, something with more punch.

EURIPIDES
    Where have I written lines like that?

DIONYSUS

I'll tell you.
"Achilles threw . . ." not a spear—but seven come
eleven!
(laughs)

All right now, on your mark, this is it!

EURIPIDES

"His right hand seized a haft heavy with iron—"

AESCHYLUS

"Chariot heaped on chariot, and corpse upon corpse—"
(His pan sinks down.)

DIONYSUS *(to Euripides)*

Look, he's outsmarted you again.

EURIPIDES

How so?

DIONYSUS

Two chariots, two corpses: Why, a hundred
Egyptians couldn't begin to hoist all that.   1290

AESCHYLUS

True, and I won't keep on playing this line for
line game. Put *him* on the scales, with his children,
His wife, and Kephison, in fact, his whole library.
Any two lines I recite will outweigh them.

DIONYSUS *(to Hades)*

Both of these men are friends of mine. I don't want
to judge or make an enemy of either.
One is a sage. I'm spell-bound by the other.

HADES

In that case, you have failed at the task you came here for.

DIONYSUS
 And if I do decide?

HADES
                    You'll leave with the man declared
 the victor; hence, your mission here won't have been wasted.   1300

DIONYSUS
 I thank you, sir.
 (to the poets)
                    Now, tell me: Do you know
 just why I came in search of a poet here?
 So that Athens would survive—and would continue
 staging works in honor of Dionysus!
 So I'll take with me whoever gives the best
 advice concerning how to save our city.
 First, Alcibiades: What should we do?
 The labor pains he's caused his mother country!

AESCHYLUS
 How does the city regard him at present?

DIONYSUS
                              How?
 It loves *and* hates him; and wants to keep him there.   1310
 But tell me, poets, what do you make of him?

EURIPIDES
 A citizen who's slow to assist his country
 and swift to cause her grief is infamous.
 Though keen to help himself, to her he's useless.

DIONYSUS
 Poseidon! Very good.
 (to Aeschylus)
                    And your opinion?

AESCHYLUS

I say the city should never have offered a
lion-cub nurture and shelter; but now that he's
grown, you should try to appease and humor him.

DIONYSUS

Zeus preserve me! Still can't quite decide!
It's either cleverness or clarity.   1320
Each of you answer one more question, would you?
What actions should the city take to survive?

EURIPIDES

I know of one and would like to speak.

DIONYSUS

                              Then do.

EURIPIDES

As soon as we trust what we now mistrust
and also *mis*trust what we now *do* trust—

DIONYSUS

Hold on, I don't quite understand your point.
Could we have more clarity and less cleverness?

EURIPIDES

If we would mistrust those we currently
consider trustworthy, and recruit those
we haven't used before—

DIONYSUS

                    Then we'd come through?   1330

EURIPIDES

Since those in charge right now have done so badly,
won't the opposite contingent triumph?

DIONYSUS *(to Aeschylus)*
>And you, what do you say?

AESCHYLUS
>>>A question. Those citizens
>now governing Athens, how far are they trusted?

DIONYSUS
>Not at all! They're despised!

AESCHYLUS
>>>The city prefers its scoundrels?

DIONYSUS
>It uses them because it has no choice.

AESCHYLUS
>How can one save such a city? No cape of
>fine silk nor uncouth woolen coat will suit it.

DIONYSUS
>If you *don't* save it, you'll be stuck down here.

AESCHYLUS
>Up there I would speak; but I'd rather not, here.　　　　1340

DIONYSUS
>But your good wishes must go up from *this* place.

AESCHYLUS
>They'll win when they think of their land as the enemy's;
>likewise, the enemy's, *theirs*. And the *fleet* as their
>wealth; and their *actual* wealth a mere hindrance.

DIONYSUS
>Fine, but the legal system gobbles that up.

HADES
Make your decision.

DIONYSUS
It is made. I choose
"The one my soul's delight would have me choose."

EURIPIDES
Do you recall the gods to whom you swore
that you would bring me back, as your true friend?

DIONYSUS
"Although my tongue was guilty of perjury,   1350
My heart dissented—." I choose Aeschylus.

EURIPIDES
What have you done, you brutal savage?

DIONYSUS
Done?
Named Aeschylus the winner. Why shouldn't I?

EURIPIDES
Shameful! How can you look me in the face?

DIONYSUS
"Why shameful if not deemed so"—by those who see it?
(gestures toward audience)

EURIPIDES
So, you're barbaric enough to leave me *dead* here?

DIONYSUS
Ah, what if "living is but dying"? Inhaling,
ingesting? And sleep, but a featherbed?
(At some point during the following, Euripides exits.)

HADES

    Dionysus, will you come inside now?

DIONYSUS

                Inside?

HADES

    We've planned a farewell banquet for you.

DIONYSUS

                     Lovely.   1360
    I have to say I'm pleased with all of this.
(Hades leads Dionysus and Aeschylus into his hall.)

CHORUS

    Fortune smiles on him
    whose mind is keen and lucid.
    Instances abound.
    This man, now proven wise,
    will wend his way back home,
    with blessings to dispense
    to those near to his heart
    because he is a sage.

    How wrong they are to sit   1370
    chatting with Socrates,
    mocking the lyric impulse,
    and scorning all that's great
    in the art of tragedy.
    To waste your foolish hours
    with gaudy rhetoric
    and quibbles over nonsense
    shows you've lost your reason.
(Reenter Hades, Aeschylus, Dionysus, Persephone, Xanthias, Charon,
and others.)

HADES

    Well then, Aeschylus, safe journey and good luck.
    Fortify the city with your useful precepts.   1380
    Instruct the simpletons—how many you will meet!
    Take this
(gives a sword to Xanthias)
             and carry it to Kleophon; and these,
    which you should give the Tax Administrators—also
    to Myrmex, oh, and Nicomachos; finally
    these hemlock leaves to Archenomos. Tell them all
    to bestir themselves and come to me posthaste. If not,
    then, by Apollo, I will brand each one and wrap them
    in chains; then speed them far below the earth, along
    with Adeimantos, son of Leucopholos!

AESCHYLUS

    All shall be done as you say. May I ask if   1390
    my throne might be granted to Sophocles? He will
    guard it in case I should ever return here.
    He's second to none but myself in our art.
    Meanwhile be sure that you don't inadvertently
    let that pestiferous charlatan sit there.

HADES *(to the Chorus)*

    Now if you will hold aloft
    torches in this wise man's honor:
    light him on his way, while singing
    his own songs and choruses.
(Aeschylus, Dionysus, and Xanthias begin to go off, followed by the
chorus.)

CHARON

    Divinities who dwell beneath the earth,   1400
    grant a peaceful voyage to the poet
    as he ascends to light and life.

May his instruction prosper our great city;
and woes occasioned by clash of arms now end.
Let Kleophon and all like him
go back to their own lands if war is what they seek.

Divinities . . .
(Curtain)

The Sexual Congress, or, Don't Call Me Late for Chow

Translated by
R. H. W. Dillard

It seems that over the last twenty-four centuries Aristophanes' *Ecclesiazusae*, like the comedian Rodney Dangerfield, just can't get no respect. Although its characters make exuberant claims of victory in its concluding lines, we don't even know how it fared in the dramatic competition in which it was first produced. It is one of only eleven of Aristophanes' forty or more plays to have survived, but it survived intact (or nearly intact) in only three manuscripts. It was annotated and commented upon minimally by the earliest scholars, and, since then, it has met mainly with either scholarly silence or abuse. And all this despite its being a very lively and funny play, with the cutting edge of its social and political satire quite as sharp as it was when it was freshly honed, and with its down-and-dirty bawdy and bathroom humor as deeply offensive and shamelessly hilarious as it was when it first drew belly laughs on the stage in Athens all those centuries ago.

I suspect that the reasons for the play's still not receiving either the acclaim or the study it clearly deserves are two: first, its structure does not conform to conventional ideas about the nature of dramatic form; and second, it has suffered from years of translations that conceal its roughness in a blue-nosed blur of "poetic" language that also manages to conceal most of its humor and much of its meaning as well.

The Sexual Congress simply does not behave itself—in any way, but especially not in accord with the conventions of comedy that we have grown used to over the years since its creation. Maybe if the only known copy of the second book of Aristotle's work, the one dealing with comedy, had not been destroyed by Jorge of Burgos at an Italian abbey in November of 1327, we might well have a different set of expectations and might have appreciated this play all along better than we have. But, be that as it may (or may not), the play does break apart in the middle, and the problems of the characters in the first part are only minimally resolved in the second part. Even that minimal resolution requires that we make a leap of faith and assume that certain characters in the second part are actually the same people we met in the first, for the manuscripts of the play are very unclear about just who is talking when. If, however, one can step away from those conventional expectations and realize that this play is not really about individual characters at all, but rather about an entire city, about men and women in general rather than in particular, and about appetite and greed as primary human characteristics, then its structure makes perfect sense, and it becomes a quite satisfying dramatic experience. It seems, in fact, remarkably up to date.

The other problem the play has had for modern readers is that, with one or two notable exceptions (Douglass Parker's very loose verse translation of 1967 and Jeffrey Henderson's quite accurate prose one of 1996),[1] even the very best and most intelligent translations of the play into English have so beclouded the play's basic scatological and sexual humor in language of such remarkable prolixity and circumlocution that a reader who has no Greek will have great difficulty even figuring out what is going on, much less why it might be funny.

The plot is simple enough: led by the boldly intelligent Praxagora, a large group of Athenian women, dismayed by the terrible condition of the city, disguise themselves as men, invade a meeting of the city's democratic assembly, and succeed in passing a set of new laws that gives over all the responsibilities and power of city governance to women. They also set up a communistic state in which women will continue to do their traditional work as well as running the city, but in which all of the other work will be done by slaves, leaving the men to become what in many ways they already were: drones who eat what is put before them, have sex in a new system of free love, and, as Chremes puts it, "just fart around all day." In the second part of the play, Aristophanes examines the aftershocks of the revolution in a set of encounters which show its effects, both positive and negative, in a variety of ways, and finally everyone goes away to dinner, dancing and singing. That's it, but, of course, there's a great deal more to it than that.

First of all, the play is a satirical critique of the sorry state of Athens at the

---

[1] Parker, *The Congresswomen* (Ann Arbor: University of Michigan Press, 1967); Henderson, *Three Plays by Aristophanes: Staging Women* (New York: Routledge, 1996).

time (roughly 392 B.C., give or take a year). The city had, only a few years before, lost the Peloponnesian War and its great navy as well. It had experimented with more than one form of non-democratic government, but has recently returned to democracy and the assembly. The people are so disheartened and disillusioned with government in general and their leaders in particular that they have to be paid (if they arrive early enough) even to attend the assembly and participate in the government. The city has also become a hotbed of corruption and greed, with the rich getting richer while the poor are homeless and living on the street; and mugging has become the norm at night. Praxagora's speech sums it up in ways that will seem remarkably familiar to disheartened American citizens at the end of the twentieth century:

> Heaven help us who can't seem to help ourselves.
> I love my country as much as any man,
> and I am saddened and hurt by the way it's being run.
> I tell you, we are in the hands of scoundrels.
> If one of them is honest for a day,
> then you'd better watch out for the ten days to follow.
> And if you back someone else, he's even worse.   (185–91)

Her radical plan to solve all the city's problems is to abolish all private property and family units and to transform the entire city into one home and one family run by the home economists who have all along been successfully running their separate homes and families—the women. Her plan seems very funny to us (and probably even funnier to the Athenians of the day, given the position of women in that society), but it also seems reasonable because the current state of events is so particularly absurd and terrible: they (we) are ruled by scoundrels; their (our) streets are no longer safe at night; their (our) poor are forced onto those mean streets by a greedy populace that chooses to look the other way or, at best, come up with ineffectual solutions to the problem. Aristophanes' ironies are compound and probably impossible for us really to understand after so very many years, but the situation of the play seems newly minted, freighted with all kinds of new ironies after our own recent experience with the long nightmare of Soviet communism and the ensuing triumph of international corporate greed. The hard core of Aristophanes' political satire remains focused and funny and chillingly accurate.

So, too, Aristophanes' comic critique of the relationships between women and men. Aristophanes may have been a man, but the men don't come off at all well in this play. With the exception of Chremes, who may not be particularly bright but at least wants to do the right thing, all of the men in the play, including the hapless youth torn between young love and civic duty, are vulgar, venal, sexually unsatisfying to their women (either by wanting too much or offering too little), and capable of being manipulated by the offer of free sex or free food. The housewives are the only capable characters in the play (and even they are not let off the satiric hook completely). Once they have taken over the city and are running it, they are replaced on stage by men (older men who are mainly concerned with their property, and one cocky young man who finds out exactly what it is to be a sex object) and by unmarried women who are either too young or too old to function effectively in the new "home economics"—a young girl who doesn't yet really know what it is she wants so badly, and three old women who know very well what they want but have been unable to get. The married women, who spoke freely if somewhat cynically about sex in the first part of the play, are now much too busy (after all, somebody's got to fix dinner and run the city) to engage in the sexual goings-on of the new order—which establishes a system of free sex, but one that requires that the young and attractive service the old and the ugly before taking pleasure with each other. The new system pleases the old and ugly but not the young and attractive; young girls in particular will be used by old women as lures for boys. The sexual satire, needless to say, is as politically incorrect as it is possible to imagine and cuts as brutally in all directions as does the more expansive gender satire in which it is embedded.

The Sexual Congress is finally a play about appetite, all kinds of appetite: for power, for money and possessions, for sex, and especially for food. The sad state of the city and the lives of its inhabitants is the direct result of either satisfied or unsatisfied appetition. Athens is a city bound by its own greed and poisoned by its own waste. How appropriate it is, then, that Praxagora's old and foolish husband Blepyrus, who is in so many ways the city personified, is cruelly bound by constipation in the first part of the play and squats center stage for a very long time desperately trying to move his bowels. How appropriate it is that he is not only tortured by the painful results of his previous greed, but is also concerned about the food that he hasn't even eaten yet:

> What am I going to do? And not just now,
> but later: how's the food I've still got to eat
> going to get out?   (375–77)

And how especially appropriate it is that his ordeal only ends when Chremes arrives to tell him that the women are now in charge of the city. His bowels finally do move, the waste is cleared from his system, and he, like the city, stands up and, however uncomprehendingly, faces the future with hope. A very good alternate title for this play would be *Athens Unbound*!

The language of the play is as raw and blunt as the dire straits of the city's inhabitants, certainly, if not the rawest of that in any of Aristophanes' plays, among the rawest. Much of the meaning of the play is located in the directness of the language and the lowness of the humor. These are not the noble figures of tragedy musing on the ways of fate (except when Aristophanes uses the high language of tragedy for comic effect); they are instead quite direct about the immediate realities of the mundane earthy moment. When Chremes approaches Blepyrus in the predawn darkness just as he has succeeded in moving his bowels (389), he says something much closer to (line 389), "You, there! What's that? Are you shitting?" than "Taking your ease, good neighbor?" as B. B. Rogers put it in his admirable but very polite Loeb translation of 1924.[2] Throughout the play, this direct speech is the norm. People in the audience are singled out directly by name for (usually gross) ridicule, and the penultimate scene between Epigenes and the three ugly old women ("old broads" as I think they should be called, rather than the usual "hags" or "crones") is a tour de force of disgusting description and sexual directness, culminating in the boy's mock-tragic speech of surrender, the nightmarish intensity of which (were it not so funny in its exaggeration) makes it worthy of Céline:

> As a fly to a wanton boy am I to the gods:
> I must fuck one crumpled bag all night and then
> all day, but once she's done, another one

---

[2] In *Aristophanes, with the English translation of Benjamin Bickley Rogers* (New York: Putnam, 1924).

> is waiting to begin, a toad with lips
> as slick and slimy as an urn of embalming fluid.
> I'm truly unlucky. No, worse than that,
> I'm cursed by Zeus himself, a poor bastard
> having to strut and fret with beasts like these!
> But if I should founder coming into port
> tugged by these two hulks, please scuttle me
> right in the channel, and take the one on top,
> coat her with tar and sink her feet in lead.
> Then set her on the shore and touch her off,
> a horrid lighthouse with her cunt my funeral urn.   (1214–27)

This speech marks not only the peak of the play's vulgarity and violence, but also an end to them. After Epigenes is dragged off by the two old broads, Praxagora's tipsy young maid enters and leads everyone on stage, male and female, old and young, off to dinner, singing and dancing. The vulgar language (like Blepyrus' constipation) is a thing of the past: there'll be no more greed, no more hunger, no more inequalities, no more insults, no more envy, no more unhappiness. In other words, the play's ending is fantastic, but it is a happy fantasy. You can call anyone anything, the play seems (with, of course, considerable irony) to suggest, as long as you don't call them late for chow.

Of course, while all this happiness is being expressed as everyone dances away to dinner, and as even the cynical sailor, Blepyrus and Praxagora's neighbor, is happily plotting how he can get in on the food without surrendering his property, there are two characters left quite unhappily out of all the joy. The arrogant Epigenes gets his comeuppance by having to satisfy the appetites of two of the old broads (and they appear to be insatiable), and the nymphet who yearned for him (and for whom he yearned) is left pouting in her house as he is dragged away to his dire duty.

Under the old law, the boy would have been subject to capital punishment had he had sex with a teenaged girl while her mother was out of the house. The new law frees them to desire each other legally and safely, but with comic cruelty it also interposes the old women between them and their satisfaction. They end up miserably frustrated, as teenagers seem to do so often in any culture under any system of laws. It offers proof (if proof were

needed) of Aristophanes' brilliance as a playwright that with them he created a relationship hitherto unknown in Greek drama because his "new
order" in the play called for it. Previously, by dramatic convention, a young
girl who directly expresses sexual desire had never been seen in a play. The
relationship of these young lovers comes to no good end in this play, but in
the comedies to follow down through the centuries their relationship moves
to the very center of comedy, and the restored order at the end of a comic
play is usually marked by a joining of two young people in marriage. Not so
in Aristophanes, but here is where it all began.

The language of Epigenes and the nymphet is also something new and
quite special. For their "love duet," Aristophanes took advantage of the
popular (and banal) love songs of the street both to make his young lovers
plausible in their inflated desire and also to make fun of that very yearning.
The girl sings,

> Come to me, come to me,
> baby, baby,
> come to my little bed,
> just for tonight.   (1050–54)

And he answers,

> Come to me, come to me,
> baby, baby,
> hurry down to the door,
> or I'll die with desire: (1063–66)

The language is the key to this scene as it is throughout the play, and it
is a translator's duty to try to render it as freshly as Aristophanes wrote it
2400 years ago (even, I might add, the longest word in the Greek language,
which I have rendered as literally as possible in our impossible language,
with a little help from a practically perfect nanny).

I used R. G. Ussher's 1973 edition of the play[3] as my text for this translation.
In almost every instance I have deferred to his decisions both word by word
and in apportioning the lines among the characters. Other decisions could

---

[3] *Ecclesiazusae* (Oxford: Clarendon Press, 1973).

be made (and have been by others), but his decisions are so thoughtfully made and so persuasively argued that, with only the rarest exception, I have trusted them completely.

Rather than attempt a direct rendering of Aristophanes' meters, I have chosen to use a five-stress accentual line. Other translators have been more strictly and formally metrical, but the meaning in every such instance has been forced to take a back seat to the metrics. I chose rather to stay as close as possible to the meaning while still writing English verse. I have rendered the choruses and songs in a variety of shorter lines, hoping to give something of the flavor of Aristophanes' poetic lines.

I have only changed or added words and lines when I felt that the literal meaning would make sense or be funny only with the addition of an explanatory footnote. I then attempted either to explain the meaning by expanding the line or to offer an alternate line that would give something of the essence of his line without actually rendering it literally. For example, Aristophanes alludes to or parodies other works, tragic dramas or serious poems, throughout the play; many of these don't entirely make sense even to a Greek scholar, and they often aren't very funny even when they do make sense. I have replaced these with anachronistic references and allusions to works with which readers today will be familiar, beginning with the King James Bible in the opening lines. Most often I have used lines from Shakespeare (our closest equivalent to the great Greek tragic playwrights), but I have dropped in references to many other works, ranging from Pope, Byron, and Emerson to Stein, Lawrence, and Eliot to Nabokov, Dylan, and Forché. I hope that this game I've played will give the reader something of the flavor of the game Aristophanes played with his audience and readers. I also hope that maybe a new postmodern (or post-postmodern) audience of readers will discover just how good a play this play is. If nothing else, they will discover how, in so many important ways, nothing at all seems to have changed over the last couple of millennia or so when it comes to human vice and folly, and to the ability of human laughter to correct that vice and folly (or at least keep them in check for a couple of hours). And I hope that you will approve of my version of this play as well, but even if you don't, remember: you can call me anything, just don't call me late for chow.

Cast

PRAXAGORA
FIRST WOMAN
SECOND WOMAN
CHORUS OF WOMEN
BLEPYRUS, husband of Praxagora
NEIGHBOR, husband of second woman
CHREMES
HERALD
UGLY OLD BROAD
NYMPHET
EPIGENES, a young man
UGLIER OLD BROAD
UGLIEST OLD BROAD
MAID TO PRAXAGORA
NONSPEAKING
    Young girls

(The play opens just before dawn on a street in Athens. Two houses front the street, and from one of them a young woman emerges, dressed as a man, shoes and all, carrying a walking stick in her left hand and a lamp in her right.)

PRAXAGORA *(with reverential awe)*
    O Lamp, which gleameth in darkness,
    hallowed be Thy flame;
    I'll hang Thee here
    and sing aloud Thy name,
    from whence Thou came
    and whither Thou shalt glow:
    the potter's wheel which spun Thee round;
    Thy nose so bright, bright as a sun.
    now send, dear Lamp, Thy promised beams abroad.

Thou alone knowest who is on the way,   10
for only Thou *should* know it all—always by the bed
when we answer nightly Aphrodite's call,
Thou from Whom we never hide
no matter how twisted we are
in love's latest position.
Thou alone hast lit the slit
between our thighs and singed
the burning bush away;
and Thou illuminate us, too,
when, skeleton key in hand, we pop   20
our husbands' pantry locks to warm
our poor spare ribs with food and drink.
Not once hast Thou ever told a living soul
and so hast earned a share in our present plans,
the ones the girls and I dreamed up
during last year's Mothers' March for Demeter.
(Growing bored with her "hymn," she peers about her in the
waxing light.)
Where are those women? They're not in sight,
it's almost dawn, and the General Assembly
is almost in session! We women have got to "grab
our seats," as Phyromachus once put it on stage   30
at a most inappropriate moment, and blend right in
with all the other asses (I mean, the men).
Maybe they haven't faked up their beards
or been able to steal their husband's cloaks . . .
but soft! what light through yonder alley breaks?
I'd better hide in case it is a man.
(She hides in a doorway. A woman with a lamp enters, leading a group
of women, carrying men's cloaks and shoes and
walking sticks. Others straggle in behind.)

FIRST WOMAN

Come on girls, hurry. When we left home
the herald and the cock were both already crowing!

PRAXAGORA *(stepping out of the doorway)*
  And I've been up all night waiting for you.
  But now let's get my neighbor up and out . . .   40
  I'll just run my nails oh so gently on her door,
  so her husband won't hear a blessed thing.

SECOND WOMAN *(coming out of the door immediately)*
  I wasn't asleep; I wasn't. I was just trying
  to tie these shoes on when I heard you scratch
  the door. My husband, you know, he's an islander,
  a real sailor; he kept putting in his oar
  all night long, so I could scarcely sleep a wink
  and only just now had the chance to pinch his cloak.

PRAXAGORA
  Hi ho! Here comes Clinarete, and here's
  Sostrata, and even Philaenete, too.   50

FIRST WOMAN
  Hurry it up now. You know Glyce swore
  the last one in will have to pay a fine,
  nine quarts of wine and a bushel and a peck of peas.

SECOND WOMAN
  Look, there's Melistiche, Smicythion's wife,
  flopping along in his big hightops!

FIRST WOMAN
  I don't think she had any trouble
  getting away from her slack-oared old man!

SECOND WOMAN
  And there's the bartender's wife,
  Geusistrata. Look, she's carrying a torch!

FIRST WOMAN

> And there's the wives of Philodoretus   60
> and Chaeretades, and other women, too.
> In fact, *all* the best people are here.

CHORUS LEADER

> I don't know about you, deary, but I
> had such a hard time getting away.
> My husband absolutely stuffed himself
> with anchovies and was up all night
> choking and wheezing, hacking and choking.

PRAXAGORA

> Now that you're all finally here, please
> be seated. I must discover whether you've
> done everything that we agreed at the Mothers' March.   70

FIRST WOMAN

> Well, I certainly have! I've let
> my armpits get gross and hairy, and whenever
> my husband went downtown, I oiled up, lay
> in the sun all day, and tried for a full-body tan.

SECOND WOMAN

> What about me? I threw my razor away
> and got so hairy I don't look a bit like a woman!

PRAXAGORA

> Have you got your beards, the ones
> we all agreed to wear when we met today?

FIRST WOMAN

> I have, by Hecate! And a swell one, too!

SECOND WOMAN

> Mine's better than an hairy man's, even Epicrates'!   80

PRAXAGORA
And the rest of you?

FIRST WOMAN
They're nodding: got 'em!

PRAXAGORA
Okay. I can see you've got the other things:
the big red shoes, your walking-sticks,
your men's cloaks, just as you were supposed to do.

FIRST WOMAN
Look, I've brought Lamias' big billy club.
I stole it while he snored away.

SECOND WOMAN
The "famous" one he leans on when he farts!

PRAXAGORA
Zeus save us, but with a night stick that big
and wearing leather like Argus, who's better equipped
to give the eye to even the public hangman?   90
But we'd better get back to business
while the stars are still out. The General Assembly
we're going to goes into session at dawn.

FIRST WOMAN
It certainly does, and we've got to find seats
down front, right below the speaker's platform.

SECOND WOMAN *(holding out a ball of wool)*
I brought this so I could get a little
carding done while the place is filling up.

PRAXAGORA *(rapping on the second woman's forehead)*
Filling up!! Is anyone home?

SECOND WOMAN

                         Artemis knows
    I can listen just as well when I'm carding
    as when I'm not. My babies need clothes!   100

PRAXAGORA

    Combing your wool! When you mustn't let
    anyone snatch a glimpse of any part of your body!
    What a fine kettle of fish if during the debate
    some woman has to climb over the seats and shows
    her woolly-woolly! But if we get there first
    and sit down front, who'll notice that we keep
    ourselves so covered up? And if we let the beards
    we're going to stick on our chins hang out,
    who would ever guess that we're not men?
    A nancy like Agyrrhius managed to pass for a man   110
    once he borrowed the beard of Pronomus,
    even though he was woman in every way but one.
    And he's the very politician who just came up
    with the dumb idea of paying men to vote!
    I swear by this good day, it's because of him
    that we must dare to dare, must do the deed
    in the high hope of taking charge, of doing
    what's best for the people. When the city's
    in the doldrums, let's join together and say,
    "Sail on, O Ship of State, sail on!"   120

FIRST WOMAN

    How can a regiment of women, mere women,
    ever speak to the General Assembly?

PRAXAGORA

                      No problem!
    Everybody knows that those who use their tongues
    the best are those who've been screwed the most.
    And, as luck would have it, naturally that's us!

FIRST WOMAN
> That may be true, but being a virgin's
> a dangerous thing in a whorehouse, and most of us
> are not exactly experienced in this oral thing.

PRAXAGORA
> Isn't that exactly why we're here? To rehearse
> our speeches? So put those whiskers on your chin,   130
> and everybody else who has practiced talking, too.

FIRST WOMAN *(sarcastically)*
> Was there ever a woman who needed practice talking?

PRAXAGORA
> Very well, why don't *you* try on *your* beard
> and be a man? I'll lay these garlands out here
> and try mine on as well, just in case
> I find I have something I might want to add.

SECOND WOMAN
> Look here, Praxagora sweety. Oh my,
> how absolutely and completely silly!

PRAXAGORA
> Silly!!

SECOND WOMAN
> Yes, we look like bearded clams!

PRAXAGORA *(acting out the opening of the Assembly)*
> First, Chaplain, purify this session;   140
> dispatch the sacrificial pussy cat.
> Delegates, be seated. Ariphrades,
> be quiet! You there in the back, come forward
> and take your seats. Now, who wishes
> to address the General Assembly?

FIRST WOMAN
    I do.

PRAXAGORA
        Then put on the garland,
    and good luck to you as you speak.

FIRST WOMAN *(putting the garland on her head)*
    So, there!

PRAXAGORA
            Please do begin.

FIRST WOMAN
                    But where's my drink?

PRAXAGORA
    You expect a drink?

FIRST WOMAN
                    If not, why's this on my head?

PRAXAGORA
    Get out of here! This is just what you would do   150
    there, too.

FIRST WOMAN
                What! Don't tell me the men don't drink.

PRAXAGORA
    The men don't drink.

FIRST WOMAN
                    By Artemis, they *must*!
    And straight up, too! When you think of the laws
    they pass, they have to be drunk. And those libations:

what other reason for those long prayers but drink?
They argue just like drunks, and when one of them
goes ballistic, the Sergeant at Arms drags him away.

PRAXAGORA
You're hopeless. Go back to your seat. Sit down.

FIRST WOMAN
Heavens above, I wish I'd never had a beard!
And this garland's made me dry as a desert!   160

PRAXAGORA
Who else among you would like to speak?

SECOND WOMAN
                                        That's me!

PRAXAGORA
Put on this other garland; we must keep at it.
Remember to act like a man, speak to the point,
and lean on your cane while you talk, like this.

SECOND WOMAN
I wish some older, wiser man had risen
to speak, and I could have sat silently and listened,
but I cannot sit by and allow the practice to continue
of keeping water in taverns, right there with the wine.
This is not fit and proper, by Persephone and Demeter!

PRAXAGORA
By Demeter and Persephone! What can you mean?!?   170

SECOND WOMAN
What's wrong? I didn't ask for a drink.

PRAXAGORA

No, you didn't, but you swore by the two goddesses,
and you forgot you're supposed to be a *man*.
(shaking her head)
You were doing so well, too.

SECOND WOMAN

Oops! By Apollo, I did!

PRAXAGORA

Okay. Okay.
But give me the garland; I'm still not going
through with this unless we get it absolutely right.

SECOND WOMAN

No, I want the garland; I'll try it again.
I'll get it right. Ahem. As I see it, sisters . . .

PRAXAGORA

You dimwit! They're *men*, and you said "sisters"!   180

SECOND WOMAN

It's all Epigonus' fault. I caught sight of him
in the audience and thought I was speaking to *women*.

PRAXAGORA

I've heard quite enough! Return to your seat.
I'd better take this garland and speak myself.
(She begins her speech.)
Heaven help us who can't seem to help ourselves.
I love my country as much as any man,
and I am saddened and hurt by the way it's being run.
I tell you, we are in the hands of scoundrels.
If one of them is honest for a day,
then you'd better watch out on the ten days to follow.   190
And if you back someone else, he's even worse.

It's hard to talk straight to men like you,
so perverse that you fear and distrust your friends
and run after those who hate and despise you.
There was a time when the General Assembly never met,
but at least we knew then that Agyrrhius
was a fraud. Now, we do meet, and those
who're paid to attend praise him to the skies,
while those who can't make the meeting claim
that those who do come ought to be shot!   200

FIRST WOMAN
    By Aphrodite, you said a mouthful!

PRAXAGORA
    "By Aphrodite," you ninny! Now won't that
    be terrific if you say it at the meeting.

FIRST WOMAN *(flustered)*
    I wouldn't do that.

PRAXAGORA
                            Then don't get the habit now.
(She resumes her speech.)
    When we were discussing the Anti-Spartan League,
    it seemed we had to have it to survive,
    but when we finally got it, nobody was happy . . .
    and its chief backer had to beat it out of town.
    Suppose we've got to build more ships, the urban
    poor are for it and join the navy, but the rich men   210
    and the farmers are opposed. Once, you hated
    the Corinthians, and they, you; now, they're bearing
    gifts, so we're the best of friends again.
    "The Argives are fools," and, natch, Hieronymus is wise.
    Once in a while we get a chance at peace,
    but then Thrasybulus, who's *out*, gets angry he's not *in*.

FIRST WOMAN
>   What a very smart *man*!

PRAXAGORA
>   That's the way to go!
> *(She resumes her speech again.)*
>   And you, my fellow Athenians, are the cause of it all.
>   You vote yourselves a salary paid for by taxes,
>   and you're scheming how to make it even more;   220
>   then you wonder why we're staggering around like Aesimus.
>   But take a chance on me, and I'll save the day:
>   let's turn the city over to the women;
>   let them run it like they run our homes.

FIRST WOMAN
>   That's terrific!

SECOND WOMAN
>   Go, *Man*, go!

PRAXAGORA
>   How are they better than we? Let me count
>   the ways. First, every mother's daughter of them
>   dyes wool in hot water in the ancient way;
>   you won't find them following every new fad.
>   And wouldn't it have saved our city a lot of woe   230
>   if we hadn't tried to fix it when it wasn't broken,
>   if change for change's sake hadn't been our motto?
>   Women follow the recipes when they cook, as ever.
>   They still carry their loads on their heads, as ever.
>   They keep secret their sacred holiday, as ever.
>   They bake their cheesecakes with honey, as ever.
>   They tempt their husbands, then deny them, as ever.
>   They hide their lovers in the bedroom closet, as ever.
>   They love to buy little things for themselves, as ever.
>   They really hate wine that's been watered, as ever.   240

And they delight in foreplay before fucking, every time.
Therefore, I move that we pass on all responsibility
of governance to the women with no shilly-shallying
or questioning what they'll do. Let them just do it.
You know they'll bend over backwards to protect
their soldier boys in harm's way, and who but a mother
would see to it that army rations are A-OK?
At getting money, who's better than women?
And they won't be cheated; remember, set a cheat
to catch a cheat. I'll skip over the other arguments   250
and conclude with this promise: vote as I say,
and you'll be happy every day in every way.

(She removes her garland.)

FIRST WOMAN

That's even better, babe! Praxagora,
where did you ever learn to talk that way?

PRAXAGORA

When we were war refugees, my husband and I,
we lived for a time on Capitol Hill. I listened to
the Delegates speak and picked up all their tricks.

FIRST WOMAN

No surprise, then, you sound so smart and smooth.
If you succeed in pulling this whole thing off,
we'll more than proudly elect you Leader of the City!   260
But what if that old crock Cephalus interrupts?
How will you handle him there on the floor?

PRAXAGORA

I'll say he's nuts.

FIRST WOMAN

But that's common knowledge!

PRAXAGORA
Then I'll say he's completely schizophrenic.

FIRST WOMAN
They know that, too.

PRAXAGORA
Then I'll say
that he's as potty as the pots he makes,
and that he's as bad a lawmaker as he is a potter.

FIRST WOMAN
What if slit-eyed old Neocleides breaks in?

PRAXAGORA
Go squint up a bitch's slit, I'll say.

FIRST WOMAN
And if they all bang away at you?

PRAXAGORA
I won't   270
be backward; I'll give them what they want up front.

FIRST WOMAN
But what if the Sergeant at Arms and his men
try to drag you off?

PRAXAGORA *(taking a martial arts pose)*
Just let 'em try.
I'll take my stance; they'll get no waist-locks
on me. I know all the holds, the take-downs and pins.

CHORUS LEADER *(very earnestly)*
If they do pick you up, why then . . . we'll just
politely ask them to put you right back down!

FIRST WOMAN *(ignoring the chorus leader)*
    This plan's a good one, I think we all agree.
    But we've yet to figure just how we're going to remember
    to raise our hands to vote when most often   280
    we find ourselves in positions where we raise our legs!

PRAXAGORA
    It's hard, I know, but in order to vote you must
    poke your right arm up till it's bare to the shoulder.
    But for now, you'd better grab your shoes and hitch
    up your tunics just like your husbands did, if they
    ever went to the assembly or even left the house.
    Then when you're dressed just right, put on your beards.
    And when they're properly adjusted, put on the cloaks
    you appropriated and drape them to the right.
    Ready? Then lean on your sticks as you go, and sing   290
    some good old country music, tunes like those
    old timers pick and sing.

CHORUS LEADER
                    Hee haw!

FIRST WOMAN *(to Praxagora and the second woman)*
                    Let's us go.
    We'll get there before the rest and maybe meet up
    with the suburban women coming straight to Capitol Hill.

PRAXAGORA
    Hurry then! Unless we get a good place in line,
    we won't even get a clothespin, much less men's pay.
    *(Praxagora and the two women leave as the other women put the
                    finishing touches on their costumes and form two
                    chorus lines.)*

CHORUS LEADER
    Well, lads, it's time we should embark,
    and "lad" *is* the word for us, don't you

forget, for we're really up Shit Creek
if even a single man discovers   300
what we've been doing in the dark.

CHORUS *(first chorus line speaking as townsmen)*
It's time to go! It's time to go!
The tocsin has been sounded,
for if we're late,
oh, if we're late,
covered with dust
and breathing garlic,
our pay will be impounded.

Step it up, Charitimides,
Smicythus and Draces get moving.   310
The stakes are high,
make no mistake,
just take your seats
and raise your hands,
our sisters we're approving.

Eeks! What did I say?
Our *brothers* all the way!
(The first chorus line files out as the second begins to speak.)

Be sure to elbow and jostle
the johnny-come-latelies from town,
who never showed   320
until the dough
rose higher; they
loafed around and had a few,
yet now they all come down
and jostle and shove for seats.

Oh, in the good old days,
yes, in the good old days,

when Myronides
was the best of men,
men brought their own lunches.   330
They did their duty
with no hint of pay.
They were workers and not the elite.

(The second chorus line leaves. From the door of Praxagora's house, an
old man enters. He is dressed in a short yellow
nighty, his penis exposed, and is having a hard
time walking in a pair of women's white shoes.)

BLEPYRUS
What is the matter? Where's she gone off on me?
It's nearly dawn, and I can't find her anywhere.
There I was, just lying in bed in the dark,
when suddenly I needed to shit, and I can't even find
my shoes or my cloak, much less my wife. I felt
around everywhere, they're gone, the Mother
of all Turds is hammering at my back door,   340
and I had to settle for her Baby Doll and pumps.
(He looks around and moves away from the house to the front of
the stage.)
Now, where's a private place to take a dump?
But then, don't all butts look alike in the dark?
Who's to see me anywhere at this time of night?
What a fool I was to get married at my age.
I ought to be whipped with nettles. I'll bet she's up
to no good at this hour. Ohh, I've got to squat!
(Another man, carrying a lamp, enters from the other house, notices
Blepyros, and walks over to him.)

NEIGHBOR
Ahoy, neighbor! Is that you, Blepyrus?

BLEPYRUS
Yes, by God, it's me.

NEIGHBOR

You're all calf-turd brown.
Some airy poet float by and hit you with a splatter?   350

BLEPYRUS

No, I had to drop a load, and all I could find
to put on was my wife's little yellow nighty.

NEIGHBOR

So, where's your cloak?

BLEPYRUS

You've got me. I searched
the bedroom, the whole house, and I couldn't find it.

NEIGHBOR

Why didn't you just ask your wife where it is?

BLEPYRUS

God knows, I couldn't! She's not even there;
she's slipped out of the house. This isn't good.

NEIGHBOR

Poseidon! If that's the case: me, too!
My wife's stolen my cloak, and what's worse,
she's taken my boots to boot! They're truly gone.   360

BLEPYRUS

By Dionysus, my good Laconian boots
are missing as well, but duty called—oh, did it call!—
so I jammed on her shoes and came out here.
I didn't want to shit on the blanket; it's just
been washed. Where could she be? Could one
of her friends have asked her to come over for breakfast?

NEIGHBOR

    That's most likely it. She's not a slut . . .
    far's *I* know. Are you trying to heave out a hawser?
    No matter, I'm off to the General Assembly once I get
    my cloak back; it's the only one I've got.   370

BLEPYRUS

    I'm going, too, if I could just get this out.
    It feels like a whole pear in there. It's really
    got me blocked!

NEIGHBOR *(as he leaves)*
                Just like a filibuster?

BLEPYRUS

    Could be: I *am* full of gas and about to bust!
(He continues groaning and talking to himself as the dawn comes up like
             thunder and lights the stage.)
    What am I going to do? And not just now,
    but later: how's the food I've still got to eat
    going to get out? The exit's been sealed up
    by this damn Deadend Kid. Is there a doctor
    in the house? By any blessed chance is there
    a proctologists' convention in town? How about   380
    Amynon: he knows his assholes, but he probably
    can't come. Or how about Antisthenes?
    Call him, somebody, please! Surely a man
    as full of shit as he is will know what to do.
    Oh, that this too too solid turd would melt!
    O Divine Eileithyia, dear goddess of childbirth,
    deliver me, poor me, so bloated and corked!
    Don't abandon me to the role of comic commode!
(He emits a wild scream of relief just as a third man enters.)

CHREMES

    You, there! What's that? Are you shitting?

BLEPYRUS *(struggling hurriedly to his feet)*
    I was, I was, but I am, thank God, no more!   390

CHREMES
    And, *really*, is that a nightgown you're wearing?

BLEPYRUS
    It's my wife's; it was dark when I put it on.
    But, not to change the subject, where've you been?

CHREMES
    At the assembly.

BLEPYRUS
               What, is it over already?

CHREMES
    It most assuredly is, and almost before
    It began. The place was packed, and what a laugh
    they had, by heavens, when they red-roped off
    the latecomers.

BLEPYRUS
             But you were paid, weren't you?

CHREMES
    Not at all! They said I was too late.
    I'm so ashamed!

BLEPYRUS
             No need to be embarrassed—   400
    until you open your wallet! Why were you late?

CHREMES
    Capitol Hill was mobbed. There's never been
    such a crowd! They were as pale and wan as shoemakers.

It was amazing to see so many pasty faces.
So, no pay for me, and for lots of others, too.

BLEPYRUS

So there's no hope for me if I went now?

CHREMES

Surely you jest! You wouldn't even have been
paid if you'd arrived by the second cock-crow.

BLEPYRUS

"Now cracks a noble heart! Good night, sweet pay,
and flights of angels sing thee to thy rest!"   410
But what pulled such a humongous crowd so early?

CHREMES

What else but the Speaker's decision to start
debate on how to save the city? First thing,
that old squint Neocleides tried to get the floor,
but he was shouted down: "You've got a nerve
to try to tell us how to prop up the state
when you can't even prop up your own eyelids!"
He squinted and shouted back, "Can I help it?"

BLEPYRUS

"Try garlic and bitter fig juice mixed with
Spartan spurge. You apply it to your eyelids   420
every night." That's what I would have said.

CHREMES

Then Evaeon, the homeless advocate, quite naked
to the naked eye, his cloak more holes than whole,
rose to say his populist piece: "As you
can see," he said, "I need some saving myself,
enough savings at least to buy me a cloak,
but nonetheless I'll show you how to save

the city. If all the local haberdashers
would donate heavy cloaks at winter solstice
to all the needy, then no more colds, and no   430
more painful pleurisy. And then let anyone who lacks
a bed or needs a blanket, after a bask
at the bath-house, be given some space at the tanners',
and if the tanners won't let him in,
then levy a heavy fine on them of three good blankets."

BLEPYRUS

By Dionysus, what a great idea! And one
no one could oppose if he'd added that millers
must give the poor three quarts of grain a day
or be damned to hell! And either way, that would
take care of that old skinflint, Nausicydes!   440

CHREMES

Well, then a pale, quite handsome young man
popped up and began to speak . . . almost as pretty
a boy as Nicias. He argued we should hand over
the city to the women to run! That mob of cobblers
began to clap and raise a ruckus, while the farm
bloc got their bowels in an uproar!

BLEPYRUS *(flinching at the mention of bowels)*
                                    I'll bet they did!

CHREMES

But they didn't have the votes, so the speaker
put them down and went on to say nothing
but good about women and nothing at all good
about you.

BLEPYRUS

                    And just what did he say about me?   450

CHREMES
  First, he said you are a villain.

BLEPYRUS
                    And what
  did he say about you?

CHREMES
                  Wait now. And then he said
  you are a swindler.

BLEPYRUS
          Just me?

CHREMES
              Just you, and then
  he added that you were a squealer as well.

BLEPYRUS
                    Only me?

CHREMES
  Only you, he said, and
  (*gesturing to the audience*)
              all of them!

BLEPYRUS
  Well, that's another story: who'd disagree?

CHREMES
  He said a woman's head is packed with brains
  and ways to make "dough," and that they always
  keep the secrets of their sacred holiday while we're
  as loose about our meetings as diarrhea.   460

BLEPYRUS
  By Hermes, he wasn't shitting you about that!

CHREMES

> And he said that women lend their dresses to each
> other, and gold jewelry and drinking glasses
> and even money without a witness, and they
> always return what they've borrowed, while men,
> he said, are always ready to go back on a deal.

BLEPYRUS

> By God, we do it even *with* witnesses!

CHREMES

> He continued to praise women in other ways:
> he said they're not informers, that they don't sue
> everybody in sight, that they don't plot   470
> against the people, but do things right.

BLEPYRUS

> And how did the vote go?

CHREMES

> > > > > Moved and passed.
> The only thing we haven't tried: to let them have it!

BLEPYRUS

> It passed?!?

CHREMES

> > > You betcha!

BLEPYRUS

> > > So everything
> we used to do, now they're going to do?

CHREMES

> You've got it.

BLEPYRUS

             So I won't have to wake early
to get paid for jury duty; my wife will?

CHREMES

    You won't even have to support your family;
she'll do it.

BLEPYRUS

             And I won't have to yawn
and groan myself awake and out of bed at dawn?   480

CHREMES

    God, no! That's women's business now.
No need to groan; just fart around all day.

BLEPYRUS

    Ay, there's the rub for men of *our* age.
Once they're in charge they'll make us . . .

CHREMES

                         What?

BLEPYRUS

    Fuck them.

CHREMES

          And if we can't get it up?

BLEPYRUS

    We'll get no breakfast!

CHREMES

              Then you'd better learn
to plow . . . to earn your early morning chow!

BLEPYRUS

But it's no fun if you're not in the mood!

CHREMES

The law's
the law, and every man must rise to the occasion.

BLEPYRUS

There *is* a saying, "When fools rush in where angels   490
fear to tread, whatever is, is right!"

CHREMES

So let it be, Pallas and all the other gods.
But now I really must be going. So long.
(Chremes walks away and exits offstage as Blepyrus calls after him.)

BLEPYRUS

Good-bye. So long. See you later, Chremes.
*(Blepyros returns to his house, and after he is in, the chorus returns from
the assembly, still dressed as men. They speak back
and forth among themselves.)*

CHORUS LEADER

Hut, two, three, four,
Keep up and keep in step.
Can anyone see a man?
Turn around, look around,
cover your flanks.
There's many a bugger   500
who'll sneak up and try
to creep up your behind!

CHORUS

Faster! Faster! And yet
remember to clip-clop along
in those boots like a man.
If our husbands should catch

us red-handed like this,
what a shame, what a shame!

Stay closer together,
look left, look right,   510
look up, look down.
Danger! Danger! Danger!

Make the dust fly; be quick!
We're near the very place
where we started out this morning.
There's the house of our leader
who dreamed up the plan
which we just voted in.

There's no more need to linger
here with beards on our chins;   520
a man might see us and see through us!
Keep alert, always alert, and then slip
deep into the shadow of the wall
and there change back to who we were.

Yes, be quick, for here she comes.
our leader's back from the assembly.
Hurry, pull off those awful hairy
hanging things that far too long
have been our very best disguise.

PRAXAGORA *(enters, pulling off her false beard)*
     Lady Luck, ladies, has smiled on us;   530
     things have worked out as we planned. But quickly now,
     before some man comes by and sees us in them,
     peel off those cloaks and get out of those shoes.
     You there, remember to untie them first!
     And ditch those canes. And you,
(to the chorus leader)

> > could you shape them up?
> I've got to slip into my house before my husband
> sees me and put his cloak back where it was,
> and all the other things I borrowed, too.

CHORUS LEADER

> You say it, we do it: everything's off
> and on the ground. Just tell us what else to do.   540
> We're yours to command; there's never ever been
> a wonder woman more totally boss than you!

PRAXAGORA

> But you've got to stay with me. I'll need you
> as my cabinet, my advisors, if I'm to do the job
> that I'm to do. At the General Assembly, you
> shrugged off the shouting, ignored the danger,
> proved that every one of you's got balls!

(Everyone clears away the discarded clothing as Praxagora moves toward
> > *her house, but just as she reaches it Blepyros comes*
> > *out the door, dressed now in his own tunic, but*
> > *barefooted.)*

BLEPYRUS

> Praxagora! Where have you been?

PRAXAGORA

> > And what business
> is that of yours?

BLEPYRUS

> > What business is that of mine?!
> Well, duh!

PRAXAGORA

> > I suppose you think I've been with a lover.   550

BLEPYRUS

> Probably more than one!

PRAXAGORA

There's a way you can

find out.

BLEPYRUS

How's that?

PRAXAGORA

Just use your nose and sniff me

for perfume.

BLEPYRUS

You're telling me a woman without perfume
cannot get fucked?

PRAXAGORA *(with a sigh)*

You ought to know: not this one.

BLEPYRUS

Then why else did you sneak out of the house
in my cloak this morning?

PRAXAGORA

A dear friend went into labor

and sent for me.

BLEPYRUS

So why not tell me you were going?

PRAXAGORA

Dear man, you'd not have me ignore a woman
in such a fix?

BLEPYRUS

At least you could have told me.
Something is rotten here.

PRAXAGORA

                                   I swear it's not,   560
    by Persephone and Demeter. I just went as I was.
    The maid she sent said, "Drop everything! Hurry!"

BLEPYRUS

    Naturally you couldn't wear your own clothes?
    Oh no, you had to pull my cloak right off me,
    replace it with your dress, leaving me
    as good as dead, practically laid out for the tomb
    in almost every way but the wreath and the perfumes.

PRAXAGORA

    It was cold, and I'm a delicate little thing,
    so I put this on to keep me warm. But I thought
    of you, dear man, and covered you snug as a bug.   570

BLEPYRUS

    And why did my cane and my boots have to go along?

PRAXAGORA

    I was afraid nightstalkers would want your cloak,
    so I changed my shoes to make like you, kicking
    my feet and whacking rocks with the walking stick.

BLEPYRUS

    I suppose you know you lost us eight liters of wheat
    that I could have bought us with my assembly wages?

PRAXAGORA

    Don't let it bug you: it's a boy!

BLEPYRUS

                              The assembly??

PRAXAGORA

    No, no, the new baby. So did the assembly
    meet? Is it already over?

BLEPYRUS

    For God's sake, I told you yesterday that it   580
    would meet today!

PRAXAGORA

            I suppose I do remember.

BLEPYRUS

    You haven't heard about the decisions?

PRAXAGORA

                      Not me.

BLEPYRUS

    You'd better sit down and chew your cud. They say
    the city's been handed over to you women!

PRAXAGORA

                      To do what?
    Woolgathering?

BLEPYRUS

              No, by God, to manage it!

PRAXAGORA

    Manage what?

BLEPYRUS

            Everything! The whole shebang!
(Chremes, returning the way he left, pauses and begins to listen.)

PRAXAGORA

    If that's so, by Aphrodite, this
    will surely be a green and pleasant land!

BLEPYRUS
>   For what reason?

PRAXAGORA
>   Lots of reasons. Now
>   jackbooted bully-boys won't be allowed   590
>   to shame the city: no more suborning witnesses,
>   no paid informing . . .

BLEPYRUS
>   Please, by the gods, not that!
>   Don't take away the way I make my living!

CHREMES
>   Be quiet, man, and let her speak her piece.

PRAXAGORA
>   No more mugging, no more envy, no more
>   poor people huddling in rags, no more
>   slander, and no more harassment for debt.

CHREMES
>   By Poseidon, that's great if that's the gospel truth!

PRAXAGORA
>   I'll explain it so that you'll be on my side.
>   *(She points to Blepyrus.)*
>   And even himself will have nothing to say against me.   600
>   *(As she prepares to speak, she removes Blepyrus' cloak and hands him the
>   cloak and his shoes.)*

CHORUS
>   Now you've got to summon up
>   all your smarts, be both wise
>   and shrewd to defend the revolution.
>   We've heard how well you can describe

the benefits for all, how all
will prosper, all be freed of fear,
but now's the time for words to turn
to deeds, so show us the new deal
we need so badly. Announce this new order,
but make sure it's really new, something   610
we've never seen or even heard of
before: you see, there's nothing a crowd
hates more than a remake of the same old play!

CHORUS LEADER
　　Now's the time, it's the time for inspiration.
　　This audience won't put up with narrative retardation!

PRAXAGORA
　　I have a grand scheme; I'm really sure I do.
　　And as to the audience, I'm only worried that they're
　　not ready for radical change and want to hold
　　to those "enduring touchstones" of the boring and old.

BLEPYRUS
　　Don't worry about that. We love what's new;   620
　　we hate what's old. That's the one thing we cling to
　　when everything else we've gambled and fumbled away.

PRAXAGORA
　　I'll brook no contradictions or interruptions
　　until you've heard and understood it all.
　　My first priority: no more private property,
　　unless there's no other way. All property
　　will belong equally to all, and to all, the same
　　income will be apportioned. No more rich;
　　no more poor. No longer will one man
　　have grand estates, while another doesn't have   630
　　even enough land for his own grave.
　　No more distinction between those with many slaves

and those without a single one. Trust me
to see that from now on there's only one standard
of living for all, each and every one of us.

BLEPYRUS

How's that possible?

PRAXAGORA

If we were eating
shit sandwiches, you'd ask for more bread!

BLEPYRUS

We'll all be eating shit?

PRAXAGORA

Of course not!
You broke in, as I asked you not to, to ask
exactly what I was just about to say.   640
And what I was going to say is that my first
executive order will be to declare that all
land, money, and other property shall belong
to all. We women will take charge of this fund
and use it, wisely and well, for the common good.

CHREMES

What about a man who owns no land
but has a fortune hidden in cash?

PRAXAGORA

He'll either
turn it in, or he'll be up for perjury.

CHREMES

I'll bet
that perjury for pay is how he got it!

PRAXAGORA

                            No matter.
It won't be of any value to him anyway.

CHREMES

                            How so?   650

PRAXAGORA

    No longer will poverty drive anyone to crime.
    Now to each according to his needs:
    bread, salt fish, barley cakes,
    cloaks to wear, wine to drink, garlands
    and chick-peas. There's no reason not
    to turn his money in. Is there?

CHREMES

    But aren't the rich the biggest thieves of all?

PRAXAGORA

    Until now, good friend, in the old order they were.
    But now that everyone will share and share alike,
    there's no reason to hoard or steal.   660

BLEPYRUS

    What if a man sees a girl and thinks
    of giving her a bit of a poke? He'll need some cash
    from the common funds. Then after they've screwed
    his revolutionary zeal will surely go limp.

PRAXAGORA

    He won't need cash; she's his for free.
    Free love's the order of the day, all for one
    and one for all, free to fuck or get
    knocked up by any man who comes along.

BLEPYRUS

    Won't every man spend all his time
    looking for the absolutely hottest babe to bang?   670

PRAXAGORA

    The pug-nosed and the homely will be right there
    with the beauties, and if a man wants to have the good,
    he must service the bad and the ugly first.

BLEPYRUS

    That's not fair to us older men! If we diddle
    the homely ones first, there'll be very little doodle
    left in our cocks for the beauty-babes later!

PRAXAGORA

    There'll be no complaints, I promise you.
    They simply *will not* complain.

BLEPYRUS

                  Who? About what?

PRAXAGORA

    About not getting laid by you—as if you could.

BLEPYRUS

    From your point of view, it makes a kind of sense;   680
    you've got it rigged so that every box will be stuffed.
    But you still haven't dealt with the men. You women
    will ignore the ugly ones and go straight for the hunks.

PRAXAGORA

    The ugly men will just have to shadow the "hunks"
    as they leave dinner, and keep an eye on the malls
    and bath-houses, because it's against the law
    for a tall, handsome man to bed a woman
    who hasn't first fucked a short, ugly man.

BLEPYRUS

You mean Lysicrates is now as tall as any man?

PRAXAGORA

By Apollo, he is! And what's more, the scheme   690
is democratic. What a joke it will be on a swell
with a signet ring on his pinky, when some nerd
in flip-flops says, "Step aside, my man,
and wait your turn, but you *can* have dibs on seconds."

CHREMES

But in this brave new world, how will a man
know his children?

PRAXAGORA

                    Not exactly a problem:
all youngsters will consider all older men their fathers.

BLEPYRUS

This means that young men will begin
to throttle all old men in earnest, since they
already choke the life out of their fathers now.   700
Under these new laws, they'll not only strangle
the "old man," they'll use him as a shit pot, too.

PRAXAGORA

Passersby wouldn't allow that! No one
used to stop a son beating up his dad,
but now if anyone sees an old man
being beaten up or dragged through an orchard
by his hair, he'll fear it's his own father
and leap quickly and surely to his defense.

BLEPYRUS

I'll grant that may be true, but how awful it'll be
if Epicurus or Leucolophus start calling me "Daddy."   710

PRAXAGORA
>There are worse things.

BLEPYRUS
>   Name me one.

PRAXAGORA
>If Aristyllus should call you "Dad" and give you a kiss.

BLEPYRUS
>If he did: Pow! Right in the kisser!

PRAXAGORA
>But you'd stink of cat shit, not catmint
>anyway! But not to worry, that buttlicker
>was born before our law was passed. He won't
>be pressing those cow-pie lips to yours.

BLEPYRUS
>Just let him try!

CHREMES
>   But who's to work the fields?

PRAXAGORA
>The slaves. The only thing you'll have to do
>is dude up for dinner when the sundial says.   720

CHREMES *(glancing pointedly at Blepyrus)*
>One might also ask, where does one get
>a cloak? Who is going to supply new cloaks?

PRAXAGORA
>We have enough on hand right now to do.
>Later on we'll weave you new ones.

CHREMES

> One other thing: what happens if I get sued
> and lose? Who'll pay court costs?
> Doesn't seem fair to take it from city funds?

PRAXAGORA

> There's not going to be any more suing.

BLEPYRUS

> Now you've done it!

CHREMES *(to himself)*

> > Looks that way to me.

PRAXAGORA *(to Blepyrus, with some exasperation)*
> My friend . . . why should there be lawsuits?   730

BLEPYRUS

> For numerous reasons, by Apollo! Here's one:
> when someone won't pay a debt.

PRAXAGORA

> > > But where did the money
> he borrowed come from? If all the money
> belongs to us all, then the lender must be a thief!

CHREMES

> By Demeter, she's on the money!

BLEPYRUS

> > > Answer me this,
> then: some drunks coming home from dinner assault
> a man on the street. They have no money, so who
> pays the fine? You've got no answer to that!

PRAXAGORA

They have a food allowance; they'll pay it out
of that. Less food will hit them where they live.   740
They'll be very unlikely to repeat the offense.

BLEPYRUS

There'll be no more thieves?

PRAXAGORA

Not a one.
Why should anyone steal what's already theirs?

BLEPYRUS

What about nightstalking muggers?

PRAXAGORA

None,
if you sleep at home in your own bed. It won't
be the way it was, even if you do
go out. Everyone will be happy with what they have.
If someone *should* tell you to hand over your cloak,
then let him have it. Just go in the morning
and have us fit you out with a better one.   750

BLEPYRUS

What about shooting craps?

PRAXAGORA

For what stake?

BLEPYRUS

So what will be our way of life?

PRAXAGORA

A life
In common with everyone else. We'll knock down walls

and join all these private houses together, so all
can go in and go out and wander about as they please.

BLEPYRUS

And where will the dining room be?

PRAXAGORA

We'll eat
in the porticos and courthouses, every one of them.

BLEPYRUS

What will you do with the witness stands?

PRAXAGORA

We'll use
them to store our wine bowls and water
jugs, and boys and girls can use them   760
to sing the deeds of heroes, and also of cowards
who will be so ashamed they won't even be able to eat.

BLEPYRUS

A great idea! But what about the lottery machines?

PRAXAGORA

We'll put them in the market-place by the statue
of Harmodius, and we'll draw lots for our dinner
seating. If you draw, say, an A, the Arcade
is where you'll eat; a T, the portico
of Theseus; a D . . .

BLEPYRUS

To dig in!

PRAXAGORA

No, *dine*!

BLEPYRUS

But what if you draw a blank? No dinner for you?

PRAXAGORA

We're not going to let that happen; we'll make sure   770
that everything's provided for everyone and all:
every man will drink 'til he's thoroughly drunk
and go home with his garland and his fiery torch.
He'll be ambushed on the way by the old and the naked,
by women calling loudly from shadowy doorways,
"Come on to my house, this way, come on over,
I've got a nymphet here you just have to see!"
"No, over here," from a second story window,
"This delicate child is so smooth and so pale.
You can fuck her little brains out, but me first!"   780
And the ugly older men will stick close to the younger
and shout, "Hey, buddy-boy, what's the big rush?
It's not as if you're going to score any tonight.
The law says the ladies, before they can fuck you,
have to first fuck the flat-nosed and the ugly.
It looks like for you it's a hand-job in the foyer,
holding it by the stump, skinning your own fig!"
Do you boys go for this picture I've painted?

BLEPYRUS

We do!

PRAXAGORA

Then it's off to the marketplace for me
to accept all the goods that people will bring in,   790
and I'll find me a woman with a big, loud voice
to be my crier. These are my duties as your duly
elected leader. And I've got to organize the dinners,
for I want to have the first of them today.

BLEPYRUS

Free eats! Today?

PRAXAGORA
>   That's what I just said.
> And then I'll clear the streets of all the whores.

BLEPYRUS *(sadly)*
>   But why?

PRAXAGORA
>   Obviously, to allow our free women
> to have their pick of the best young men themselves!
> It's not right that painted whores in a house
> of love should rob free women of the boys   800
> that they deserve. Since they're slaves, let them sleep
> with slaves and only shear their shaggy bushes
> to the scratchy texture of a sheep's shorn hide.

BLEPYRUS
>   I'll come along and be seen right by your side,
> so everyone can say, "Look, it's the Leader's husband!"
> *(Praxagora and Blepyrus depart.)*

CHREMES
>   I'd better look over my things and get them together.
> And make a list, if I've got to turn them in.
> *(Chremes exits. The chorus would here have sung a song, but it has been*
> >   *lost. As they finish, Chremes returns with two*
> >   *slaves who carry his household goods. Following his*
> >   *instructions, they line them up along the street as*
> >   *though they were a ritual procession.)*

CHREMES
>   You come first, my lovely sifter, most precious
> of all my belongings. You'll be the pretty girl
> who usually bears the Basket; you're so nicely powdered   810
> from all the sacks of flour I've poured through you.

And who's to bear the Chair? Let's see. Of course,
my cooking pot. By God, you're very black!
It's almost as if Lysicrates had mixed
the dye for his hair in you! And you, come here
and stand by her. And you be the Maid-in-Waiting.
And you be the Water-Bearer and hold this jug.
And this rooster shall be the Musician, yes, you
who've crowed me up too early more than once
in the dark of night on days when I went to Assembly.   820
Whoever has the sacred Honey Pot,
step up! And put the olive branches
right beside it. And next the Tripod and the Flask
of Oil. And now, bring out the rest, the odds
and ends, the little things to bring up the rear.
(While he is lining up his "procession," the Neighbor, the second
woman's sea-faring husband who had found
Blepyrus at his labor earlier that morning, comes
out of his house.)

NEIGHBOR *(to himself)*
So, am I to surrender *my* goods?
Fat chance! I'd be finished if I did and a total
fool! By Poseidon, not me! First,
I've got to check things out and take
my bearings. I'm not about to heave my cargo   830
overside, all that hard work
and all that saving, and with no security!
Not until I've checked this whole thing out.
(He notices Chremes' curious behavior and speaks to him.)
Ahoy there! What are all these pots
and pans doing here? Are you moving, or getting
ready to pawn them off?

CHREMES
Neither one.

NEIGHBOR
 So why are they all lined up? It's not
 a procession to Hiero's Flea Market, is it?

CHREMES
 God, no! I'm obeying the law. We're carrying
 these things to the marketplace to hand them over.   840

NEIGHBOR
 You're going to pay up?!

CHREMES
                    Of course.

NEIGHBOR
                                   Zeus
 save you, you *are* a sad sack.

CHREMES
                         Just how?

NEIGHBOR
 That's easy.

CHREMES
                    Is it? Aren't we supposed
 to obey the law?

NEIGHBOR
                         The law? What a dork!

CHREMES
 The law that's just been passed.

NEIGHBOR
                              Just been passed?
 You're a dimwit!

CHREMES

A dimwit?

NEIGHBOR

Well, aren't you?
In fact, is there anyone anywhere anyway any dimmer
than you?

CHREMES

Because I obey the law?

NEIGHBOR

So *that's*
what a smart man's supposed to do.

CHREMES

Absolutely.

NEIGHBOR

No, that's what a *moron's* supposed to do!   850

CHREMES

Then you're not going to turn in your stuff?

NEIGHBOR

I'm just keeping out a weather eye;
first, I'll see what other people do.

CHREMES

Why, everybody's turning in their things!

NEIGHBOR

That I'll believe when I see it.

CHREMES

That's what
everybody's saying at any rate.

NEIGHBOR

                    Oh, aye,
    that's what they'll say.

CHREMES

                They promise to turn in all
    their possessions.

NEIGHBOR

                Oh, aye, that's what they'll promise.

CHREMES
    Your distrust will be the death of me!

NEIGHBOR
    Oh, aye, everyone will be distrusting.   860

CHREMES
    Goddam you!

NEIGHBOR

                Oh, aye, they'll damn the plan
    for sure. Do you believe that anyone with half
    a brain will give up their things? That's not the way
    we do things here. God knows we're meant to get,
    not give. Just like the gods themselves. Look at
    the hands on their statues; whenever we ask their help,
    there they are with their hands held out, palm up,
    poised not to give blessings, but to receive.

CHREMES
    Please, buddy, just let me get *something* done.
    We've got to bundle all this up. Now where's   870
    that strap?

NEIGHBOR

                You're actually going to do this?

CHREMES
God knows it. There, I've got my tripods
tied up already.

NEIGHBOR
It's so foolish not to lie at anchor
and see what all the others are going to do.
And then and only then . . .

CHREMES
Then what?

NEIGHBOR
Oh . . . wait some more, and later, wait some more!

CHREMES
But why?

NEIGHBOR
There might be bad omens:
an earthquake, or a lightning strike, or maybe
a cat will cross the road. That'll stop
this turning in of stuff, you whacko!   880

CHREMES
That'll be another fine mess you've gotten
me into, if I wait until there's no more room!

NEIGHBOR
That's what's bothering you? Don't worry.
There'll be plenty of room day after tomorrow.

CHREMES
What's that supposed to mean?

NEIGHBOR *(indicating the audience)*
>   I know this crowd.
>   They'll vote for any law, but they won't obey it.

CHREMES
>   They'll bring them in, pal.

NEIGHBOR
>   And if they don't?

CHREMES
>   Don't *you* worry. They will.

NEIGHBOR
>   And if they don't?

CHREMES
>   We'll make them.

NEIGHBOR
>   What if they're stronger than you?

CHREMES
>   I'll just leave my things and come home.   890

NEIGHBOR
>   What if they sell your stuff?

CHREMES
>   Get stuffed!!

NEIGHBOR
>   And if I get stuffed?

CHREMES
>   It'll be a favor to all.

NEIGHBOR (*shaking his head incredulously and angrily*)
    You really want to turn your stuff in.

CHREMES
    I do. And there's my neighbors carrying theirs.

NEIGHBOR
    I'm *sure* Antisthenes will dump his load;
    a month-long diarrhea would relieve him better.

CHREMES
    Shit-head!

NEIGHBOR
                    And Callimachus the poet, what's he got?

CHREMES
    More than a spendthrift playboy like Callias.

NEIGHBOR (*to the audience*)
    He's going to lose the shirt right off his back.

CHREMES
    That's pretty strong.

NEIGHBOR
                    No, it's not. There are   900
    Always new laws like this. Don't you
    recall the price controls on salt?

CHREMES
                            I do.

NEIGHBOR
    And remember the silver-copper sandwich coins?

CHREMES

> Yes, that was terrible for me. I sold my grapes
> and headed off to the market for flour, my mouth
> crammed full of copper, but just as soon as I opened
> my sack, the herald shouted: "No more copper
> coins should be accepted; we're back to silver!"

NEIGHBOR

> And more recently, didn't we all believe
> that the two and a half percent property tax   910
> of Euripides would balance the budget, how everyone
> thought he was God's gift? But then we looked
> that gift horse in the mouth, it was the same
> old thing again. It didn't do the job, and then
> they almost tarred and feathered Euripides.

CHREMES

> But times have changed, my friend. Back then *we* were
> in charge of things, but now the *women* are.

NEIGHBOR

> By Poseidon, they'll never sit on my face!

CHREMES

> I have no idea what you mean.
> Slave, pick up that bundle over there.   920
> *(The new female herald enters and cries out her announcement in a big,*
> *loud voice.)*

HERALD

> Friends, Athenians, countrypersons, lend
> me your ears! All of you, under the law,
> you all must hurry straight to the place appointed
> by our new Leader, there to draw lots
> to determine where you will go this evening for dinner.
> The tables are set and heavy with the best food

you've ever had, and the couches are freshly recovered
and cushioned. The wine's already being mixed in bowls,
and slave girls are lined up to spray you with perfume.
The fish are being grilled; the rabbits are spitted;   930
and cakes are rising in the oven. Garlands are being
woven while rich desserts are being prepared.
Lovely girlies, the youngest there, are bringing
their soup to a boil. Smoius is there to be helpful,
dressed and ready for riding, lickety-split!
And old Geron is there in the coolest of fashions,
his worn-out clothes and orthopedic shoes
tossed in the trash. It's all for you! Come along!
Come along! The slaves are there with the food you need!
All you have to do is open wide.   940
So don't say I called you late for chow!
(Herald exits.)

NEIGHBOR

If that's the way the wind is blowing, I'm lifting
anchor! Let's go eat; it's the will of the state.

CHREMES

And exactly *where* do you think you're going? You've not
even tried to turn in your belongings.

NEIGHBOR

To eat!

CHREMES

Not a chance, unless they've lost their minds,
the women won't feed a scofflaw and shirker like you.

NEIGHBOR

Hey . . . I'll do it.

CHREMES

When?

NEIGHBOR

I won't get

in anyone's way.

CHREMES

That's supposed to mean?

NEIGHBOR

Others will be even later than I'll be.   950

CHREMES

You really mean to go to dinner anyway?

NEIGHBOR

How can I not? All good men must come
to the aid of their country!

CHREMES

And if the women bar

the door?

NEIGHBOR

I'll lower my prow and ram my way in.

CHREMES

If they have you beaten like a runaway slave?

NEIGHBOR

I'll sue!

CHREMES

What if they laugh in your face?

NEIGHBOR

I'll stand by the door.

CHREMES
   What good will that do?

NEIGHBOR
                    I'll steal food
   from people who've brought it to share with all!

CHREMES
   You'd better come *after* me in that case!
(He turns to his slaves.)
   Sicon and Parmeno, gather up all my things.   960

NEIGHBOR
   Looks like you need some help there.

CHREMES
   I think not. I don't need your help in claiming
   to the Leader that a big part of my things are yours!
(Chremes and the slaves exit, carrying his goods.)

NEIGHBOR
   God knows I need a good scheme to hang onto the things
   I already have while getting my share of the dinner.
(He pauses and muses, hand on chin, then brightens.)
   Eureka! That's it! I've got to follow them, and quick!
*(Here the chorus would have sung another song, but it too has been lost.
              The scene shifts to a street in front of another two
              houses. An old woman, bawdily made-up and
              dressed, appears in one doorway. A young girl
              then appears in the upstairs window of the house
              next door.)*

UGLY OLD BROAD
   What's keeping all those men? The dinner's got
   to be over by now. And here I stand, ready
   and waiting, my face all painted snowy white.

I'm wearing my yellow gown and whistling like a bird,   970
ready to pounce on the first to pass by. O Muses!
touch my lips with a lewd Ionian air.

NYMPHET *(at an upstairs window)*
You think, you rotten old thing, that you've gotten
the jump on me. You thought to strip the vines
when everyone's back was turned and hook a man
with your stupid song. Just sing, and then I'll sing
a somewhat livelier tune. And if the audience thinks
this will be boring, I promise there'll be one thing
quite comic and then something else quite sweet.

UGLY OLD BROAD *(flipping her the bird)*
Take this, little sweetie, and go play with yourself!   980
(She speaks to the flautist in the orchestra.)
Hey, Mister Flute Man, play a song for me,
one that's good enough for both of us:

Whoever wants a good time
let him come to me.
What do young girls know
of the ripening of love?
Who could love you better,
give you pleasure longer
or deeper or truer than I . . .
and never away to fly?   990

NYMPHET
Don't deny a young girl
her pleasure; she's so soft
and so smooth, with her apples
just budding, so easy to touch.
You've plucked out so much hair
and slapped on so much paint,
you look quite ready for bed . . .
on the night of the living dead!

UGLY OLD BROAD

> I hope your hole seals up,
> and when you're ready to fuck,   1000
> no one can find the seam!
> I hope when you're kissing
> with your hand on his jake . . .
> you'll discover that it's a snake!

NYMPHET

> Oh, what's to become of me?
> There's not a boy in sight.
> And I'm here all alone,
> my mom has gone out,
> and nobody cares for me.
> And where's my dear Nanny   1010
> with her toy, "Big Dick,"
> that makes her so wet and so slick?

UGLY OLD BROAD

> Poor little baby's so hot
> that she's begging for a dildo,
> or maybe a lady from Lesbos
> where with women there is sucking!
> But you'll never take my fun away
> or lure a man from me,
> no, from me you'll never steal . . .
> for I'm quite as young as I feel.   1020

> Sing any song you like, like a kitten in heat,
> no man will ever get to you before me.

NYMPHET

> At least not for my funeral. That's one on you!

UGLY OLD BROAD

> Oh, sure, as if I haven't heard it.
> It's not my *age* that's your problem.

NYMPHET
What, then? Your wonderful makeup job, Pink-cheeks?

UGLY OLD BROAD
Are you talking to me?

NYMPHET
That you, skulking there?

UGLY OLD BROAD
Me? I'm singing a song for my boyfriend, Epigenes.

NYMPHET
You have a boyfriend? Apart from that geezer, Geres?

UGLY OLD BROAD
I'll prove it even to you. He's on his way.   1030
And look, he's coming now.

NYMPHET
But not for you.

UGLY OLD BROAD
Oh, yes he is, you snotty little brat!

NYMPHET
We'll see who's right, you withered old fig. I'm going
back inside.
(She moves away from the window but still where she can see.)

UGLY OLD BROAD
I'll step inside myself.
I'm sure we'll soon find out who's right and who's wrong.
*(She walks haughtily inside her door but reappears as soon as she thinks
the nymphet is out of sight. Epigenes, a young man,
enters, wearing a garland and carrying a torch.)*

EPIGENES

>If only I could tumble a dear
>little dolly and not have to ball
>an ugly old broad when I do it.
>It's no way for a free man to have to behave!

UGLY OLD BROAD *(to herself)*

>You'll ball and you'll like it, by God!   1040
>the sad days of Charixena are over.
>You're free all right: to obey the law.
>And, like it or not, this city's still free!
>But I'll slip out of sight and see what he's going to do.

(She moves into the shadows of her doorway.)

EPIGENES

>Dear gods, let me find my little
>girl alone. She's driven me to drink!

NYMPHET *(reappearing at her window)*

>I've totally fooled that awful old woman; she's gone
>   into her house, sure now that I'm indoors, too.
>But there's the boy we were just talking about!

(She begins to sing.)

>>Come to me, come to me,   1050
>>baby, baby,
>>come to my little bed
>>just for tonight.
>>What is this desire
>>that sets me afire,
>>awhirl like the curl
>>in your tangling hair?
>>I'm burning with yearning,
>>I'm aching, I'm quaking,
>>and praying to Eros   1060
>>to give me, to bed me
>>this boy so rare!

EPIGENES

> Come to me, come to me,
> baby, baby,
> hurry down to the door,
> or I'll die with desire:
> let me spank your bottom
> instead of my monkey.
> O Aphrodite,
> I'm crazy with love!   1070
> And Eros, have mercy:
> lead her to my bed,
> I can't even tell you
> the burning I feel.
> Please, darling,
> please, baby,
> come open the door
> and give me a squeeze,
> I'm hurting so bad!
> Light of my life,   1080
> Fire of my loins,
> Aphrodite's darling,
> Muses' honeybee,
> Graces' baby,
> You walk in beauty.
> O hottest baby,
> Come open the door,
> let me in, let me in.
> Come hold me tight:
> I hurt so much!   1090

(He begins to knock loudly and urgently on the door. The nymphet leaves
the window, but before she get to the door, the old
broad yanks open her door and enters.)

UGLY OLD BROAD

> What's that knocking? Looking for me?

EPIGENES

>No way!

UGLY OLD BROAD

But you just knocked me up!

EPIGENES

>I'm damned if I did!

UGLY OLD BROAD

What else could you be doing? You're carrying a torch!

EPIGENES

I'm looking for a jerk from Friggonia.

UGLY OLD BROAD

>By what name?

EPIGENES

Not Diddleus, whom *you're* looking for.

UGLY OLD BROAD

By Aphrodite, you'll diddle, like it or not!

EPIGENES

I don't take on cases that are dated over sixty.
They must be carried over to another session.
I only examine cases under twenty.

UGLY OLD BROAD

That was when the men were in charge, Sweetcakes,   1100
but now you've got to handle the old cases first!

EPIGENES

In the game of hearts, you can always pass.

UGLY OLD BROAD

                                                      You sure
weren't playing hearts when you sat down to dinner.

EPIGENES

What *do* you mean? I've got to knock on this door.

UGLY OLD BROAD *(pointing to her crotch)*

Knock on any door, but this one's first!

EPIGENES

I really have no need for a colander.

UGLY OLD BROAD

You know you love me. You're just surprised
to see a lady at her door. So, give me a kiss.

EPIGENES

I can't; I'm afraid of your lover.

UGLY OLD BROAD

                                                   What lover?

EPIGENES

The greatest of painters.

UGLY OLD BROAD

                                   I wonder who you mean?   1110

EPIGENES

The grim one who paints the funeral urns.
You'd better hustle, or he'll find you out of doors.

UGLY OLD BROAD

I know what you want.

EPIGENES

And I know what you want, by God!

UGLY OLD BROAD

For Aphrodite, who sent you to me, I will
not let you go!

EPIGENES

You're a senile old bat!

UGLY OLD BROAD

Don't be silly. I'm taking you to bed.

EPIGENES

I wonder why we buy bucket-hooks
when we could lower a crooked old crone like this one
down the well; her chin could hook the bucket.

UGLY OLD BROAD

Enough of your sarcasm, my boy. Get over here.   1120

EPIGENES

I'm not yours unless you've paid the tax.

UGLY OLD BROAD

By Aphrodite, oh yes you do. There's nothing
I like better than fucking a boy your age.

EPIGENES

And I hate fucking someone like you.
I will never ever agree to do it!

UGLY OLD BROAD *(pulling out a copy of Praxagora's decree)*
The law says, by God, you'll do it.

EPIGENES

What's that?

UGLY OLD BROAD

> The law that says you've got to come with me.

EPIGENES

> I dare you to read it out loud.

UGLY OLD BROAD

>   I certainly will:
> "The women have decreed that if a young man
> desires a young woman, he shall not have   1130
> intercourse with her until he first services
> an old woman. Should he refuse and go
> to the young woman, then the old lady has
> the legal right with all impunity to catch
> and drag him away by the most obvious handle!"

EPIGENES

> Woe is me! I'm to be stretched out like Procrustes!

UGLY OLD BROAD

> The law's the law. You must obey the law.

EPIGENES

> What if one of my fraternity brothers or a friend
> puts up my bail?

UGLY OLD BROAD

>   No man can now enter into
> a deal where the money's more than the price of a bushel   1140
> and two pecks of barley. The tables are turned!

EPIGENES

> I swear I'm sick!

UGLY OLD BROAD

>   You'll not wiggle out.

EPIGENES

    I swear I'm a merchant, exempt from the law.

UGLY OLD BROAD

                                Slacker!

EPIGENES

    What can I do?

UGLY OLD BROAD

                Just follow me and see.

EPIGENES

    I've got to?

UGLY OLD BROAD

           When Duty whispers low, *Thou must* . . .

EPIGENES

    Oh, well. Begin by spreading asafetida leaves
    over the bier and broken vines for firewood.
    Decorate it with ribbons, set the urn beside it,
    and the jug of holy water outside the door.

UGLY OLD BROAD

    And what about my wedding bouquet?

EPIGENES

                      A waxen   1150
    funeral wreath, by God, is what you'll need,
    because you'll fall to pieces once I start!
(The ugly old broad starts pulling Epigenes toward her door as the
                nymphet finally pops out of hers.)

NYMPHET

    Where are you dragging him?

UGLY OLD BROAD

                  I'm taking my husband home.

NYMPHET

    Not a good move. He's too young to sleep with you.
    You'd make him a better mother than a wife.
    If you start enforcing this law, you'll make the whole
    city a complex of Oedipuses and Jocastas.

UGLY OLD BROAD *(quite distraught, as she goes into her house)*
    You nasty little slut, you're emerald with envy,
    and that's why you've thought this whole thing up.
    I'll get you, my pretty!

NYMPHET

              And my little dog, too?   1160

EPIGENES
    By All-Saving Zeus, my darling dearest, you've saved me
    from that ugly old witch! I'll give you a *huge* reward
    once I've spread you out like the evening against the sky!
(As he is talking and embracing the nymphet, she begins to lead him to
            her door, but a bigger and even uglier old woman
            enters behind them.)

UGLIER OLD BROAD *(to the nymphet)*
    Hey, little missy! Just where do you think you're going?
    That's against the law. It says specifically
    he's got to fuck me first!

EPIGENES

                Oh, no. What hole
    did you pop out of? She's uglier than the first.
    This dog has got to be the Hound of Hell!

UGLIER OLD BROAD
    You! Come here!

EPIGENES *(to the nymphet, who is edging nervously away toward her*
                    house, into which she eventually disappears)
                    Don't leave me, baby, and let
       this monster drag me away!

UGLIER OLD BROAD

                              It is the law, not I   1170
       who drags you away.

EPIGENES

                         No, it's a vampire from the grave,
       blistered in blood!

UGLIER OLD BROAD *(pulling him away)*
                         Move it, chicken! This way.
       Step it up. That's more than enough clucking!

EPIGENES

       Hold it! I need to go to the crapper first.
       I've got to get myself together. If you don't let me,
       something's going to happen. I'm so scared,
       I'll strike mud right here!

UGLIER OLD BROAD

                              Just you hold it.
       You can let it go indoors.

EPIGENES

                         I'll have to let go
       in more ways than I want to, I'm sure. Look,
       I'll put up twice whatever you want in the way of ransom.   1180

UGLIER OLD BROAD
       I don't want ransom, just you!
       (A third old woman enters, even uglier than the second.)

UGLIEST OLD BROAD

You, there!
Where are you going with her?

EPIGENES

I'm not *going*;
I'm being harassed! But bless you, dear girl, whoever
you are, for stepping in to stop this torture.
(He finally sees that it's not another young girl who has spoken.)
O Heracles! O Pan! O Corybants!
O Dioscuri! She's even worse than this one!
What kind of monster is this? A gorilla made up
in drag? Or a rotten corpse puked up by Hell?

UGLIEST OLD BROAD *(grabbing Epigenes' free arm)*
Enough teasing, honey. You come with me.

UGLIER OLD BROAD *(pulling on his other arm)*
Not so! This way.

UGLIEST OLD BROAD

I'll never let you go!   1190

UGLIER OLD BROAD
And I won't either!

EPIGENES

You're going to tear me in two,
You crazy bitches!

UGLIER OLD BROAD

According to the law,
you've got to come with me.

UGLIEST OLD BROAD

Not if an even
uglier and older woman comes along.

EPIGENES
>   Now, listen. If you two kill me, how'll I
>   ever get to get to my pretty dolly?

UGLIEST OLD BROAD
>   That's your problem, but this is your legal duty.

EPIGENES *(sighs)*
>   Okay, which of you two do I do first
>   in order to go my way?

UGLIER OLD BROAD
>   That's plain to see;
>   you come with me.

EPIGENES
>   If *she'll* let go of my arm.   1200

UGLIEST OLD BROAD
>   Step right this way.

EPIGENES
>   But first *she's* got to let go!

UGLIER OLD BROAD
>   I won't, by God!

UGLIEST OLD BROAD
>   Me neither!

EPIGENES
>   You two are rougher
>   than ferrymen!

UGLIER OLD BROAD
>   How so?

EPIGENES

You tear your passengers apart
before you ever get them in the boat.

UGLIER OLD BROAD

Enough joking! Come with me.

UGLIEST OLD BROAD

This way!

EPIGENES

This is just like Cannonus' law: I'm shackled
before the court, but I've got to fuck my chains!
And how am I going to row two boats at once?

UGLIER OLD BROAD

You can do it. Just have some oysters and ginseng.

EPIGENES

Woe is me! They've dragged me right to the door.   1210

UGLIEST OLD BROAD

There's no saving you now! There's room for three.

EPIGENES

God, no! Not the toothless twosome together!

UGLIEST OLD BROAD

By Hecate, your fate is sealed. We've got you now.

EPIGENES

As a fly to a wanton boy am I to the gods:
I must fuck one crumpled bag all night and then
all day, but once she's done, another one
is waiting to begin, a toad with lips
as slick and slimy as an urn of embalming fluid.

I'm truly unlucky. No, worse than that,
I'm cursed by Zeus himself, a poor bastard   1220
having to strut and fret with beasts like these!
But if I should founder coming into port
tugged by these two hulks, please scuttle me
right in the channel, and take the one on top,
coat her with tar and sink her feet in lead.
Then set her on the shore and touch her off,
a horrid lighthouse with her cunt my funeral urn.
(The two old broads drag him through the door and close it behind them.
Praxagora's maid, a bit tipsy and quite cheerful,
enters immediately after.)

MAID

Happy are the people, and how happy I am, too,
and, too, my mistress, the luckiest one of all,
and, too, all of you who've gathered at our door,   1230
and, too, all our neighbors, and our whole city,
and I'm really happy, just a maid
with perfume in her hair, thanks be to almighty Zeus!
But sweeter than perfume is the giddy heady aroma
of the wine of Thasos, the way it hits you
and the way it lingers, while others fade and vanish
like water. There's nothing better, not a bit
better, thanks be to God! And drink it straight.
It'll make you cheery all night long
if you pick the wine that smells the very best!   1240
But tell me, ladies, do you know where my master is?
I mean, the husband of my mistress, where is he?

CHORUS LEADER

If you stay here, he's bound to pass this way.
(Blepyrus enters in the company of a group of young girls.)

MAID

Oh, there he is on his way to the dinner. Yoohoo!
Master! What a very lucky man are you!

BLEPYRUS

Who, me?

MAID

Yes, you, by God! You're the luckiest man
of all! Who could be luckier? Out of thirty
thousand citizens, you're the only one
who hasn't eaten dinner yet. Just you!

CHORUS LEADER

Oh, that makes him *really* lucky, I suppose.   1250

MAID

Are you going now?

BLEPYRUS

I'm late for chow!

MAID

By Aphrodite, you'll be the very last.
But my mistress has asked me to bring you along,
you and these girls she knew you'd have with you.
There's some good Chian wine and lots of food
left, so hurry, hurry! And any of you
in the audience who're on our side, and any judges
who aren't glancing around with your minds made up,
come join us. It's all on the house, and it's good!

BLEPYRUS

Why don't you be a lady and invite them all?   1260
The short and the fat and the tall? The old man,
the boy and the tot? There's plenty of dinner
just waiting for them all—if they'll go home!
(*He laughs raucously at his stale joke.*)
But I'm off to get my dinner now.
(*He embraces one of the young girls.*)

And luckily I've just acquired this bright little match
to light my way and keep me stepping lively!

CHORUS LEADER

Well now, pick her up or put her down,
but don't waste even more precious time.
Shake a leg, and take along these girls!
And while you're making your exit, I'll sing a song   1270
in anticipation of *our* victory dinner.
But first, a little bit of advice to the judges:
if you're deep judges, judge me for my depth of thought;
if you like a laugh, judge me for my jokes.
And, therefore, that's almost every one of you!
So please don't let it count against me, the luck
of the draw that made my show the first in line,
and don't forget me while you watch the other plays.
Hold to your oath and judge all fairly. Don't act
the whore and only remember the last to come.   1280
And, now, girls, all together:

CHORUS

We've only come to say
we really must be going,
so shimmy and shake your booty,
we're dancing the Cretan Boogie!

BLEPYRUS

I think I've got it! By Zeus, I think I've got it!

CHORUS

Then lead these women here, so limber
and so light, so marvelously slender,
keep in step and keep in time,
for soon they're going to serve us: 1290

Supercalifragilistic
expialidocious

saltfishsharksandfilleteddogfish
otherfishandpickledmullet
thrushontopofblackbirdpigeons
cocksandwagtailsroastedlarksand
chickenwingletsroastedrabbits
soakedwithsilphiumandhoney
oilydressingsoverall!

Now that you know what's waiting for us,   1300
take a bowl and hurry, hurry,
and maybe bring some oatmeal, too,
just in case, old man, you need it,
for they're all bound to be chowing down!
(Everyone, Blepyrus and his girls, the maid, the chorus and the chorus
leader, all leave singing and dancing.)

Let's step it up,
hooray!
We're off to eat,
hooray!
We've won, we've won,
hooray!   1310

Callooh! Callay!
Hooray! Hooray!

About the Translators

ALFRED CORN's seventh book of poems, entitled *Present*, appeared in 1997, along with his novel *Part of His Story* and a study of prosody, *The Poem's Heartbeat*. He has published six earlier volumes of poetry and a collection of critical essays entitled *The Metamorphoses of Metaphor*. Fellowships and prizes awarded for his poetry have come from the Guggenheim Foundation, NEA, the Academy and Institute of Arts and Letters, and the Academy of American Poets. He has taught at the City University of New York, Yale, the University of Cincinnati, U.C.L.A, Ohio State, and the University of Tulsa. At present he teaches in the Graduate Writing Program at Columbia. A frequent contributor to the *New York Times Book Review* and the *Nation*, he also writes art criticism for *Art in America* and *ARTnews* magazines. He lives in New York City.

R. H. W. DILLARD has published five volumes of original poetry (most recently *Just Here, Just Now*), two novels (most recently *The First Man on the Sun*), a book of short fiction entitled *Omniphobia*, and four books of criticism (most recently *Understanding George Garrett*), in addition to numerous critical articles and a translation of *Cistellaria* (or *The Little Box*), by the Roman comic playwright Plautus. His honors include a Woodrow Wilson Fellowship, a DuPont Fellowship, the Academy of American Poets Prize, and an O. B. Hardison, Jr. Poetry Award from the Folger Shakespeare Library. A graduate of Roanoke College, he received his M.A. and Ph.D. degrees from the University of Virginia. Since 1964 he has taught at Hollins University, where he is currently Professor of English.

X. J. KENNEDY has published thirteen collections of original poetry and poetry in translation (including *Dark Horses: New Poems*), as well as more than a dozen books of verse for children (including *Uncle Switch*), and is editor or coeditor of several influential college textbooks on literature and writing (including *The Bedford Guide for College Writers*). He has studied at the University of Michigan, the Ecole Supérieure des Professeurs de Français à l'Etranger, Sorbonne, Columbia University, and Seton Hall University. Before turning freelance in 1977, he taught at Tufts University, Leeds University, University of California at Irvine, Wellesley College, University of North Carolina, and University of Michigan. Widely recognized for his work, he is the recipient of the Michael Braude award for light verse of the American Academy and Institute of Arts and Letters, the *Los Angeles Times* book prize for poetry, a Guggenheim fellowship, the Shelley Memorial Award, an NEA grant, the Lamont Award of the Academy of American Poets, and the Bess Hokin prize from *Poetry* magazine.

CAMPBELL MCGRATH has published three collections of poetry: *Capitalism, American Noise*, and *Spring Comes to Chicago*. A fourth, *Road Atlas*, is forthcoming, and his play, *The Autobiography of Edvard Munch*, premiered in 1984. His poems have appeared widely in such journals as *Ohio Review, TriQuarterly, Shenandoah, Paris Review, Ploughshares*, and elsewhere. He has won the Academy of American Poets Prize (three times), an Illinois Arts Council Literary Advancement Grant, the Pushcart Prize, the Kingsley Tufts Poetry Award, a Guggenheim Fellowship, and the Witter-Bynner Fellowship from the Library of Congress. He has taught at Columbia University, University of Chicago, and, since 1993, Florida International University.